**Arms Transfer Limitations and
Third World Security**

sipri

Stockholm International Peace Research Institute

SIPRI is an independent international institute for research into problems of peace and conflict, especially those of arms control and disarmament. It was established in 1966 to commemorate Sweden's 150 years of unbroken peace.

The Institute is financed mainly by the Swedish Parliament. The staff, the Governing Board and the Scientific Council are international.

The Governing Board and Scientific Council are not responsible for the views expressed in the publications of the Institute.

sipri

Stockholm International Peace Research Institute
Pipers väg 28, S-171 73 Solna, Sweden
Cable: PEACERESEARCH STOCKHOLM
Telephone: 46 8/55 97 00

Arms Transfer Limitations and Third World Security

Edited by
Thomas Ohlson

sipri
Stockholm International Peace Research Institute

OXFORD UNIVERSITY PRESS
1988

Oxford University Press, Walton Street, Oxford OX2 6DP
Oxford New York Toronto
Delhi Bombay Calcutta Madras Karachi
Petaling Jaya Singapore Hong Kong Tokyo
Nairobi Dar es Salaam Cape Town
Melbourne Auckland
and associated companies in
Beirut Berlin Ibadan Nicosia

Oxford is a trade mark of Oxford University Press

Published in the United States
by Oxford University Press, New York

© SIPRI 1988

British Library Cataloguing in Publication Data
Arms transfer limitations and Third
    World security
    1. Munitions—Developing countries.
    2. Munitions. 3. Developing Countries
    —Commerce
    I. Ohlson, Thomas. II. Stockholm
    International Research Institute
    382'.456234   HD9743.D44
    ISBN 0-19-829124-8

Library of Congress Cataloging in Publication Data
Data available

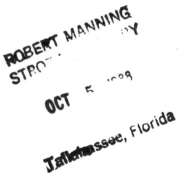

Set by Wyvern Typesetting, Bristol
Printed and bound in
Great Britain by Biddles Ltd.,
Guildford and King's Lynn

Contents

Part II. Supplier control   73

Part III. Recipient control   173

Preface

SIPRI has for nearly 20 years studied the global arms trade, with particular emphasis on the trade in major conventional weapons and weapon technology between industrialized and Third World countries. The Third World countries build up their military arsenals in two ways. One is a more recent phenomenon—the creation of domestic arms industries—which was treated in the 1986 SIPRI publication entitled *Arms Production in the Third World*. The second, and the main, route to acquiring weapons is through arms imports. In 1987, in *Arms Transfers to the Third World, 1971–85*, SIPRI described and analysed this crucial aspect of the armament processes in the developing countries. These two books were written in the classic SIPRI tradition of presenting the facts and figures in order to make the world military sector more transparent.

This third volume in the trilogy on the facts and implications of Third World arms buildups takes a somewhat different approach and addresses the crucial question of whether limitations can be put on arms transfers.

Since the early 1970s, arms transfers have played a prominent role in international relations and have been a focus of global concern. By the mid-1980s, arms transfers had also become a serious problem for policy makers and governments in many countries, largely owing to the structural changes this market has undergone and to the behaviour of the actors on this market. Political control of the arms trade has declined in recent years: short-term commercial and political gains have frequently clashed with longer-term foreign policy goals. This has potentially destabilizing effects on both arms supplier and recipient states, perhaps most clearly illustrated in the case of arms transfers to the two belligerents in the now seven-year war between Iraq and Iran.

Arms Transfer Limitations and Third World Security assesses past attempts, current proposals and future possibilities for limiting the trade in weapons and weapon technology with Third World countries. Because arms transfer limitations are also intimately related to such broader concepts as development and security, the subject cuts right across North–South and East–West issues. This makes it not only an urgent and a tremendously complex subject of study, but one in line with another goal of SIPRI studies: to facilitate arms control and disarmament efforts.

The contributors to this publication were carefully chosen. They represent the North and the South. They combine academic expertise with practical political insight and experience. Their assessments and recommendations are thus not presented in a vacuum; they are tabled with political feasibility in mind.

Apart from the contributors, special acknowledgement is due to Michael

Brzoska, who participated in the early stages of planning for this book; he provided many valuable comments and suggestions for all the chapters. Comments on sections of the book were contributed by Ian Anthony, Aaron Karp, Evamaria Loose-Weintraub and Elisabeth Sköns. Elisabeth Sköns also prepared the bibliography. Finally, the editorial expertise of Connie Wall is gratefully acknowledged.

Thomas Ohlson
SIPRI
September 1987

About the authors

Muthiah Alagappa is a Research Fellow at the Institute of Strategic and International Studies, Kuala Lumpur, Malaysia. Two of his most recent publications are *The National Security of Developing States: Lessons from Thailand*, and *Towards a Nuclear-Weapons-Free Zone in Southeast Asia*.

Nicole Ball is a Senior Analyst at the National Security Archive in Washington DC, specializing in arms transfers and security assistance. She is the author of *Third-World Security Expenditure: A Statistical Compendium*, *Converting Military Facilities*, and *Security and Economy in the Third World* and co-editor of *The Structure of the Defense Industry: An International Comparison*.

Anne Hessing Cahn is Director of the Committee for National Security, Washington, DC. She has served as Chief of the Social Impact Staff of the US Arms Control and Disarmament Agency and as Special Assistant to the Deputy Assistant Secretary of Defense for Coproduction Policy. She is co-author of *Controlling the Future Arms Trade* and other publications on arms transfers, a comprehensive test ban and general arms control policy.

Jacques Fontanel is Maître de Conférences at the University of Grenoble, France, and Deputy Director of the Centre d'Etudes de Défense et Sécurité Internationale (CEDSI). He was consultant for the United Nations Experts Group on Reduction of Military Budgets. He has published on disarmament and development, economics of defence, the arms industry and economic arms.

Jean-François Guilhaudis is Professor at the University of Grenoble, France, and Director of the Centre d'Etudes de Défense et Sécurité Internationale (CEDSI). He is the author or co-author of several books, among them *Le Droit des peuples à disposer d'eux mêmes*, *Désarmement pour le Développement, un pari difficile*, *Le mouvement de paix en France* and *Le désarmement pour le Développement*.

Björn Hettne is Professor in peace and development research at the University of Gothenburg, Sweden, where he holds a PhD degree in economic history. He has specialized in Indian colonial history and development theory, and on the relationship between peace and development. He also co-ordinates a project on European perspectives for the United Nations University.

Jo L. Husbands is a Research Associate with the Committee on Contributions of Behavioral and Social Sciences to the Prevention of Nuclear War of the US National Academy of Sciences. She has written extensively on security issues, with special emphasis on the Third World, arms transfers and nuclear non-proliferation.

Michael T. Klare is the Five College Associate Professor of Peace and World Security Studies and Director of the Five College Program in Peace and World Security Studies. He is also an Associate Fellow of the Institute for Policy Studies in Washington, DC, and Defense Correspondent for *The Nation*. He is the author of several books on US foreign and military policy, including *War Without End* and *American Arms Supermarket*.

Joachim Krause is Research Associate at the Stiftung Wissenschaft und Politik, Research Institute for International Affairs, Ebenhausen, FR Germany. He is also a Resident Fellow at the Institute for East–West Security Studies, New York. Among his recent publications are *Die Sowjetische Militärhilfepolitik gegenüber Entwicklungsländern* and articles on international arms transfer issues, West German arms export policy, international security and arms control.

S. D. Muni is Professor at the School of International Studies, Jawaharlal Nehru University, New Delhi, India. He has previously served as Visiting Research Fellow at the School of International Service, American University, Washington, DC, and the School of Advanced International Studies, The Johns Hopkins University, Washington, DC. Among his publications are *Arms Buildup and Development: Linkages in the Third World* and *Domestic Conflicts in South Asia*.

Thomas Ohlson was a Researcher and the Project Leader of the SIPRI arms trade research programme until 1987. He is the co-editor of *Arms Production in the Third World* and co-author of *Arms Transfers to the Third World, 1971–85*. He is a political scientist and an economist, specializing in problems of development, underdevelopment, militarization and security. He is currently a Researcher at the Centre of African Studies in Maputo, Mozambique.

Frederic S. Pearson is Professor of Political Science and Fellow at the Center for International Studies, University of Missouri–St Louis. He has written widely on the international arms trade and international military intervention. He is co-author of a textbook entitled *International Relations: The Global Condition in the Late Twentieth Century* and author of *The Weak State in International Crisis: The Case of the Netherlands in the German Invasion Crisis of 1939–40*.

John Simpson is a Senior Lecturer in Politics at the University of Southampton, UK, and Deputy Director of its Centre for International Policy Studies. He participated in the UN Secretary-General's Study on Conventional Disarmament in 1983–85 and has since 1984 co-ordinated a study of North–South Security Relations in the 1990s. He has written widely on British defence and nuclear policies, and nuclear non-proliferation.

Chris Smith is a Researcher at the Institute of Development Studies, University of Sussex, UK. His academic interests include the security dilemma in the Third World, the transfer of military technology to developing countries, nuclear proliferation and alternative defence and security. His main geographic area of interest is the Indian subcontinent. He has previously been fellow of the United Nations University in Delhi, India.

Noordin Sopiee is the Director-General of the Institute of Strategic and International Studies, Kuala Lumpur, Malaysia. His field of research is political and economic issues in the Asia–Pacific region, particularly South-East Asia. He is a member of the Standing Committee of the Pacific Economic Co-operation Conference and the International Council of the Asia Society, New York.

K. Subrahmanyam is Director of the Institute for Defence Studies and Analyses, New Delhi, India. He is a member of the UN intergovernmental experts group on the relationship between disarmament and development and Chairman of the United Nations study group on nuclear deterrence. His recent publications include *India and the Nuclear Challenge* and *Security without Nuclear Weapons*.

Augusto Varas is Senior Researcher at the Latin American Faculty of Social Sciences in Santiago, Chile. He has served as consultant to UNESCO, the Department of Disarmament Affairs of the United Nations, and the United Nations University. He is co-ordinator of the regional study group on armed forces and society of the Latin American Council of Social Sciences and the International Sociological Association, and is Director of the Latin American Centre for Defence and Disarmament. He has published *Militarization and the International Arms Race in Latin America* and *Soviet–Latin American Relations in the Eighties*.

Introduction

THOMAS OHLSON

Multilateral attempts to limit transfers of conventional weapons to Third World countries have by and large been unsuccessful throughout the post-war period. Except for the 1977 UN mandatory arms embargo on South Africa, no international treaty or other formal inter-state arrangement aimed at reducing the level of conventional armaments is currently in force, but many efforts have been made, and much can be learned from them. The main purpose of this book is to present a critical assessment of past attempts, current proposals and future possibilities to limit the transfer of weapons and weapon technology to the Third World. The basic assumption is that arms transfer limitation is not a dead issue. On the other hand, realism is essential: the feasibility of limitation measures is largely determined by a wide variety of strategic, political, economic and military factors inherent in the current functioning of the international system as well as in individual regions and countries. These factors must be taken into account: they limit the scope for choice, but they do not preclude choice altogether. Realism means, among other things, taking account of the fact that states behave in a rational and self-interested way. Under certain circumstances, arms transfer limitations may be seen to be rational behaviour.

Arms transfer limitation is only one factor—not always decisive—in the broader problem of enhancing Third World security. However, the subject is topical and sufficiently well defined to merit separate investigation. While the papers in this volume also refer to related and more general issues—such as East–West and North–South relations, conflicts and security in the Third World, and so on—the book focuses primarily on the more narrow subject of arms transfer limitations. It investigates whether the prevailing view of the mid-1980s—that there is no future for such limitations—can or cannot be challenged.

I. Notes on the history of past proposals

Details of earlier proposals to limit the arms trade have been dealt with at length by others.[1] However, it is instructive to review these early proposals since new attempts have to be based, among other things, on the experiences gained from these past failures. What were the underlying reasons for these proposals and attempts, and why did they fail?

The history of arms transfer control proposals can be divided into three periods, with respect both to *when* and *why* they were put forward. During the first period, from the 1880s until World War I, various combinations of colonial powers reached a series of agreements to regulate the export of arms and other military equipment to their respective African colonies. The most important of these agreements was the General Act for the Repression of the Slave Trade, known as the Brussels Act of 1890. The Act was essentially concerned with the slave trade, but there was a section on arms trade which prohibited, with some exceptions, the delivery of arms and ammunition to the larger part of the African continent.[2] The Act had two goals with respect to arms transfers: to maintain a stable military balance between the colonial forces in Africa, and to prevent armed insurgencies by the native populations. It was by definition a discriminatory agreement, aimed at preserving the *status quo* of colonialism in Africa.[3] The other agreements during this period were of a similar nature but were less comprehensive in terms of the number of signatories. These agreements were only partly successful, mainly due to often extensive arms smuggling by private arms merchants.

The second period, from the end of World War I until the mid-1930s, was the heyday of arms transfer control proposals. There was a widely shared perception that the arms races before 1914 were fuelled largely by private arms merchants and that this was a major cause of the war. Concern focused on the problem of restraining the activities of private arms traders. This was to be accomplished by publicizing and regulating the international arms trade. With few exceptions, the arguments and proposals made since World War II are identical to or were derived from ideas advanced during the second period. Among them were: the inequity argument (i.e., the discriminatory effects of imposing restrictions on the arms trade but not on arms production), the need for proper licensing procedures and publicity for all arms production, standardized international rules governing the arms trade as well as mechanisms for supervision, and qualitative and quantitative restrictions on deliveries to conflict-ridden areas.

These measures were presented and discussed in several multilateral forums during the period: the 1919 Covenant of the League of Nations, the 1919 St Germain Convention, the Geneva Arms Traffic Convention of 1925, the 1932 Disarmament Conference of the League (at which the Committee for the Regulation of Trade in the Private and State Manufacture of Arms was set up), the Permanent Disarmament Commission of the League, and so on.[4] Numerous unilateral proposals were also put forward and measures taken, for example, by France, Spain and, not least, the United States. Most of the actual measures were in the form of embargoes on countries at war, such as in connection with the Chinese Civil War in the 1920s, the Chaco War between Bolivia and Paraguay in 1934, the 1935 war between Italy and Ethiopia, and the Spanish Civil War in 1936–39.

Most of the agreements and conventions proposed during this period were never ratified or never entered into force. Most of the embargoes proved to be very ineffective. There were a number of reasons for this. Most importantly, much of the effort was the product of a general outburst of moral rage over what was going on—with special reference to the private 'merchants of death' and their allies in government and the military. There was little understanding of the *systemic* nature of the arms trade problem, that is, the economic and political forces at various levels which encourage exports and imports of arms. There was a gap between disarmament rhetoric and the real world of politics, economics and insecurity. This—in combination with loose control mechanisms, the continuing activities of private arms dealers and the breadth of the supply-side of the arms market—rendered these attempts ineffective. The subject disappeared altogether from the international agenda in the rising tide of international tension and rearmament processes in the late 1930s.

The third period commenced after World War II. A bi-polar international system emerged, dominated by US and Soviet efforts to expand their influence. As part of its programme of containment, the United States, with its allies, sought close co-operation with the 'forward defence areas'—Third World countries bordering on or geographically close to the USSR. This ambition was paramount among the factors behind the Tripartite Declaration by the United States, France and the UK in May 1950 regarding security in the Middle East. The three countries, at the time enjoying almost total control of arms supplies to the Middle East, were opposed to an arms race between Israel and the Arab states. Regional compliance at a comparatively low level of armament was sought by the parties to the Declaration. Arms would be sold only in combination with commitments not to attack any other country in the region. Effectively, this meant that only countries willing to accept an open or tacit military alliance with the Western countries would receive major weapons. This policy was more clearly reiterated in the Four Power Statement on a future Allied Middle East Command.[5] Through the Near East Arms Co-ordinating Committee, Britain, France and the USA successfully regulated the flow of arms to the Middle East between 1950 and 1955. However, this arms transfer control measure served mainly as a tool in the race for global hegemony. Consequently, all control efforts were eradicated and effectively reversed when the Western arms monopoly in the Middle East was broken by Egypt's order for weapons from Czechoslovakia and the Soviet Union in 1955–56.

The later, from time to time recurring, control initiatives were often dominated by the United States. The US initiatives in this period had two prime features: first, the USA advocated restraint by Third World recipients on a regional level; and second, the USA was prepared to support unilaterally such restraint, while hoping that other suppliers would follow suit. It can be argued that there were two major reasons for these US initiatives. First, the United States re-lived the moral indignation of the 1930s. It was not, as in the 1930s, directed against private arms traders. Members of Congress instead criticized the Administration, claiming that it was not in line with long-term US national interests to be so heavily involved in arming the Third World, in, for example, the Fulbright and Eximbank hearings in 1967.[6] Later, in the early and mid-1970s, there was also much congressional concern about US conduct in the Viet Nam War and the virtually unrestrained flow of major weapons to the Middle East—in particular to Iran—and there were the Lockheed and the Northrop bribe scandals.

Second, there were the Third World policies, pursued—at least on the level of declaratory policy—by the Kennedy and Carter Administrations. In the early 1960s the Kennedy Administration argued that improved social and economic conditions in Third World countries were the best guarantees against Soviet advances in the Third World. At the time, most of the arms transferred by the USA were for the maintenance of internal security. Later, the Carter Administration initially challenged the Nixon–Kissinger assumption that global détente was an exclusive function of improved relations between the USA and the USSR. President Carter did not advocate an international system characterized by superpower hegemony and *realpolitik*. In its early years, the Carter Administration argued that the need for rearmament and global security alliances were not or should not be the main driving force of international politics. The Carter Administration re-affirmed the Kennedy belief that economic and social problems are a greater threat than military problems. They argued that global stability is best enhanced by increased political and economic co-operation between the USA, Western Europe, Japan and the Third World. Against this background, the Carter arms export policy stated that the unrestrained spread of conventional weapons threatened stability in every region of the world and that the United States—as the largest supplier—bore a special responsibility to slow down the international trade in arms.[7]

During this period, there were several unilateral and implicit Soviet measures for arms export restraint, most often having to do with the risk that Third World conflicts might lead to a superpower confrontation. The USA and the USSR also attempted jointly to find ways of bringing about a slow-down of the international traffic in arms.[8] The leading, more commercially oriented, suppliers in Western Europe did not pursue any major efforts at arms transfer control during this period.

II.   Lessons

This overview of arms trade control proposals illustrates that there is an extremely important link between explicit/implicit, multilateral/unilateral limitation measures, on the one hand, and national interests on the other. During the first two periods, for example, proposals for multilateral measures were often made. Governments had little control over arms flows, and it was in their interests—individually as well as jointly—to check the activities of private arms merchants. Their activities often contradicted government policies. After World War II the situation changed. The arms trade was government-controlled and thus integrated in the respective foreign policies of the arms-supplying countries. It became a feature of their rational and self-serving behaviour mentioned above. More unilateral and implicit restraints therefore appeared during the third period. Similarly, it became more difficult for suppliers to agree on proposals for explicit, multilateral arms transfer control, owing to the disparity of foreign policy goals. The exceptions occurred in times of war or other crises.

The initiatives during these periods also show some common features. First, they were initiated by supplier countries.[9] There was a lack of proposals from the recipient countries, but this was due largely to the fact that it is easier to reach consensus among a relatively small number of suppliers than among a larger number of recipients. In addition, the sellers could more easily than during the late 1970s/early 1980s dictate the terms on the market. The arms market was a seller's market until at least the mid-1970s. Global demand tended to be higher than available supplies. Consequently, recipients had little interest in self-restraint. A second common feature is that attempts at arms transfer limitations were expressions of vested interests. Proposals seldom reflected a sincere conviction that positive results would accrue from some measure of disarmament, nor were they based upon thorough appraisal of the driving forces of the arms trade. Third, there are no examples of a co-operative response on the part of the recipients. In some cases, they simply did not have a say; in other cases they argued against arms transfer controls.

III. The current situation

Despite severe economic problems, Third World countries continue to receive about two-thirds of the global flow of major weapons. Almost half of this flow was, by the mid-1980s, directed towards five nations—Iraq, Egypt, India, Saudi Arabia and Syria. The imports of major conventional weapons by all other Third World countries have declined by one-quarter over the past 10 years.[10] While the USA and the USSR still dominate global arms sales, their joint share is declining in favour of the shares of more commercially oriented suppliers—particularly those in Western Europe but also in the Third World and China. Fierce competition among a growing number of producers and exporters thus coincides with a global reduction in the demand for major weapons, owing largely to the world-wide economic recession thus far in the 1980s. This shift towards a buyer's market has led to structural changes in the arms market.

With few exceptions, the main producers/exporters—arms industries and government decision makers—are pushing harder than ever to sell their products. The national security doctrines of these states normally emphasize the importance of retaining a broad arms production base in order to be able rapidly to respond to domestic needs in case of war or other crises which disrupt international trade. When at the same time pressures are mounting to make cuts in peacetime domestic military procurement expenditures, arms exports are seen as a way to preserve a strong military–industrial base. Export efforts are further strengthened by competition from new suppliers: fears of losing market shares, civilian trade and political influence in the recipient countries reduce the willingness of suppliers to control and restrain the arms trade.

The recipients, for their part, oppose supplier restraint, which is seen as paternalistic and discriminatory. It is also argued that the legitimate security needs of Third World countries are not taken into account.[11] It is no wonder that proposals for supplier control are regularly received with suspicion in the Third World. Were they carried into effect, the existing gap between the *haves* and *have-nots* in the field of conventional armaments would widen considerably. International hierarchies among countries, in so far as arms suppliers are concerned, would become legalized, not only between industrialized arms-producing countries and non-producers in the Third World, but also between states belonging to military alliances and non-aligned states. The gap would also widen between those Third World countries that have sizeable arms production, those with only limited production and those totally dependent on foreign supplies.

Furthermore, the increasing number of arms producers has made attempts to control the proliferation of conventional weapons even more difficult. Even if some measures of supplier control were to be implemented, the multitude of available suppliers and the technological know-how already acquired in most industrialized and many Third World countries would enable the recipients to continue to purchase or produce weapons. Conflicts and wars may be prolonged through enhanced capabilities to sustain war efforts via domestic production of 'war consumables'.

Control and limitations are necessarily the responsibility of governments, but governments are not the only force that shapes the arms trade. Industrial offsets, counter-trade, civilian and military technology transfers, barter agreements, and so on, in connection with arms transfers have commercialized and privatized the arms market, just as the growing number of producers has diversified it and led to fierce supplier competition. The civilian sectors—in both supplier and recipient counties—are now more easily drawn into arms sales. Commercial ambitions, in companies and in governments, often get the upper hand of what would seem to be sound political judgement. Still, it has been a widespread belief among many observers that the greater part of the arms trade occurs as a result of politically controlled government-to-government negotiations. This may be true, but it is becoming increasingly clear that commercal aspirations and political considerations do not always pull in the same direction. The use of private arms dealers, middlemen, obscure shipping lines and false end-use certificates occurs throughout the arms market as a result of commercialization and competition.

Nowhere is this more clear than in the arms trade with Iraq and Iran since 1980. The specific demand created by this war has been a real boost for hard-pressed arms manufacturers, coming as it does in a period of relative slack in arms sales to the Third World as a whole. The market has experienced a revival, in both the legal and illegal sectors. The Iraq–Iran War also shows that no state selling arms can fully influence how, by whom or against whom these arms will eventually be used. In general, weapons are now being used rather than just stockpiled: the number of conflicts has increased during recent decades, and the use of war as a means of conflict resolution is not diminishing. During 1986, for example, 36 armed conflicts were waged, involving over five million soldiers from 41 nations.[12] The levelling-out of the volume of arms transfers observed during the 1980s is not to any significant extent due to a reduction in what can be called real demand; it is due largely to shortages of foreign exchange. It can therefore be argued that arms transfers will again increase if the international economy establishes an upward momentum.

On the other hand, it can be argued that most tensions within and among Third World countries result largely from local or regional economic, social and political problems. Such problems might be exacerbated through arms imports and domestic arms production via diversion of scarce resources or distortion of the domestic industrial structure. However, the current international system lacks effective institutions for conflict resolution. Rather, weapons are used as the universal coin of power. The question arises: Are more arms transfer limitations desirable?

IV.   Are more limitations desirable?

Any discussion of limitations of conventional arms transfers must take into account the fact that weapons are acquired with the declared aims to deter armed aggression, to defeat aggression when it has occurred and to maintain internal order. Conventional arms also facilitate—though at great costs—other subordinate objectives of countries involved in the process of nation-state building: independence, prestige, power and political viability. Furthermore, arms import programmes can function as regime stabilizers in many societies marked by under- or maldevelopment and political instability: in some cases they simply serve to buy the military off; in others they are seen by the military as a means of remaining in power.

However, all the contributors to this volume underline that more arms transfer limitations are desirable. They argue that the accumulation of arms by one state unavoidably provokes reciprocal action by others. The ensuing instability may decrease the feeling of security of all participants in the arms race, instead of strengthening it. Another important point made throughout this book is that security is too often thought of in military terms alone, while in fact real security can never be achieved without social and economic stability and progress.

Clearly, in a world of sovereign nation-states, and given the present international system, it is unrealistic to argue in favour of the total cessation of arms acquisitions. It is not unrealistic, however, to strive for significant reductions, so as to discourage the initiation of hostilities between rival nations, to lower the degree and mitigate the consequences of violence and destruction in wars that may break out, to reduce the wasteful use of resources and to contribute to political stability.

A major problem, however, is that the potential benefits of arms transfer limitations have to be pointed out more forcefully. This is a difficult task. The level of conflict and instability in the world is fuelling traditional security thinking. Pressures to export arms will continue to be strong as long as military research, development and arms production in the supplier countries remain at current levels. Similarly, there will be continued pressures to import arms and arms technology for reasons of national security or to fulfil other aims. As pointed out by Subrahmanyam (paper 2), the endeavour to close the military–technological gap between industrial and Third World countries will remain prominent among those developing countries that have attained or aspire for regional power status. The global diffusion of power and the slow shift towards a more multi-polar world generate new regional conflict formations and rivalries. For example, distrust between neighbours may increase as regional powers acquire more and better weapons than their weaker neighbouring states.

For reasons of economic necessity, some Third World countries have made deep cuts in planned procurement programmes, but there are few, if any, examples of political processes to accompany these cuts. As noted by Fontanel and Guilhaudis (paper 13), some Third World countries instead hail the idea of channelling resources from the military sectors of industrialized countries to the Third World via a disarmament fund for development. This is not an expression of interest in arms control; it is simply a way of securing more civil aid at unchanged levels of armaments. Substantial efforts are therefore needed in order to identify, research and more concretely test the benefits to be derived from arms transfer limitations. However, the bulwark of conventional security thinking is a formidable barrier against even minor modifications in attitudes towards traditional concepts of security.

There are potential benefits on several levels. First, on the level of national security policy in the Third World, arms import limitations might contribute to the defusing of conflicts and, in particular, to insulating these conflicts from unwanted outside interference. Obviously, arms imports are not the main cause of Third World conflicts, and arms transfer restraint is not the main solution. But arms imports can aggravate tensions and, as noted by Ball (paper 3), they may tilt the balance between latent conflict and open warfare in crisis situations.

Second, arms imports retard economic development in the Third World. Arms imports incur direct foreign exchange costs and indirect follow-on costs as a result of necessary downstream investments in infrastructure, training, and so on. More than 5 per cent of all Third World imports and as much as 20 per cent of all Third World imports of machinery and transportation goods consist of weapons and semi-fabricated goods for arms production. Up to 10 per cent of the total Third World debt burden has been incurred for the purchase of military goods.[13] Arms transfers and domestic arms production thus contribute, in many cases significantly, to the hampering of economic development.

Third, in so far as high levels of arms transfers are a burden for recipient countries, suppliers of civilian goods to the Third World would benefit from arms transfer limitations. Two things would result: a redistribution of trade earnings from the most important suppliers of arms to those countries—such as FR Germany and Japan—which sell mainly civilian products, *and* an increase in the total volume of world trade, which would benefit everyone. This is so because the higher multiplier effects in civil trade as compared to military trade would enhance the longer-term potential for growth and development, and thus for trade in general. Resources can only be used once, either for arms or for civilian use. The opportunity-cost argument could thus gain weight among many suppliers: theoretically speaking, there are economic motives in favour of arms transfer restraint also for supplier countries.

Fourth, on the level of superpower security concerns, Husbands and Cahn (paper 7) argue that arms transfer restraint could help to decrease the danger of horizontal escalation of Third World conflicts. The huge flow of arms to their Middle Eastern allies, for example, has in the past taken the superpowers to the brink of direct confrontation. Also, arms transfers to the Third World which serve the interests of superpower rivalry have often heightened tensions between them. Several contributors mention the famous statement by US National Security Council Advisor Brzezinski about SALT II being buried in the sands of Ogaden. Moreover, the growing commercial considerations even in the arms transfer policies of the superpowers may further loosen their control of conflict escalation. Finally, there is also the fear of illegal or unintended transfers of high-technology items ending up in the hands of 'the other side'. Such fears are obviously exacerbated in a situation where superpower leverage in world affairs is on the decline.

There are, consequently, sound arguments for more arms transfer limitations. However, they carry little weight with political decision makers in the industrialized and Third World countries. First, owing to the size and diversity of the arms market, all arguments are not valid for all actors on the market. Second, the arguments compete with political, economic and security considerations and forces pulling in the opposite direction. Third, they are not so easily quantifiable. More research is needed to test the validity of the above arguments. This could affect their persuasiveness and political attraction.

These problems and issues are neither new nor dead. In 1987, for example, a UN Special Conference on Disarmament and Development was held. As mentioned above, there is also a large body of proposals for limiting the international arms trade. What appears to be lacking are sincere efforts at linking diagnosis to policy prescriptions. Diplomats and politicians argue that, since there is little hope of changing the current situation, such efforts are not worthwhile. In the academic field it is felt that, although many good proposals have been made in the past, there is a profound lack of political will to try them. Put another way, the gap between perceived political and economic feasibility on the national level, on the one hand, and UN disarmament rhetoric, on the other hand, is too wide and still widening. Most people, including the political and economic decision makers, would probably theoretically subscribe to the proposition that it is better if the same level of security could be maintained at lower levels of armament. But in reality they do not, for the simple reason that the above-mentioned gap is too wide. There appear to be two ways of bridging or closing this gap: by emphasizing proposals that are politically realistic and feasible and, second, by gradually modifying the attitudes towards such concepts as 'security'. For one thing, in order to be successful, any arms transfer limitation must offer what is seen as unequivocal advantages for all parties—no agreement will be reached in this field just for the sake of reaching an agreement. Such advantages may be found in the growing awareness, enhanced by the bad performance of the world economy in recent years, that security (national, regional, common or global) not only includes the absence of foreign military intrusion and domination, but also includes certain minimum levels of economic and social well-being. Disarmament, to be sure, does not automatically generate development, but—in a world of scant and finite resources—it may in many cases be an important prerequisite for development.

V.   Issues and questions

Arms transfers can, on the one hand, be seen as a perfectly legitimate aspect of international relations. Just as it is natural that states that do not have an automobile-manufacturing industry import motor cars, buses and lorries to fulfil transportation needs, it is also natural that states without a substantial arms industry import arms for reasons of national security, and so on. According to this view, mutual benefits arise from arms transfers for both suppliers and recipients; and what is good for the individual actors on the market cannot be bad on the global scale.

Arms transfers can, on the other hand, be seen as inherently harmful. The likelihood of wars and the level of destruction in wars are, it can be argued, a direct function of the magnitude of the international arms trade. Third World countries waste scarce foreign currency on non-productive military investments instead of buying more security through increased spending on basic human needs.

Both of the above approaches are simplistic and inadequate from the point of view of academic assessment. SIPRI has, along with many other observers of the arms market, taken the view that arms transfers are essentially a *systemic* phenomenon. Arms transfers do not occur in a vacuum. They result from national political, military and economic motivations and considerations in both supplier and recipient countries. There are also sub- and supra-national factors at work. It is therefore not so easy to stop trading arms. Simply put, there are various national and international sub-systems in the international system. One such sub-system, or set of sub-systems, is the economic system— the production and consumption of goods and services. Political and bureaucratic systems regulate and administer the economic systems, and military systems guarantee (or threaten to topple) the continued existence of the other systems. Arms transfers can neither be understood nor judged without insight into the dynamics of this complex web of systemic interaction between and within interest groups and states.

Another important issue concerns what is meant by arms transfer limitations. First, the concepts of 'limitation' and 'control' are used synonymously in this book, even if limitations would appear to be more neutral—control is often taken to mean something exercised by producers/suppliers over non-producers/recipients. Second, limitations can assume many forms. These include, most prominently, *reductions*, strictly meaning actual cuts in traded quantities (or less than one-for-one replacements of force levels) at unchanged or lower qualitative levels; *restraint*, meaning—at a minimum—a decrease in growth rates of quantities and qualities traded; and *regulation*, meaning —at the least—the formalization and bureaucratization of an existing situation.

These distinctions are useful from an analytical point of view. Also, the judgement of future limitation prospects is obviously affected by the choice of definition. However, at this stage and for the purposes of this book, it seems sufficient to note that there are such distinctions.

Aside from conceptual matters and choice of approach, two main prerequisites for arms transfer limitations are realism and modifications of attitudes. From this arise some more basic and concrete questions which this book sets out to answer. They are, for example:

1. Is the arms trade completely out of control or are there vestiges of control?
2. What are the major hurdles against more limitations?
3. Are there any positive signs of wider acceptance of arms transfer proposals? Which pre-conditions would increase such accceptance? Which are the proposals most likely to gain such acceptance?

VI.   The contributions

The papers comprise four main parts. The first part presents different and often contradictory assessments of the desirability, feasibility, pre-conditions and possibilities for limiting arms transfers to the Third World, thus illustrating the magnitude of the problem and the diversity of views on the subject. In the second part the papers deal with supply-side control. The authors were asked to assess past attempts at limiting arms transfers to the Third World from a particular supplier or group of suppliers. This includes a review of policies aimed at arms export control and the factors, concerns and interest groups that shaped these policies. It also includes an assessment of the circumstances currently facilitating or hampering control efforts as well as of the future possibilities for such efforts. There is a special paper on the Conventional Arms Transfer Talks (CATT) between the USA and the USSR in the late 1970s.

What are the main lessons from this recent attempt at bilateral superpower arms export control?

The third part consists of papers taking a regionally oriented recipient perspective. The history of political and academic proposals from within the regions towards limiting the inflow of weapon technology is presented. Regional reactions and positions on such proposals coming from outside the region are also treated. Again, the papers include assessments of the factors that currently influence the propensity to implement limitations in the region and of the possibilities for such limitations in the future. There is also a special paper on the potential of the non-aligned movement with respect to arms import limitations. The fourth part contains two papers dealing with attempts to link supplier and recipient incentives for arms transfer limitations. One of them looks at the disarmament–development issue in North–South relations, and the other investigates whether the NPT regime offers a possible model for conventional armament restraint. Finally, the concluding chapter assesses the contributions. The proposals that seem most feasible for the future are identified along with the pre-conditions necessary for these proposals to find fertile ground.

Notes and references

[1] See, for example, Harkavy, R., *The Arms Trade and International Systems* (Ballinger, Cambridge, MA, 1975), chapter 7; and SIPRI, *The Arms Trade with the Third World* (Almqvist & Wiksell: Stockholm, 1971), chapter 2.

[2] The Act was signed by the United States, 13 European states, Iran, the Congo Free State and Zanzibar. See also *Treaties, Conventions, International Acts, Protocols and Agreements between the United States of America and other Powers 1776–1909*, vol. II (Washington, DC, 1910), quoted in SIPRI (note 1).

[3] See also Harkavy (note 1), p. 213.

[4] For details, see Harkavy and SIPRI (note 1).

[5] See also SIPRI (note 1), p. 160.

[6] See Sampson, A., *The Arms Bazaar* (Hodder and Stoughton: London, 1977) and Harkavy (note 1), pp. 225–38.

[7] Changes in US arms export policy *vis-à-vis* Third World countries are described in Brzoska, M. and Ohlson, T., *Arms Transfers to the Third World, 1971–85* (Oxford University Press: Oxford, 1987), pp. 46–59 and the bibliography p. 372 ff; see also paper 5.

[8] The CAT Talks are described in paper 7.

[9] The one major exception was the Ayacucho proposals put forward by the Andean countries in 1974. These proposals are discussed in paper 10.

[10] See Ohlson, T. and Sköns, E., 'The trade in major conventional weapons', SIPRI, *SIPRI Yearbook 1987: World Armaments and Disarmament* (Oxford University Press: Oxford, 1987).

[11] The terms 'regional security' and 'national security' are most often defined differently in the Third World and in the Western industrialized countries. The characterization of the problems related to the concepts of 'security' is, however, not primarily of a semantic nature. Rather, different definitions reflect a deep divergence in the experience of Western and Third World states, for example, with respect to (a) the history and duration of the process of nation-state formation in the West and in the Third World, and (b) the pattern of élite recruitment, regime establishment and maintenance in the Third World and in the West. These differing concepts of security pose a number of significant and substantial hindrances in the way of joint supplier/recipient action to limit the international arms trade. For descriptions of the concept of security in the Third World, see Ayoob, M. (ed.), *Regional Security in the Third World* (Croom Helm: London, 1986); or Buzan, B., *People, States and Fear: The National Security Problem in International Relations* (Wheatsheaf: Brighton, 1983).

[12] SIPRI (note 10), chapters 7 and 8.
[13] Brzoska, M., *The Accumulation of Military Debt*, Universität Hamburg, Forschungszentrum Kriege, Rüstung und Entwicklung, Arbeitspapiere no. 7.

Part I.   Controversies

Paper 1.   Third World arms control and world system conflicts

BJÖRN HETTNE

I.   Introduction: dimensions of global militarization

Arms transfers are one dimension of global militarization along with others such as the horizontal spread of arms production, the growing number of military regimes (or regions controlled by the military), and dissolution of the state monopoly on violence manifested in the growth of subnational and transnational armed actors (for example, local guerrilla groups and international terrorist groups).

This paper explores the argument that global militarization is inherent in the present world order and that global structural changes consequently are a prerequisite for successful arms control, being one dimension of demilitarization. A structural analysis of conflict formation and conflict patterns tends to be deterministic and should be combined with more normative, voluntaristic and actor-oriented approaches in order to counter this bias and not lead to paralysis and pessimism.[1] Ultimately, structures are nothing but stable regularities in human behaviour, and one must believe that changes in these behavioural patterns are possible as their inherent destructiveness is revealed: not in the final holocaust, but in a more piecemeal fashion, which nevertheless can be traumatic.

According to the *SIPRI Yearbook 1986*, world military expenditures have reached $850 billion per annum, which means that a substantial part of the gross world product is being used for the creation of the means of destruction. This misallocation of resources contributes to the world economic crisis and strangles a number of national economies, at the same time as, for example, millions of Africans are facing starvation. For this reason it seems appropriate to speak of a new international 'anarchy' (in the sense of chaos) resulting from the disintegration of an old economic order, while the old military order remains largely intact. The military dominance of the two superpowers is overwhelming, and there is no way in which their military power could be challenged. However, their economic power is on the decrease and their normative power seems exhausted. This implies a leadership problem for both the capitalist and the socialist worlds. Therefore the conceptualization of the world as 'anarchic' has again become more relevant but perhaps rather as a description of a transition phase than as a way of understanding the international system as such. This transition phase is characterized by increasing tensions on various levels of the world system.

The global conflict pattern indicates underlying structural contradictions, even if not manifested in repeated wars among nations. The technology of collective violence and the sophistication of the means of destruction have tended to make countries that possess this technology avoid war among themselves but not necessarily intervention against countries which are less advanced in this respect.

This tendency to avoid war as a means of demonstrating strength is not a peace-factor in the positive sense of the term. Instead it leads to growing militarization on all levels of the world system. By 'militarization' is implied a multi-dimensional process containing phenomena such as rearmament, the growth of armed forces, an increasing role for the military in the decision-making process, an increasing role for force in conflict resolution, and the spread of militaristic values. In general, albeit somewhat simplistic terms, militarization is a process whereby the 'civilian' sphere is becoming increasingly militarized towards a state of excess, usually referred to as 'militarism'.

It is a fact that the greater number of developing countries have small imports in relative terms, and their rank order changes constantly. In spite of, or perhaps because of, the fact that most countries started from fairly modest military establishments after the break-up of the colonial system, it is (until recently) in the Third World that the most dynamic market, as far as conventional weapons are concerned, has been found. There is, for instance, a strong connection between the process of nation-state building and militarization; this is part of the explanation for Third World rearmament. However, there are also specific reasons which explain the unevenness of this process. The major share of military imports goes to the Middle East, not only because this region is particularly conflict-ridden but also because there is the money to buy the arms. However, since the early 1980s there has been an overall stagnating trend obviously related to the financial crisis.

Another important dimension of militarization is military influence on, or outright control of, political decision making. It is difficult to establish an overall trend in this respect, since there are contrasting trends in various regions owing to changing patterns of conflict and because repression and domestic political violence may characterize civilian as well as military regimes. Besides, the state monopoly on violence is loosening up as the disintegration of many nation-states continues in the Third World and the terrorist challenge in the industrialized world becomes increasingly serious. The militarization of political power is most visible in the Third World. Between 1960 and 1985, 138 successful military coups occurred. Of 78 independent Third World countries, 22 were under military-controlled governments in 1960. Fifteen years later there were 57 military-controlled out of 114 independent states.

Turning to the dynamics of global militarization, it is seen in the many mutually supportive links that exist between the various dimensions of militarization, which thus can be conceived of as a vicious circle. It is inherent in the intricacy of vicious circles that it is difficult to distinguish between causes and results. Increased tensions on various levels of the world system reinforce conventional security thinking ('realism') and in general strengthen the position of military establishments and the urge for rearmament. Production for military ends is today a high-technology area in a relatively small number of producers; and for the much larger number of importers, military hardware is inhibitively costly and a heavy drain on foreign currency reserves. What all this amounts to is an overall strengthening of the conventional 'mainstream' pattern of development which tends to generate more conflicts, military coups and militarization.

This paper is outlined as follows: the first section describes a structural approach (rather than an actor-oriented approach) to an understanding of the global conflict pattern. It is derived from the imperialism, dependency and world-system theory traditions in development studies as well as structural violence and dominance theory traditions in peace studies. The main objective is to provide an inventory and classification of conflicts that are inherent in the structure of the world system.

The following three sections analyse the specificity of the conflict pattern on three structural levels: the global, the regional and the national/subnational. On the global level the superpower relations, the question of hegemony and world order, and the meaning of the 'new' cold war are considered. On the regional level, the *eigen-dynamik* of regional conflicts versus the structural interpretation of the specific role of the region—and so-called regional powers in particular—in the world system as a whole is discussed. On the national/subnational level, various challenges to the nation-state coming both from the growing transnational web of relations and the simultaneous growth of ethno-regional identities are explored.

The final section discusses—rather tentatively—whether a regionalizaton of the world system might not be a firmer, or at least less unstable, foundation for peace than the 'interdependence' scenario.

II. A structural approach to international conflicts

The arms races on various levels of the world system are fed, but not necessarily created, by the cold war or the East–West conflict. We need to understand the total conflict pattern in the world in order to grasp the dynamics of the global arms race and the process of militarization. One way of structuring this problem is to relate various types of conflict to the world system model.

According to what has become known as World System Theory (WST) the capitalist world system first emerged in embryonic form in the 15th century, gradually incorporating a growing number of previously more or less isolated and self-sufficient societies into a complex whole of functional relations. As a result of this expansion, a limited number of *core states* transformed a huge *external arena* into a *periphery*. Between the core states and the periphery, the world system theorists identify *semi-peripheries*.[2]

Without necessarily adopting the WST in all its implications, the model seems to provide a useful framework and a taxonomy for comparing global conflicts and their impact on militarization. World system conflicts are basically of two types: (*a*) between the world system and the external arena, and (*b*) within the world system. The first type can be subdivided into (i) conflicts associated with the process of peripheralization (i.e., incorporation of external regions into the world system), and (ii) conflicts associated with attempts at breaking out and staying out of the system.

The second type can be subdivided into (iii) horizontal conflicts between states on the same structural level, and (iv) vertical conflicts between countries on different structural levels of the world system hierarchy. The horizontal category covers competition between state actors for the same structural space. The vertical category covers two closely related aspects: control and emancipation. Thus some of these vertical conflicts result from efforts to control states on a lower structural level, whereas other conflicts relate to ambitions of certain states to improve their position in the hierarchy and become so-called semi-peripheral states or core states. The different conflicts can be summarized as in figure 1.1.

The world system is not a static structure. There are both secular trends and cycles which maintain and transform the structure of the system. The secular trends are: the expansion of the size of the system; the interrelated increases in proletarianization, commodification and capital concentration; and the increase in mechanization.

The basic cyclical processes are: long waves of economic growth and stagnation; long-term cycles of the distribution of power among core states

Figure 1.1. Types of world system conflict

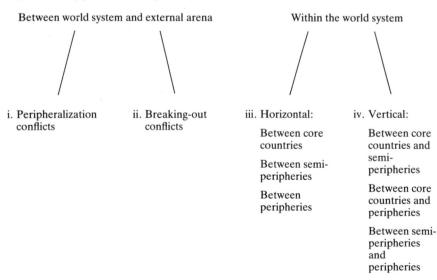

Between world system and external arena		Within the world system	
i. Peripheralization conflicts	ii. Breaking-out conflicts	iii. Horizontal:	iv. Vertical:
		Between core countries	Between core countries and semi-peripheries
		Between semi-peripheries	Between core countries and peripheries
		Between peripheries	Between semi-peripheries and peripheries

between periods of rivalry and hegemony; and alterations in the core–periphery control structure between colonial control and informal control. These cycles seem to be empirically correlated. Periods of economic stagnation lead to competition among core powers and more direct colonial-type controls. Thus the dynamics of the world system should also be related to conflicts. We shall return to this in the following sections, which deal with the specificity of each level in terms of its conflict potential.

It is a well-established fact that there is a strong causal link between the structure of the world system and war. Peter Wallensteen, in a study of wars between 1920 and 1968, found that the typical war, particularly after World War II, was that of a core country intervening in a peripheral country and, furthermore, a peripheral country forming part of the sphere of interest of the core country in question. Istvan Kende, who made a statistical analysis of wars during 1945–70, termed these 'local wars'.[3] This has been the typical kind of war after 1945. This picture is certainly not contradicted by the development of the 'new' cold war since the late 1970s, with even stronger military control over the spheres of interest of respective superpowers and the interventions in Afghanistan and Grenada.

The relationship between the structure of the world system and the pattern of global conflicts can of course not be understood in static analysis. It could be concluded from such an analysis that certain structural positions imply a conflict potential, but it is only when the processes of change are included in the analysis that the understanding of how conflicts are generated is really enhanced.

Recently there has, for instance, been a new interest in the cycles of war, a depressing subject since the recurrence of such a cycle in the future spells the end of human civilization. However, without being deterministic, it is legitimate to ask what problems the present global security arrangement may face in the future. The basic question in cycles of war seems to be changes in hegemonic power—the capability of a great power or a political bloc of powers to impose their order upon the world system. It is the displacement process that gives rise to major wars.[4]

Moving downwards to the regional level of the world system, there are good arguments for dealing with regional security as an issue in itself, but from the point of world system theory the semi-peripheral countries (which typically are prominent in a certain region) fulfil specific functions in the world system, and therefore conflicts on this level are also essentially world system conflicts.

There are recent wars that can be seen as manifestations of vertical and horizontal regional types of structural conflicts: the Falkland/Malvinas War and the war between Iran and Iraq. Conflicts over the same structural and geographical space tend to be particularly serious, illustrated by the Iraq–Iran War. The war between the United Kingdom and Argentina can be seen as a challenge from a semi-peripheral state against a core country declining from its previous structural position.

On the third of the three levels, the national one, many conflicts are also world system-related since the nation-states constitute the building-blocks of the world system. The fact that WST rejects the state-centred tradition in the study of international relations in no way diminishes the role of the nation-states for the functioning of the world system. The problem here is precisely to what extent the nation-states actually are nation-states in any meaningful sense of the word. The role that states can play in the world system, the position they can take in its hierarchical structure, is a function of their internal coherence. In most countries there are contradictions between state and people owing to the vulnerability of peripheral state formations. These contradictions are further reinforced by external shocks, as a result of the *modus operandi* of the world system.

Different patterns of development create different tensions and conflicts, which in turn have an impact on the organized violence or the role of force. Taking the point of departure in the world system approach presented above, a distinction could be made between: (*a*) attempts to gain an improved position within the capitalist world system, and (*b*) attempts to break out of or at least reduce the dependence on the capitalist world system. Among the countries trying to improve their position within the capitalist world system, it is possible to distinguish between two different strategies: (*a*) the strategy of seizing the chance, and (*b*) the strategy of promotion by invitation. Among the countries trying to reduce their dependence on the capitalist market, it is also possible to distinguish between two different strategies: (*a*) the strategy of self-reliance and non-alignment, and (*b*) the strategy of orientation towards the socialist bloc.

Different patterns of development are related to different forms of violence. Development strategies aiming at improving a country's position in the capitalist world economy create tensions and conflict of both an external and internal nature. The fact that not all countries can 'seize the chance' or successfully invite foreign capital tends to establish a certain amount of rivalry between countries. This is most obvious in the case of 'seizing the chance' which implies very active state action. Capitalist development also creates internal social inequalities and, consequently, increased political tension. In the case of 'promotion by invitation' the political stability required to attract foreign capital makes the role of force crucial, particularly within the country. Self-reliant strategies also create internal and external violence in spite of their inward orientation, simply because they challenge the world order and the hegemony which defines the rules of the game—the principles under which economic transactions take place.

III.   The new cold war and the question of hegemony

The most crucial level of the world system is naturally the world level, since the general rules of transactions and interactions are set by the main hegemonic power. During the post-war world order this power has been the United States. The decline of hegemonic power implies growing disorder and increased opportunities for conflicts on other levels of the world system to manifest themselves more openly. This is not necessarily a negative development, but, as was pointed out above, the decline of hegemonic power and ensuing succession struggles also mean that the risks of war are increasing. There have been several such 'drop-out contests': Spain and Portugal were replaced by the Netherlands; subsequently England took its place and entered a successful hegemonic contest with France; and towards the end of the 19th century FR Germany and the United States emerged as new challengers. Today, the Soviet Union is challenging the USA, but Soviet-based hegemonic power could hardly be seen as comprehensive enough. According to Senghaas, 'we are presently living in a time in which it might be possible to interrupt the hitherto existing cycles of major wars and periods of hegemonic peace; e.g. we are living in a time of structural change which implies considerable dangers for peace as well as new chances for a new international order'.[5]

The concept of hegemony is an ambiguous one, and in spite of its recent popularity it is very often left undefined.[6] One reason for this is the unfortunate gap between political and economic analysis in the social sciences. Implied in most discussions on hegemony is the understanding that both economic strength and military power (and also often ideological or normative power) make up hegemonic status; but in spite of this, most analyses approach hegemony from one angle or the other. It seems necessary to distinguish between different dimensions of hegemony, since they may undergo changes independently of each other. A further problem is the lack of empirical cases to draw on. Strictly speaking, there are only two phases of hegemony in modern capitalism—the British and the US—and there are more similarities than differences between the two. What is relevant in this context is that British hegemony had a stronger economic content, whereas the US ambition to defend and expand what was called 'the free world' (precisely that area within which US hegemony counted) also contained strong security considerations. The USA faces a challenge from an alternative socio-economic system, established by the Soviet Union. Soviet world hegemony would therefore imply a revolutionary change of the world system. Much of the current security debate is centred on the question of whether the Soviet Union is attempting to achieve hegemony. If this is not the case, one could argue that the USA exploits the communist threat in order to maintain its hegemony and rationalize interventions made to this effect. The same accusation could be made against the Soviet Union for its maintenance of hegemony within the socio-economic system of its own creation. In terms of arms transfers, hegemony implies centralized control which does not exclude arms transfers but subsumes this diffusion under the hegemonic interest. In a transitional phase, the whole process of arms production and arms transfers tends to get out of control owing to the relative political autonomy of other levels in the world system hierarchy, particularly the semi-peripheral level where indigenous arms production tends to emerge.

There is a complex connection between the decline of US hegemony and the decline of détente, which is the same as the rise of the 'new' cold war from 1979 onwards.[7] The reasons for this change in the international climate are still under debate. To list a number of relevant factors is one thing; to specify their relative importance is another. Furthermore, the continuity versus discontinuity between the two cold wars raises problems. *This reflects two different phases in the structural evolution of the world system.* Of relevance here is the catching up of Western Europe and Japan with the United States, the increasing economic relations between Eastern and Western Europe, and the growing restlessness among the Soviet allies in the WTO. The increasing tensions were therefore not only related to East–West rivalry but also to intra-bloc tensions, creating a need for the superpowers to insist on discipline. The best argument for this is of course the threat posed by the opposite bloc.

Thus the most obvious difference between the 'old' cold war of the 1950s and the 'new' one of the 1980s is that, whereas both the USSR and the USA were after World War II on the move towards hegemony and therefore perceived each other as competitors, today they are in a process of decline and therefore fear that one of them will 'bury' the other.

What then is the reason for the decline of superpower hegemony? The two powers are not materially or militarily weaker in any absolute way, but rather the structure of the world system, in which the two superpowers have had hegemonic power, is changing—a change that implies a weakening of their structural position and, by implication, their economic and ideological normative hegemony.

The manifestations of the 'new' cold war, as far as the superpowers are concerned, are rearmament, ideological fundamentalism, political pressure on allied countries and intensified struggle for influence in the non-aligned countries. This is not really a new policy, but rather a sudden accentuation of existing contradictions, caused by underlying structural changes. Thus, the weakened economic and political position resulting from these changes is compensated for by rearmament and military adventurism.

Since both superpowers tend to identify their own interests with the two political blocs they control, they have also put pressure on the allies to rearm. In the case of the Warsaw Pact this has been most forcefully resisted by Romania. However, all Warsaw Pact countries are for economic reasons very reluctant to spend more money on arms. More or less the same attitude is prevalent among the European NATO countries towards US proposals that Western Europe assume more responsibility for its own defence—and of course a greater part of the cost burden.

There are also cases where the USA has exerted pressure on other countries in sensitive regions to militarize, for example, in the two cases (the only two) of relatively demilitarized societies, Japan and Costa Rica. Japan had until recently a long tradition of spending less than 1 per cent of its gross national product (GNP) on defence. However, since Japan has initiated larger weapon procurement programmes, its defence expenditure will increase in the 1980s.

Officially the USA has made it clear that Japan must decide about its defence, but it is no secret that the USA would like Japan to do better.

The case of Costa Rica is more flagrant since the country is—in a more or less clandestine way—encouraged not only to increase its very low military budget (formally it has no army) but also to abandon its traditional neutrality.

Thus the East–West conflict is a major factor behind global militarization. The reliance on coercive power (relative to remunerative and normative power) is more evident in the case of the Soviet Union, and its leaders are therefore particularly sensitive about perceived changes in the military balance of power. The sources for global militarization are manifold, and it is not possible to explain them only by reference to the superpower conflict. There are at least two more important underlying causes: regional conflicts that are (more or less) independent of the superpower struggle, and political decay leading to the breakdown of states. There are two major reasons to focus on these levels: first, because future drop-out contests are unlikely, simply because there are no strong contenders for hegemonic power in the foreseeable future. A hegemonic war would in any case imply destruction of the present world system. The second reason is that the decline of hegemonic power would increase the relative autonomy of other hierarchical levels. Therefore, it is important to investigate the specificity of these levels in terms of conflict potential.

IV.   Regional conflicts and regional powers

There has been a recent growing interest in regional security and regional conflicts as a specialized field of academic interest. How autonomous are regional conflicts? And, depending on the answer to this question, how important is the region as a political arena for conflict resolution and arms control?

The relative autonomy of the regional level of course differs. For example, in the drawn-out war between Iran and Iraq no external power seems interested in victory for either of the belligerents. In the conflicts in Southern Africa, South Africa is basically acting on its own through destabilization and clandestine warfare. In the conflicts in South Asia and South–East Asia, the USA, the USSR and China are heavily involved, but one could still say that the basic dynamics of the conflict are the relations between the countries in the region. In the case of Central America the regional conflict is more related to the internal breakdown of the states. The fact that governments in the area are rejected by the populations disturbs the political relations between the countries and presents a security problem for the USA, whose involvement further intensifies the regional conflict.

The internal crises in Third World countries often have external implications, because international relations are still based on the inter-state system. Very strong conservative forces are released to preserve this system as soon as it is threatened. Therefore there are, so far, few examples of national disintegration leading to the creation of new political formations. Bangladesh is one example. Lebanon may be difficult to reconstruct. Eritrea will hardly be reconquered. However, all these conflicts constitute threats to the regions concerned.

It has been argued that 'the lack of a stronger sense of regional security subsystems is a major weakness in contemporary analyses of international relations'.[8] It is true that there is a tendency to concentrate either on the global system level or the national level. However, emphasizing the regional level is not the same as granting it autonomy in terms of conflict generation or conflict solution. Rather, the problem is to understand the interrelations between general world system dynamics and the specific security problems on each level. To start from both ends is one way of avoiding the determinism inherent in cruder forms of world system analysis.

As Väyrynen points out, the world system imposes homogeneity and at the same time heterogeneity on regional subsystems because various subsystems are located in different structural positions.[9] Furthermore, these regional subsystems are influenced by both national and sub-national factors. Thus a region constitutes a vertical structure of domination in which the top-dog position is occupied by semi-peripheral countries or regional powers. The mode of domination tends to be politico-military since the economic division of labour in most regional subsystems is still underdeveloped (in contrast to the world division of labour). This also implies certain constraints as far as autonomous conflict resolution within the respective regions is concerned.

A second problem in this regard is the fact that the regionally dominant powers are usually considered as threatening rather than helpful leaders. South Africa is of course the extreme example, but even a case like India illustrates that a regional power tends, much to its own surprise, to instil fear and suspicion in the smaller nations within the region. Nevertheless, stronger regional autonomy and conflict resolution capability may offer a route to a more stable peace for the world system at large. The Contadora experiment is an illustration of both the possibilities and the problems involved. Let us now take a closer look at the most crucial actor in the regional context: the regional power.

Some regional powers base their new status on strategic resources, others on successful experiments in export-led industrialization, while a third category combines one or both of these criteria with a powerful position within their own region, due to geographical size and/or military capacity. It is therefore to be expected that future powerful nations are to be found among countries combining all three criteria.

A semi-periphery holds an intermediate position in the world economy and is conceived as a stabilizing force, since a world system consisting of only core and periphery would be more polarized. This is true as long as we are dealing with a stable world order. However, the stability is not permanent. The intermediate category consists of very different types of countries, some on their way down from a previous core position, others working themselves up from a previous peripheral position. With declining hegemonic power, the relative autonomy of the regional level will increase, and semi-peripheral countries will struggle among themselves and challenge core countries.

These positional shifts within the structure of the world system are its most dynamic feature. They are, also a highly destabilizing element, since they constantly challenge the status quo. They are, furthermore, crucially related to authoritarian tendencies within the states. Since semi-peripheral states are the most heterogeneous category, it is necessary to find relevant criteria for structuring this group in a meaningful way. Arms production capacity is, for example, one important criterion for semi-peripheral status. Consequently, moves towards establishing indigenous arms production indicate ambitions towards such a status.

Thus a secular strengthening of regional powers within their regional context and a relative decline in superpower control over sensitive regions seem to be inherent in the present transformation of the world system. The scenario of superpower control through regional powers ('sub-imperialism') may not have lost its relevance but cannot be regarded as a stable situation in most regions. Regional 'security complexes' will rather have a dynamic of their own. In the absence of stable regional orders, there will be regional arms races that are more or less independent of conflicts on the world level.

V. The weakening of the nation-state and the rise of ethnopolitics

Conventional security theory is based on the integrity and permanence of the nation-state and on the idea of balance in an inter-state system made up of sovereign states. Today the sovereignty of the nation-state is threatened by external and internal forces. The challenge to the nation-state is not uniform. There are different types of challenge and different types of vulnerability as far as the states are concerned. In this context we are mainly interested in changes with implications for Third World arms control.

Arms control presupposes an agreement or at least an understanding between states. The state monopoly over violence and the means of destruction is taken for granted. To the extent that this monopoly is broken, the whole issue of arms control looks very different. This can, for instance, be seen in the phenomenon of international terrorism.

Of greater importance with respect to the quantitative impact on arms transfers is the growing ethno-regional identification in most parts of the world.

From the Canadian glaciers across to the moors of Britain and to the high Pyrenees, down through the broad belt of Black Africa, the arid hills of Turkey, Iraq, and the southern USSR to the riverbanks and deltas of South Asia, *peoples* are challenging *nation-states*. In one of the most perplexing trends of the second half of the 20th Century governments are being hounded, cajoled, and defied by minorities within their societies—by ethnonationalism.[10]

Max Weber once gave the classic definition of the state as 'a human community that [successfully] claims the monopoly of the legitimate use of physical force within a given territory'.[11] In many parts of the Third World the process of state-formation and nation-building (mistakenly viewed as a sort of 'natural history' in conventional social science) has been arrested and replaced by a disintegrative tendency, so marked that the future of the nation-state as a mode of political organization cannot be taken entirely for granted. It is true that the separatist ethnic struggle usually aims at establishing a new state carved from the territory of the old, but more often the struggle ends up in a stalemate that is devastating for the effectiveness of state power.

The reason why so few states have actually broken down is precisely because the world is organized as an inter-state system and because conventional security doctrine stresses the need to maintain territorial integrity in order not to be swallowed up by stronger state formations. Military defence towards the external world and firm control over the domestic territory are the twin principles of state survival. In fact, adherence to these principles may speed up the disintegration process, as the survival of the state (an abstract expression for what more often is the survival of the ruling elite) becomes the dominant concern, leading to repression and the militarization of society. As physical force erodes and gradually replaces legitimacy and national identification as the cohesive factor, the disintegration of the state has already been initiated and becomes a vicious circle. The repressive machinery of the state fights the domestic challengers with the same determination as if it were under foreign attack. The distinction between internal and external security can no longer be maintained. This is of course particularly true when the ethnic conflict becomes internationalized, which is what usually happens. In fact the internationalization of ethnic conflict is a logical continuation of the process of politicization of ethnicity, since the latter process implies a polarization which necessarily has an impact on the country's external relations. The ethnic group that is threatened by genocide may have ethnic relatives in neighbouring countries, and the conflict is easily manipulated for destabilization purposes. Very few ethnic conflicts, if any, are without international implications—primarily for regional security but also as a possible battleground in the cold war. If the ethnic challenge to the existing system of nation-states is assuming increasingly greater importance, which seems to be the case, the prospects for arms control are slim.

A clear distinction must be made between two forms of domestic unrest: *ethnic conflicts*, representing a horizontal challenge to the state, and *class conflicts*, representing a vertical cleavage and challenging the state only in certain respects. A social revolution implies changes in the *form* of the state, as expressed in its concrete institutional manifestations, whereas the ethno-nationalist challenge concerns the very *idea* and essence of the state. The security implications of these two forms of domestic unrest are different, as are the implications for arms control. The social conflict is the one that most easily becomes part of the global East–West conflict, whereas the ethnic conflict has a more distinct regional quality. Its impact on regional security depends on the nature of the 'ethnic balance'. This point requires some elaboration.

Ethnic identity has many sources, and there are always different levels of identity where the crucial boundaries are drawn. The crystallization of mobilized ethnicity (the *an sich* to *für sich* transition) is furthermore historically and contextually determined. The elusiveness of ethnic conflict, however, does not imply that a structural analysis lacks meaning. There are certain patterns of ethnic stratification which are important for understanding the conflict dynamics.[12]

Some important patterns are: (*a*) a politically dominant majority versus a subordinate minority (Sinhalese vs. Tamils in Sri Lanka); (*b*) a politically dominant minority versus a subordinate majority (whites vs. blacks in South Africa); (*c*) a dominant core versus an aggregation of minorities (the Hindu belt vs. minorities in India); (*d*) a balance between one politically and another economically dominant group (Malays vs. Chinese in Malaysia); and (*e*) a politically dominant group versus an economically strong 'pariah' minority (Africans vs. Indians in East Africa).

While this list is not exhaustive, it does illustrate the way in which patterns of ethnic stratification shape the dynamics of conflict. The first pattern is explosive to the extent that the subordinate minority can count on support from outside—not an uncommon situation. The second is even more explosive if the minority is well armed and believes in a 'civilizing mission'. The third assumes balancing skill on the part of the state, in the absence of which it easily gets transformed into a pattern of the first type, but with several subordinated minorities. Neither is the fourth pattern stable, since those who control the state would like to control the economy as well. The fifth usually leads to expulsion and mass emigration, since the economically strong minority has the resources to move and is small enough to make migration a viable if not an unproblematic solution.

These types of conflict and the structural patterns which shape their dynamics are obviously on the increase. Their roots lie in the historical development of the world system, but the contradictions that trigger them must be sought on the lower levels of the system outside the scope of superpower control. This also indicates where the solutions are to be found.

VI.   The rationale and prospects for a regionalized world system

In this final section a more constructivistic approach is chosen, though without shifting from a structural to an actor's perspective (which in fact would be necessary to get a full picture of the possibilities for a more peaceful world in general and for arms control in particular). From a structural perspective, the armament process is a function of conflicts that are inherent in the structure of the world system—or 'structural violence', as peace researchers would say. To the extent that the world system is a real system, that is, if there is a high degree of interdependence within the system, different types of structural conflict also become interdependent, thus creating an explosive situation in the world system as a whole.

This argument may be countered by the more optimistic 'interdependence' thesis, suggesting that all countries—whether rich or poor—benefit from increasing economic relations in that part of the world economy where allocation takes place in accordance with the market principle. The point is that the mutual vulnerabilities implied in a situation of interdependence would make peaceful behaviour among states rational. However, there is a whole tradition of dependency literature which denies that this is the case. Even if there are cases of successful adaptation to the global marketplace, which cannot be explained from a rigid dependency position, the overwhelming number of poor countries fail to so adapt.[13] Thus the argument that there is an incompatibility between interests of North and South seems to be stronger than the interdependence argument.[14] Whether the latter argument makes better sense with regard to East–West relations is a different matter and the answer less obvious. It depends on whether the domestic political situation in the socialist countries at present is stable enough to absorb external stocks. Evidently there is a need for internal reforms in these countries before they can open up their economies to any significant degree. Poland illustrates the problem, but there is no uniform situation among the socialist countries. For instance, Hungary and Poland are both intertwined with West European economies, but the shock-absorption capacity of the former is obviously greater. The North–South relation is thus more illustrative with regard to structural violence.

War is one way of exercising power and, as noted above, there is a strong correlation between structural topdog–underdog relations and manifest overt conflicts. However, a situation of structural dependency and weak peripheral state structures can also be used to exercise power and influence without the use of direct violence. This method is called *destabilization*.

Because of the secret nature of destabilization, it is difficult to point out confirmed cases. The most well-known case, and something of a model, is of course Chile under Allende. Other Latin American cases that are reasonably clear are Peru (1968–76), Jamaica (1975–80), Grenada (1979–83) and Nicaragua (1979–   ). In the cases of Grenada and Nicaragua, the destabilization policy gradually changed from structural violence to direct violence. Looking closer at these countries it is evident that they had something in common. They all tried to pursue policies of self-reliance. Thus there seems to be a logical connection between self-reliance and destabilization. In fact all types of development strategies have security implications, and the issues of peace and development are therefore closely related. However, the actual relationship is often conceived in a simplistic way.

The unsuccessful attempts at self-reliant development can be explained by the overwhelming difficulties for a single country to break out of the system and restructure the internal economy in a situation of external hostility and internal opposition. Restructuring is of course not possible without opposition since all significant changes of a social structure imply that some groups gain while others lose. If self-reliance shall succeed it must be realized on several levels of the world system simultaneously, which implies a systemic change of the system as such, starting with a process of regionalization.

In this process Europe plays the key role since the division of Europe is by far the most important manifestation of East–West conflict, even if similar divisions can be found in most other regions of the world. But in most cases the East–West conflict is mixed with other conflicts that are specific to the respective regions, whereas in Europe the East–West or superpower conflict is basic. In fact, the superpower status of both the USA and the USSR presupposes the subordination of Europe. Therefore an autonomous Europe (the great obstacles in its way are recognized) implies a regionalization of the superpowers (i.e., they will be reduced to regional powers) and a step towards a regionalized world without world powers.

It will of course be a world with regional powers which probably will pose a threat in their respective regions. It could, nevertheless, be a less explosive situation for the world as a whole. Furthermore, self-reliance and autonomy (of a selective kind) cannot be confined to the regional level but must characterize the nation-state and sub-national levels as well. At present the states in many parts of the world are weak because they respond to the ethno-regional challenge with desperate violence. Only by accommodating these interests through the development of federal political structures with a high degree of autonomy can these states remain viable units. This may sound utopian, but the ethno-regional challenge is nevertheless a reality which cannot be wished away. The response can be either political reforms or civil wars. Reforms require viable states (in the sense that they are more legitimate), and viable states are necessary for comprehensive regional co-operation. Civil wars and disintegration of nation-states are, on the other hand, a threat to an interdependent world system.

A regionalized world system is not compatible with a liberal world economy but would need a kind of (benign) mercantilist economic structure. Many would instinctively associate mercantilism with a more war-prone system whereas liberal economics is conventionally assumed to be particularly peaceful. The relationship between security system and economic system is much too complicated to be so simplistically explained.[15] The prevalent social paradigms of peace and development are of course not unrelated to the post-war global power structure. Therefore neo-mercantilist arguments are dismissed by the conventional wisdom of the academic world and outside. However, neo-mercantilist solutions to the problem of security and welfare have never been tried constructively but have only appeared as destructive components in an already chaotic and disintegrating order, ultimately caused by the inherent instability of a liberal world economy. A regionalized world system would, so far as arms control is concerned, be preferable to a polarized system which has a tendency to break down. Today arms control is to ask the wolves to act as shepherds.

Notes and references

[1] For a more comprehensive discussion, see Hettne, B., *Approaches to the Study of Peace and Development. A State of the Art Report*, EADI Working Papers no. 6, Tilburg, 1984.

[2] Wallerstein, I. M., *The Modern World-System: Capitalist Agriculture and the Origins of the European World Economy in the Sixteenth Century* (Academic Press: New York, 1974); Wallerstein, I. M., *The Capitalist World Economy* (Cambridge University Press: Cambridge, 1979); 'The future of the world economy', T. Hopkins and I. Wallerstein (eds), *Processes of the World System* (Sage Publications: Beverly Hills, 1980).

[3] Wallensteen, P., *Structure and War: On International Relations 1920–1968* (Rabén & Sjögren: Stockholm, 1973); Kende, I., 'Twenty-five years of local war', *Journal of Peace Research*, no. 1 (1971).

[4] Modelski, G., 'The long cycle of global politics and the nation-state', *Comparative Studies in Society and History*, vol. 20 (Apr. 1978).

[5] Senghaas, D., 'The cycles of war and peace', *Bulletin of Peace Proposals*, vol. 14, no. 2 (1983).

[6] See the discussion in Mjøset, L., *Developments in the Postwar World Economy: 1. The Rise of US Hegemony*, PRIO Working Paper 15/1983, Oslo, Norway.

[7] Halliday, F., 'The new cold war', *Bulletin of Peace Proposals*, vol. 14, no. 2 (1983).

[8] Buzan, B. and Rizvi, G. et al., *South Asian Insecurity and the Great Powers* (Macmillan: London, 1986).

[9] Väyrynen, R., 'Regional conflict formations, an intractable problem of international relations', *Journal of Peace Research*, vol. 21, pp. 337–59.

[10] Shiels, F. L., *Ethnic Separatism and World Politics* (University Press of America: Lanham, 1984), p. 1.

[11] Geerth, H. H. and Mills, C. W., *From Max Weber: Essays in Sociology* (Routledge & Kegan Paul: London and Boston, 1970), pp. 77–79.

[12] Rothschild, J., *Ethnopolitics, A Conceptual Framework* (Columbia University Press: New York, 1981).

[13] Blomström, M. and Hettne, B., *Development Theory in Transition. The Dependency Debate & Beyond: Third World Responses* (ZED Books: London, 1984).

[14] For this argument, see Krasner, S. D., *Structural Conflict: The Third World Against Global Liberalism* (University of California Press: Berkeley, 1985).

[15] Buzan, B., 'Economic structure and international security', *International Organization*, vol. 38, no. 4 (1984).

Paper 2.   Third World arms control in a hegemonistic world

K. SUBRAHMANYAM

I.   Introduction

The international system today consists of 159 nations. Of these, 126 nations are categorized as Third World nations. Around 80 per cent of these are decolonized nations which have become sovereign over the past 40 years—especially in the past 25 years. In the international community 37 nations have populations of 1–5 million, and 35 have less than 1 million each. Of these 72 nations, barring five, the rest are Third World nations at various stages of development. Of more than 170 major inter- and intra-state conflicts that have occurred since the end of World War II, over 160 have occurred in the developing world.[1] Major regional conflicts are taking place today in Central America, Western Sahara, Southern Africa, West Asia, South-West Asia (the Iraq–Iran War and Afghanistan) and South-East Asia. In addition, there are insurgencies in the territories of a number of Third World countries. As an illustration, there are ongoing insurgencies in Burma, Indonesia (East Timor), Malaysia, the Philippines, Thailand, Angola, Chad, Ethiopia, Mozambique, Sudan, Uganda, Bolivia and Peru. In other words, the Third World consists largely of recently decolonized, relatively small or weak nations, still in the process of evolution as nation-states in an overall atmosphere of turbulence and insecurity. Half of the developing nations can be categorized as small, mini and micro states.

II.   Analysis of military expenditure in the developing world

According to the *SIPRI Yearbook 1986*, the industrial market economies (20 nations) accounted for 53.1 per cent of the world's military expenditure, and the non-market economies (12 nations) for 29.6 per cent. The share of the major oil-exporting countries (11 nations) was 8.2 per cent and that of the rest of the world (116 nations) was 9.0 per cent. In the last category of nations, the military expenditures of only 12 nations (Egypt, Syria, India, Pakistan, South Korea, Malaysia, Taiwan, Thailand, Argentina, Brazil, Chile and Peru) account for 55 per cent of that share. South Africa, Israel and Viet Nam—which are not included in the above category—account for approximately 15 per cent, and the balance of 100 nations incur around 30 per cent of the 9.0 per cent share of world military expenditures. Therefore, when mention is made of growth in Third World military expenditure, the reference is to the 11 oil-exporting nations and the 12 developing nations listed above plus North Korea and Viet Nam. Given that South Africa and Israel are classifiable as developing nations—which is debatable—they should also be included.

In this study, we are primarily concerned with high military expenditures and arms production and imports. We are not dealing here with militarization in Third World countries. A country can be under military rule or have a government dominated by the military without incurring high military expenditure or having significant arms production or imports. Imposition of military rule and sustaining it do not require such very sophisticated armaments as multi-role fighter aircraft, ships, submarines, tanks, medium guns and missiles. Machine-guns and armoured personnel carriers are the most effective means employed for keeping populations subjugated by the military.

Therefore, any study of Third World arms control has to focus on 26 countries—Argentina, Brazil, Chile, Cuba, Egypt, India, Indonesia, Iran, Iraq, Israel, Kuwait, North Korea, South Korea, Malaysia, Nigeria, Oman, Pakistan, Peru, Saudi Arabia, South Africa, Syria, Taiwan, Thailand, the United Arab Emirates, Venezuela and Viet Nam—which spend more than $1 billion each on annual defence expenditure. There is a clustering pattern among these high defence-spending countries. Argentina, Brazil and Chile form one cluster. Egypt, Israel, Syria and Saudi Arabia form another. Iran, Iraq, Kuwait, Oman, Saudi Arabia and the United Arab Emirates form a third. Thailand, Viet Nam, Indonesia and Malaysia constitute a fourth. Another notable feature is high defence spending by nations which have emerged out of a partition—North and South Korea, Taiwan, and India and Pakistan. Except for Brazil, Chile, Peru and Venezuela, all the other nations listed above have been involved in major wars or are situated very close to war zones, or have had to fight major civil wars or face a threat from a great power. It is therefore difficult to maintain that arms acquisitions by these countries are for prestige purposes and are not directly related to the security threats they actually face. Except for the cases of the four Latin American countries mentioned above plus Argentina—which is involved in a decolonization dispute—and Nigeria, the other 18 developing nations have security problems arising out of either direct confrontation with the great powers of the world (Taiwan *vis-à-vis* the USA, India *vis-à-vis* China) or interaction between great-power interplay and the local conflict situations (North–South Korea, South-East Asia, West Asia and South-West Asia). In the Western strategic literature there is a trend to underestimate the sense of insecurity of developing nations which have been involved in wars in the recent period, while accepting the sense of insecurity among the rival blocs of industrialized nations which have not had a war for more than 40 years and the leaders of which have not fought a war in all of history except for a minor clash in 1918.

III.   Regional conflicts and great-power confrontation

The linkages between the major-power confrontation and the conflict situations in the developing world are well established. Dr Brzezinski talked of SALT II lying buried in the sands of Ogaden.[2] Both at the 1986 Geneva summit and the recent Reykjavik talks, the USA tended to give as much importance to regional conflicts as to arms control between the two major military blocs. The Chinese leader Deng Xiaoping considered the Kampuchean situation as the most important obstacle to the improvement of relations between the USSR and China—more important than even the reduction of Soviet forces in Mongolia and along the Chinese border.[3] Even as SALT II was being successfully negotiated, the talks between the USA and the USSR on the transfer of conventional arms to Third World countries and deployment of navies in the Indian Ocean area failed.[4] It is therefore obvious that arms control in the Third World cannot be considered in isolation from the interaction and rivalry among the global powers in various parts of the world and the policies they pursue. There is no region in the world where the great powers are prepared to concede that they have no interests and where they will adopt a policy of mutual restraint and total non-interventionism. Successive US Administrations have highlighted that the most important difference with the USSR relates to the lack of responsible behaviour on the part of the latter in maintaining the international system, especially in the developing world.[5]

IV.   Arms control in the developing world

In these circumstances, problems of arms control in the Third World are different from those arising between the two structured alliances headed by the two great powers (the USA and the USSR) which carry out defence research and development (R&D) on the frontiers of technology and which can conclude agreements without any external factors impinging on them or influencing them. In the case of the developing nations, any arms control agreement would have to take into account not merely the local arms balance as it exists in a particular situation but the impact of policies likely to be adopted by the great powers. It is difficult to imagine a local arms control agreement in West Asia without the involvement of the great powers. One of the reasons why the Camp David process did not lead to stabilization in the Middle East was the exclusion of one great power (the USSR) from the process.

Unlike the relationship between the central great-power adversary systems, which is currently uni-dimensional, some developing countries face security problems in more than one direction. Egypt has to take into account both Israel and Libya. Pakistan has Afghanistan, Iran and India to consider. In the Indian view the country has to provide for threats from China and Pakistan. Viet Nam, too, faces a two-front situation. While confidence-building measures are certainly feasible, limited to one or the other or both fronts, comprehensive arms control measures—limiting the overall sizes of the forces and the nature, types and numbers of weapons to be acquired between two adversaries facing multiple threat problems—are much more complex than the negotiations between the two major alliances in Europe.

After all, the history of arms control between the two alliance systems in Europe, which are in a position to negotiate without unduly worrying about extraneous factors, has not been very confidence inspiring. While they were able to reach agreements on strategic arms (with their enormous capabilities for national means of verification), they have not been able to do so in respect of conventional forces. One wonders whether there is not an element of patronization in the advocacy of arms control among the Third World countries which have experienced recent wars and which are not able to act without worrying about external factors, by those who are unable to achieve arms control agreements in respect of conventional arms even after more than 40 years of peace.

V.   Arms transfers to the developing world

All the developing nations have to varying degrees to depend on imports of armaments from the arms producers in the industrialized world. Although a few developing countries have started producing armaments, the overwhelming proportion of arms trade with the developing world originates in the industrialized world. In discussing armament control in the developing world one faces a problem somewhat akin to drug control. In some quarters it has become fashionable to take the easy way out and preach that young people who are exposed to the lure of drugs should simply say 'no'. The more pragmatic line is to attempt to destroy or at least constrict the sources of supply. Society holds drug pushers more responsible than the victims—the users. In the arms trade, too, one has to concentrate more attention on arms pushers, their *modus operandi* and motivations. Unfortunately, an ever-increasing amount of literature on the subject tends to be devoted exclusively to the demand side.

Most of the Third World arms producers are not original designers of equipment but are beneficiaries of licences made available by the armament firms in the developed world. The *SIPRI Yearbook 1986* chapter on military R&D does not list any of the arms-producing developing countries listed above, except for India, as having significant military R&D. It lists the heavy involvement of armaments firms from the USA, the FRG, the UK and France in licensing subsystems for the Brazilian Tucano aircraft and the Osorio tank.[6] North Korean and Egyptian arms production is based on Soviet designs, and their export performance is linked to Iraqi demands for Soviet-designed weapons and ammunition in the ongoing Iraq–Iran War. Brazil, Singapore, South Korea and Taiwan export equipment and ammunition produced under licences obtained from the major Western industrial countries. In effect, this is an offshoot of the arms export policies of the industrialized countries and cannot be considered an independent phenomenon at this stage.

The demand for armaments from the major military spenders of the developing world often results from two externally generated stimuli. First, there is the cycle of modernization in conventional weapons that occurs every 15–20 years in the industrialized countries. The high military R&D spending in the industrialized world is the main engine driving this cycle of modernization of weaponry. As and when new generations of conventional weaponry are introduced into the developed countries of the world, this poses a dilemma for the middle powers in the developing world which incur significant military expenditure. As pointed out, these countries are in clusters in areas of high tension and mutual suspicion and where wars frequently occur. The normal expectation is that—whether it is on the initiative of an advanced industrialized supplier country or of an industrializing recipient country of the region—the new advanced equipment will sooner or later come into the area. Such a diffusion of advanced-technology weapons cannot, however, take place without the industrialized supplier's active consent. The higher the technology and sophistication, the greater are the controls on arms transfers. For the recipient nations, the earlier the new equipment is inducted into the armed forces, the longer will be the period of currency of the equipment before it becomes obsolescent. This is an external stimulus arising from the pace of technological advancement.

The second stimulus is one imparted by arms transfers on a selective basis to a particular country in a region of tension by a major industrial power in pursuit of certain policy aims. For instance, it appears to be a policy of the USA to ensure supply of high-technology weapons to Israel to enable it to maintain a distinct margin of superiority over its Arab neighbours, though this is often rationalized as sustaining an *existing* balance which has been in favour of Israel for the past three decades. This compels the Arab states around Israel to seek sophisticated arms either from the USA or, if that is not possible, from the USSR or West European countries. Similarly, the supply of sophisticated arms to the Shah of Iran stimulated the demand for weapons of analogous levels of technology from Iraq, Saudi Arabia and other Gulf states.

Current reports about the impending US supply of airborne warning and control system (AWACS) aircraft to Pakistan fall into the same category of externally induced arms competition, since India will be compelled to seek similar systems.[7] No doubt the nations demanding such sophisticated systems lobby hard to get equipment which will give them a distinct advantage over their local adversary. However, in a case such as that of the AWACS aircraft, the recipient nations are in no position to threaten to go to a rival producer of analogous equipment.

The arms transfer policies of the USA *vis-à-vis* the developing countries are closely inter-linked with the strategic stakes it has in various areas of the world. The United States has created its Central Command with jurisdiction for contingent operations by the Rapid Deployment Force over 19 nations, extending from Pakistan to Kenya. Creation of this Command necessitates access to naval, ground and air facilities in the nations of this area. In turn they are in a position to press the USA for the supply of arms. At the same time those nations which fall under the operational jurisdiction of the Central Command and fear direct or indirect military intervention by the USA or US-supported regional powers are compelled to seek arms from the rival great power, the USSR. It is generally recognized that this is the area in receipt of the major share of arms flows to the developing world. Is it a realistic proposition to conceive of local arms control arrangements in this part of the world without involving the two great industrial powers—the USA and the USSR?

VI.   Developing nations and confrontation with the great powers

North and South Korea and Taiwan figure in the list of significant military spenders with their security problems rooted in a larger national entity, having been divided on ideological grounds through great-power intervention. US troops are physically present in South Korea. Continued US arms supplies to Taiwan are a point of contention between the United States and the People's Republic of China. The levels of military spending of Viet Nam and Indonesia are related to their threat perception *vis-à-vis* China. China invaded Viet Nam to teach that country a lesson in 1979, and there has been continuous tension on the Sino-Vietnamese border ever since. The Vietnamese sense of insecurity has led to their making available to the Soviet Union the US-built facilities at Cam Ranh Bay. The interplay of great-power influences in the region and the Vietnamese overthrow of the genocidal Pol Pot regime have generated a significant sense of insecurity in Thailand and Malaysia.

The South Asian subcontinent is surrounded by China, the USSR and the US Central Command, the jurisdiction of which extends into the subcontinent since Pakistan is included in it. While the USA and the USSR are leaders in conventional weapon technology, China has also launched a programme of defence modernization, which has recently received support from the United States as well.[8] The naval activities of extra-regional powers are on the increase in the Indian Ocean, and particularly in the Arabian Sea.[9] There are also reports of the modernization of Chinese-supplied aircraft to Pakistan, refitted with US engines, avionics and weapon systems.[10] The subcontinent abuts the Gulf area where a prolonged war has been raging since 1980. To the immediate west of the subcontinent is the area of highest density of weapon deployment in the developing world. To the east of the subcontinent is the volatile South-East Asia, which has seen wars continuously since the 1940s. Under the circumstances India has undertaken a defence modernization programme. Pakistan has a similar justification for its defence modernization over and above its 'sibling rivalry' to keep up with its much larger neighbour, India, with whom it has fought four wars in the past four decades.

Among the other large defence spenders in the developing world, Cuba has an immense security problem in having to survive US hostility. The high military spending of Argentina, Brazil, Chile, Peru, Venezuela and Nigeria, however, cannot be directly linked to external threats. Except for Venezuela, the other five have until recently had or continue to have military-dominated governments. Some of them face serious domestic turbulence. Nigeria has experienced the secession of Biafra and a consequent civil war. While some of the security problems these countries face may have had indigenous origins, they have now been enveloped by great-power strategic interaction, and it is hardly possible to conceive of local arms control initiatives being taken independently of these great powers.

It is also to be noted that out of the 26 developing countries which are significant military spenders (above $1 billion per annum) only six have populations of less than 10 million (Israel, Kuwait, Oman, Saudi Arabia, Syria and United Arab Emirates); eight states have populations of 10–20 million (Chile, Cuba, Iraq, Malaysia, North Korea, Peru, Taiwan and Venezuela); and another nine states have large populations of 20–100 million (Argentina, Egypt, Iran, Nigeria, Pakistan, South Africa, South Korea, Thailand and Viet Nam). Three have very large populations—India, Indonesia and Brazil. Except for the four oil exporters, Israel and Syria, the balance of 20 significant military spenders in the developing world are within the 40 developing nations with populations above 10 million. In other words, there is—with few exceptions—a rough proportionality between military spending and the size of the population.

VII.   Medium powers in the developing world

An impression of disproportionality in defence spending by developing countries has been created by aggregating the very high spending of some oil-exporting countries with the expenditure of the rest of the developing countries. A more appropriate perspective is as follows. Today's international system is dominated by the industrialized world, consisting of 30 countries. They and China are responsible for nearly 82 per cent of the world's military expenditure. The developing world attempts to challenge this status quo in two ways. At the basic level a universalized nation-state system embodied in the UN has emerged as a result of decolonization. This has resulted in nearly 100 new sovereign nations. This democratization process itself is a challenge to the domination by a minority of industrialized nations. Within this generalized challenge it is the larger nation-states of the developing world which generate immediate pressures on the established international order dominated by the developed nations. Twenty out of 26 significant military spenders in the developing world are among the 40 large developing nations with populations above 10 million. Although these 20 countries spend only a small part of the world military expenditure, given their populations, areas, growing industrialization and their political role in the international system, their military capabilities are seen as a potential challenge to the world order dominated by the present set of developed countries: hence the excessive and somewhat distorted focus on military spending by the developing countries in the strategic literature of the industrialized world.

VIII.   Interventionism in the developing world

The developing countries, on the basis of their historical experience over the past four decades, have every reason to take adequate measures to safeguard their nascent nation-state building and consolidation processes from the threats posed to them both externally and internally. As mentioned above, more than 160 major intra- and inter-state conflicts out of around 170 that have taken place in the world since 1945 have taken place in the developing countries. It has been estimated that, of these, 120 conflicts took place in the first 25 years and in two-thirds of them there was direct or indirect intervention by the developed world.[11] This trend continues to persist in significant measure, although the percentage of internal wars and interventions by developing nations have increased in the past 15 years.[12]

The demonstrative use of force without war has been studied extensively by Barry Blechman, Stephen Kaplan and Philip Zelikow. According to them the United States demonstrated the use of force without war on 259 occasions from 1945 to 1982.[13] The figure for Soviet resort to demonstration of force without war is 167 occasions from 1945 to February 1979.[14] In the case of the USA demonstrative use of force was directed against developing nations on 83 per cent of the occasions in the first 32 years since 1945 and 92 per cent of the occasions in the next five years.[15] In the case of the USSR the figure for the first 32 years was 48 per cent in respect of developing nations.[16] Similar demonstrative uses of force have been resorted to by France, China and the UK. While perhaps all developing countries run the risk of being subjected to such coercive diplomacy, only the larger developing countries are in a position to attempt to safeguard themselves from such action and take steps to lower the risks of coercive diplomacy.

Decolonization has transferred the responsibility for security of the developing nations from the hands of the erstwhile imperial powers to the governments of the concerned developing nations. In a sense this means in accounting terms a reduction in defence expenditure of the leading Western developed countries and an increase in the defence expenditures of the developing countries. Therefore the so-called increase in the defence expenditures of the developing countries is a natural phenomenon. Further, there are overhead expenditures in respect of each defence establishment, and the requirements of a number of independent nations in terms of equipment and personnel are more than what would have been required for a single colonial power administering a number of adjacent colonies. Therefore one has to expect an increase in the defence expenditures of the developing countries significantly over and above what was incurred by the colonial states. However, the increase has been very much more than could be explained by these factors. This is partly explained by the fact that the superimposition of great-power rivalry on the developing world coincided with the decolonization process. The more important reason is the problems of security arising internally and externally in the developing world out of the process of nation-state building, consolidation and development.

IX. Nation-state building and insecurity

Colonialism froze the political, economic and social development of vast populations in the world, and decolonization has unleashed great turbulences in the erstwhile colonial societies in a climate of rapidly rising political consciousness. The attempts being made to evolve and stabilize nation-states come into conflict with traditional ethnic, tribal, linguistic, religious and sectarian loyalties since the concept of the nation-state demands that it should be the primary focus of loyalty for citizens, superseding other loyalties. There are also conflicts between traditionalist and authoritarian political cultures and demands for more representational forms of government. As development proceeds, disputes arise about the shares of the resources distributed to different sections of the populations and areas of a country. Some of the borders inherited from the colonial period have divided populations across international borders, and in a climate of rising political consciousness this has led to demands to revise some of the borders. There are also hegemonic ambitions of some rulers. These are not new problems in the evolution of traditional societies into nation-states. Europe underwent all these problems in the past three centuries, and the first half of this century witnessed two world wars. Today there is peace in the industrialized world under the threat of nuclear annihilation. Yet there are still problems arising out of sectarian differences, such as Northern Ireland; Basque separatism in Spain; secession-ism in Yugoslavia; disputes between Greece and Turkey, and so on. Viewed in this perspective the process of nation-state evolution, consolidation and development in the decolonized world is likely to be a highly turbulent one, giving rise to both inter-state and intra-state violence. The basic security problem of most of the developing countries, especially the medium- and larger-sized ones in terms of population, is how to shield their developmental process—social, economic and political—from both internal and external threats posed by the pressures arising out of the nation-building process as well as the present hegemonistic international milieu where use and threat of use of force continue to be resorted to as part of coercive diplomacy by nations—especially by those which lead the international community because of their military, economic and technological power.

X. Towards attenuation of violence in the developing world

Underlying the advocacy of local arms control arrangements within the developing world are usually two sets of perceptions. Very often there is among the leaderships of the developing world an inadequate understanding of these global linkages and the deep-rooted phenomenon of the problem of insecurity arising out of the nation-state building process. Such leaderships are often influenced by the literature generated in the developed world that exhorts the developing nations not to waste their resources on armaments, but instead concentrate on development. The other set of perceptions are in the developed world, where there is a strong subliminal urge to disown the responsibility of the developed nations for their part in generating insecurity in the developing world. This results in underplaying the global linkages in regard to the phenomena of arms transfers to and arms production in the developing world. There is also an element of ethno-centrism which regards arms production in the developed nations as not so dangerous as that in the developing nations.

Arms control makes sense among blocs of nations which are locked in permanent hostility and are engaged in continuously perfecting new generations of nuclear weapons which cannot be used in wars. Arms control measures are truces in the continuous arms race.

Arms control has also worked relatively more successfully with highly visible and easily monitorable nuclear strategic systems. It was neither successful with respect to naval armaments before World War II nor is so far with conventional forces, even among blocs of industrialized nations which claim to have concluded some strategic arms control measures. Even if such conventional arms control measures are accepted between the military alliances in Europe, it will not be a readily transferable experience because conventional arms control within the overall framework of nuclear deterrence is a very different concept from that to be achieved outside the context of nuclear deterrence, as in the case of most of the concerned countries in the developing world.

The recent disclosures of US arms supplies to Iran show that—even where major industrialized powers profess to keep out of a regional conflict—there are covert resupply operations which keep the war going. In view of both belligerents lacking the capacity to produce the weapons and equipment required to sustain high-intensity hostilities, it was all the time evident that there had been large-scale covert resupplies from the industrialized countries and some developing countries with significant arms production capabilities.[17] A revealing aspect of some of the recent disclosures on the link between covert arms transfers to Iran and funding of arms supplies to the contra insurgents in Nicaragua is the complexity of the network arrangement to introduce arms into the tension areas of the developing world. It has been reported that countries like Brunei were persuaded to put up the money, and the Chief of Staff of the Philippines, General Fabian Ver (who has since fled the country), signed the end-use certificate to get the arms to contra rebels. This surely is not an isolated instance.[18]

So long as the confrontation between the two major blocs of the world has a global dimension, some of the developing countries in areas of high strategic interest for the major powers are in a position to extract arms supplies from the latter. The United States, in pursuance of its policy of enabling the Afghan tribals to continue their insurgency against the Soviet-supported Kabul regime, is prepared to waive the Symington Amendment which prohibits military and other assistance to countries known to be developing nuclear weapons.[19]

The South Pacific nations have concluded among themselves a nuclear weapon-free zone arrangement. The USA and the UK have refused to accept the status of the nuclear weapon-free zone.[20] The South-East Asian nations have initiated a proposal to have a nuclear weapon-free zone but have been told that it would not be conducive to stability.[21] These instances illustrate that no regional arrangement will be permitted if that is considered to affect adversely the interests of a great power. Wherever such regional arrangements have developed—ASEAN and the Gulf Co-operation Council—it is under the patronage and implicit security guarantee of a great power and in turn results in countries outside such arrangements adopting countervailing security measures, thereby stepping up arms inflows into the area as a whole.

The only hope of reversing the present trend is in the decline of the hegemonism of the foremost of the two militarily capable powers and assertion of a large group of middle-tier nations (from both Western and Eastern Europe, China, Canada, Japan and more than a score of large developing nations) of their collective will in the international system to steer the world away from the present conflictual approach to international relations and move towards a more co-operative approach.

The hegemonic power of the USA is on the decline, but its power has been diffused not to another country but to a number of countries. The USSR is the countervailing military power. FR Germany and Japan are the major contenders in the realm of technology and trade. Politically, the rise of the developing nations has been the major challenge. As it is increasingly realized that a nuclear war cannot be fought and won—consequently, the sense of insecurity among the developed nations decreases and their security dependence on the great powers declines—the economic factors will come to the forefront and the task of tackling non-military threats to security will attract greater attention. This in turn will call for greater co-operative action among the middle-tier nations of the world. With the further consolidation of nation-state systems in the developing world, greater awareness that war is no longer a viable instrument of politics and increased pressures towards global integration through further developments in transportation and communication technologies, it is likely that the world may move towards attenuation of inter- and intra-state violence. Under those conditions compulsions of development may lead to increased interest in a regional approach. No doubt regional co-operation—in the few instances where it has come about—has had a shared security perception as the main motivating force. This will change with the decline of hegemonism at the top, with the consolidation of nation-states in the developing world and decrease in regard to security concerns in terms of military security among the middle-tier nations.

While that will be the longer-term perspective, the developing world is bound to be turbulent for many decades to come until the nation-state building is completed in a majority of them. Perhaps Latin America and parts of Asia may move into that stage earlier than some other parts of Asia and Africa. What is called for today is a global approach to violence in the developing world. Since it cannot be totally eliminated it should be attenuated. Towards this end both the industrialized powers (especially the leading intervening powers, such as the USA, the USSR, France and Britain) and the major developing nations which deploy troops outside their territories (Cuba, Israel, Pakistan and Libya) have to exercise restraint and observe a code of conduct of non-interventionism. The two great powers have to reach agreement that they will observe the Helsinki spirit not only in the industrialized world but also in the developing world. This no doubt will call for them to denuclearize the territories in and oceans adjacent to the developing world and confine their nuclear capabilities to the NATO and Warsaw Pact areas as a first step. A code of conduct in regard to arms sales and deputing personnel to developing countries beyond a certain limited number (say 20) will have to be observed by the two great powers. Since 50 per cent of arms transferred to the developing world are related to the Middle East situation and there cannot be a solution of that situation without the participation of all arms-supplier countries, an international conference is urgently called for.

Notes and references

[1] Kende, I., 'Wars of ten years (1967–76)', *Journal of Peace Research*, vol. 15, no. 3 (1978); and 'New features of armed conflicts and armament in developing countries', *Development and Peace*, Spring 1983. The figures have been approximately updated.

[2] Brzezinski, Z., *Power and Principle* (Weidenfeld & Nicolson: London, 1983), p. 189.

[3] *XINHUA*, 3 Oct. 1986.

[4] The failure is described in 'SALT without linkage', in Brzezinski (note 2), ch. 5.

[5] Brzezinski (note 2), p. 148. Confirmation Hearings of George Shultz, *Facts on File*, 1982, p. 505.

[6] For details see SIPRI, *World Armaments and Disarmament: SIPRI Yearbook 1986* (Oxford University Press: Oxford, 1986), pp. 338–39.

[7] Singh, J., 'US arms for Pakistan: AWACs and its implications', *Strategic Analysis*, vol. 11, no. 9 (Dec. 1986).

[8] Dutta, S., 'Emerging Sino-US military cooperation', *Strategic Analysis*, vol. 11, no. 12 (Mar. 1987).

[9] For the naval deployments of the USA, the USSR, France and Britain, see IISS, *Military Balance 1986–87* (IISS: London, 1986), p. 1. See also *International Herald Tribune*, 6 Apr. 1987.

[10] *Jane's Defence Weekly*, 7 Feb. 1987.

[11] Kende (note 1).

[12] Subrahmanyam, K., 'Insecurity of developing nations and regional security', *Strategic Analysis*, vol. 9, no. 11 (Feb. 1986), p. 1153.

[13] Singh, J., 'Threat of nuclear weapons', in *India and the Nuclear Challenge*, ed. K. Subrahmanyam (Lancers International: New Delhi, 1986).

[14] See note 13.

[15] Note 13, p. 70.

[16] Note 13, p. 70.

[17] *New York Times*, 11 Apr. 1987.

[18] See *FBS (Asia & Pacific)*, 12 Jan. 1987; see also *Baltimore Sun*, 7 Dec. 1986.

[19] Crawford, M., 'Glenn asks Reagan to halt Pakistan aid pending review of nuclear program', *Science*, 13 Mar. 1987; and 'Pakistan thought to possess the atom bomb', *Science*, 6 Mar. 1987.

[20] For refusal of the USA and the UK to sign the South Pacific Nuclear Free Zone Treaty (SPNFZ), see *International Herald Tribune*, 12 Feb. 1987; see also *Defense and Foreign Affairs Weekly*, 30 Mar.–5 Apr. 1987.

[21] *International Herald Tribune*, 12 Feb. 1987.

Paper 3.   Third World arms control: a Third World responsibility

NICOLE BALL

I.   Introduction

A survey of the arms control negotiations currently in progress gives the impression that arms control is solely of interest to the members of NATO, the WTO and a few neutral and non-aligned countries in Western Europe. It is by no means surprising that the arms race among the major powers has been accorded such attention. Since 1950, the members of NATO and of the WTO have accounted for no less than 70 per cent of all military expenditure recorded by SIPRI, and in many years they have been responsible for a good deal more. The United States and the Soviet Union have accounted for between one-half and three-quarters of this expenditure.[1]

At the same time, the increase in the developing countries' share of global military expenditure, the rapid rise in the value and volume of the arms trade with the Third World since the early 1970s, the amount of government resources devoted by many Third World states to the security sector, and the number of inter- and intra-state conflicts that have occurred in Africa, Asia, Latin America and the Middle East over the past four decades suggest that arms control has a role to play in the less-developed world as well. Since only a handful of countries in the Third World possess the technology to produce nuclear weapons, arms control and arms limitation efforts in this portion of the world have been oriented towards the acquisition of conventional weaponry.

In general, it can be argued that Third World governments and leaders have not paid sufficient attention to the need for arms control and have been unwilling to accept a degree of responsibility in this sphere commensurate with their power at the national and regional levels. They have been only too eager to place the blame for rising Third World arms imports and the failure to resolve conflicts in Asia, Africa, Latin America and the Middle East on the major powers, primarily the two superpowers. In reality, arms control has had a very low priority for nearly all Third World governments, and none of the attempts since the end of the World War II to limit the availability of weapons to countries in the Third World has successfully overcome the major obstacle confronting all arms control initiatives: how to convince governments to take actions that they do not perceive to be in their interests. Expressed in the simplest terms, past attempts at limiting the supply of weapons to the Third World have failed owing to the lack of political consensus for control within and among supplier and recipient governments. It is notable, for example, that 'discussions on conventional arms trade in the United Nations' General Assembly and in the Committee on Disarmament in Geneva have always met a negative, or even hostile reaction from most non-aligned members . . .'[2] To some extent, this negative attitude derives from an inequality inherent in all proposals to limit the arms trade. The Third World is dependent on imports for its weapons; the industrialized countries are, for the most part, not. Despite the growth of arms production capabilities in the Third World during the past decade or two and the increased transfer of production technology in recent years, this basic equation remains valid. Third World governments feel that they are being discriminated against when arms control proposals deal solely with the transfer of weapons and leave the issue of production untouched.[3]

Perhaps more important, the reluctance of Third World governments to discuss reductions in the arms trade is a reflection of the fact that, just as suppliers have what they believe to be compelling political and economic reasons for transferring weapons, Third World recipients have strong reasons for wishing to acquire arms. It was, for example, reportedly the Egyptian Government that first contacted the Soviet Union in 1951 in an effort to circumvent the restrictions on arms purchases imposed by Britain, France and the United States under the Tripartite Declaration of 1950, although it was not until at least mid-1953 that the Soviet Government evinced interest in entering the Middle Eastern market.[4]

This paper focuses first of all on the reasons why Third World governments procure weapons. It then briefly discusses why these governments would benefit from arms control and concludes by examining some of the ways in which Third World arms control might be promoted.

II.   Why arms are bought

Without a clear understanding of the forces that drive the arms trade, it will be impossible to effect reductions in the sale of weapons. Forces propelling the suppliers are dealt with elsewhere in this volume. On the demand side, the two most important 'pull' factors are probably the involvement of the recipient in an ongoing internal or external conflict and the availability of financing. Table 3.1 lists the 20 Third World countries that together imported more than three-quarters of all the major arms supplied to the Third World between 1971 and 1985, according to SIPRI data. A number of these countries received this weaponry from the superpowers either free of charge or on very favourable terms. Even more noteworthy is the effect of the increase in the price of petroleum during the 1970s, which enabled several OPEC member states to equip arsenals with a large quantity of high-quality weapons and to subsidize the purchases of other states. It may have been in the interests of the suppliers to recycle petro-dollars, but a number of the oil-wealthy states needed no convincing of the desirability of purchasing weapons. The sizeable increase in weapon imports recorded by Iran, Libya, Saudi Arabia, Algeria, Venezuela

Table 3.1. Leading importers of major conventional weapons in the Third World, 1971–85

Country	Value[a]	Share[a]	Cumulative per cent
Iraq	22 771	8.0	8.0
Iran	22 085	7.7	15.7
Syria	20 585	7.2	22.9
Egypt	20 476	7.2	30.1
Libya	20 250	7.1	37.2
India	17 491	6.1	43.3
Israel	15 143	5.3	48.6
Saudi Arabia	12 435	4.3	52.9
Viet Nam[b]	8 796	3.1	56.0
Argentina	7 213	2.5	58.5
Algeria	5 690	2.0	60.5
Pakistan	5 678	2.0	62.5
Taiwan	5 646	2.0	64.5
South Korea	5 519	1.9	66.4
Peru	5 436	1.9	68.3
Jordan	4 833	1.7	70.0
Brazil	4 741	1.6	71.6
South Viet Nam[c]	4 690	1.6	73.2
Morocco	4 298	1.5	74.7
Venezuela	4 086	1.4	76.1
Cuba	3 766	1.3	77.4
Kuwait	3 335	1.2	78.6
Indonesia	3 309	1.2	79.8
Ethiopia	3 165	1.1	80.9
Nigeria	3 142	1.1	82.0
Subtotal	*234 579*		*82.0*
Third World total	**285 818**		**100.0**

[a] Figures are based on SIPRI trend indicator values as expressed in US $ m., at constant (1985) prices. Shares are expressed as a percentage of total imports of major weapons by the Third World.
[b] Covering North Viet Nam (1971–75) and Viet Nam (from 1976).
[c] Effectively covering the period 1971–74.

Source: Brzoska, M. and Ohlson, T., SIPRI, *Arms Transfers to the Third World, 1971–85* (Oxford University Press: Oxford, 1987), p. 7 and appendix 7.

and Iraq (before the war with Iran) occurred to a large extent because of the increases in petroleum-derived income after 1973. Several other countries have had their weapon imports subsidized by the oil-rich countries—Syria, Egypt, Jordan, Morocco and Iraq (after the war with Iran began).

Over three-quarters of the main importers of major weapons since the beginning of the 1970s have been party to conflicts of many years' duration. Iran and Iraq have been at war since 1980. Egypt, Syria, Israel and Jordan have been directly involved in the Middle East conflict, Saudi Arabia and Algeria less directly. Morocco has sought to gain control over former Spanish Sahara, and Algeria and Libya have been indirectly involved in this conflict. Libya has also been an important participant in the civil war in Chad. India and Pakistan went to war with each other in 1971, and relations have yet to be fully normalized. Viet Nam has been at war for most of this period, first with the United States and then with the Pol Pot forces in Kampuchea and in smaller skirmishes with China. Argentina engaged in a short but costly war with Britain in 1982. South Korea is still technically at war with North Korea and has armed itself accordingly. Peru is currently fighting a serious internal insurgency against the Sendero Luminoso guerrillas, while Cuba has some 30 000 troops in Angola.

In addition to threats from abroad and from within, Third World armed forces sometimes acquire weapons to protect against what they perceive to be potential threats. In Latin America, for example, most wars have resulted from border disputes that governments have been unwilling to resolve peacefully. The US-sponsored system of hemispheric defence which grew out of World War II defence agreements caused intra-regional disputes to subside but did not resolve them. The weakening of this system in the 1960s and the development programmes pursued by a number of South American governments in border regions caused these disputes to re-emerge, thereby raising tensions in the region. In response, some governments increased their purchases of weapons, which caused tensions to rise even further and provided additional justification for arms purchases. The value of major weapons imported by countries such as Argentina, Peru, Brazil, Ecuador and Chile increased significantly during the 1970s and early 1980s.[5]

Some governments purchase weapons in order to bolster their claims to regional-power status. The Shah of Iran envisaged his country becoming a second-order power, 'guardian of the Gulf'. During the 1970s, Nigerian governments began to see their country as having a 'claim to regional dominance and as an arbiter in the region'.[6] While such countries may be encouraged to assume this role by one or the other of the major powers—as Iran was by the USA during the Nixon years—there can be no denying the interest their governments have in becoming the dominant power in their respective regions.

In the 1950s and 1960s, decolonization was an important source of increased demand for weapons, primarily in Africa and Asia. As countries became independent, they created armed forces where none had existed previously and began supplying these forces with weapons. In the early 1970s, SIPRI reported that 'quantitatively, the establishment of armed forces had been the major factor responsible for the growth of major weapon imports to Sub-Saharan Africa. The main reason for the 500 per cent increase between 1950–54 and 1965–69 is the emergence of 27 new importing nations'.[7] Since the late 1960s, decolonization has declined in importance as an explanatory factor in the arms trade.

Related to decolonization is the psychological support said to be provided by arms purchases for the nation-building process. Many countries in Africa, Asia and the Middle East that became independent after 1945 included within their borders several, and sometimes a sizeable number of, different ethnic, racial and religious groups with which the new state was forced to compete for its citizens' loyalties. Government institutions were also weak, rooted as they were in foreign systems and having only recently been introduced into these regions. Under such conditions, the armed forces, equipped with as modern weapons as possible, came to be regarded by many governments in the Third World as a symbol of unity and independence and as tangible evidence that the government intended to defend its sovereignty. The actual utility that these weapons might have in any conflict in which the importing country could reasonably expect to become involved was often of secondary importance.

During the period up to 1962, the main military contingency for which India was preparing was the possibility of a war with Pakistan. Indian purchases of major weapons between 1954 and 1958 were mainly a reaction to the acquisition of weapons by Pakistan under the US military assistance programme after 1954 . . .

Yet there are reasons to suppose that India's attempts to match Pakistan's weapons were not based on contemplation of their use. First of all, India chose to purchase mainly prestige weapons . . .

Secondly, India totally neglected the backing required to support these prestige weapons . . .[8]

The fragility of Third World political systems and the concentration of political and economic power in the hands of relatively few individuals have resulted in the inability of governments to reconcile the various demands of different segments of the population and in the tendency of individuals in power to give the fulfilment of their own needs higher priority than those of the general public. As a result, governments have frequently been forced to rely on the armed forces to maintain themselves in power. One means of gaining or rewarding this support has been by purchasing weapons. In Saudi Arabia, for example, 'modernizing pressures promoted by the depotism and extravagance of the ruling family and the requirements of the Yemeni Civil War, which broke out in 1962, culminated in the deposition of King Saud by his brother King Faisal in 1964, with the implicit support of the army. A programme of military expansion was then embarked upon'.[9]

These, then, are the most important causes of internally generated demand for weapons in the Third World. Together with the supply-side factors, they determine the amount of weapons which countries in the Third World wish to procure. None of these factors is mutually exclusive, although one may be dominant at any given point in time (for example, a sudden increase in income or the activation of a dormant conflict). Consider Syria: it is involved in the Arab–Israeli conflict, aspires to establish itself as a regional power, has a politically active military, acts as a proxy for the Soviet Union in the Middle East and finances many of its weapon purchases with subsidies provided by Saudi Arabia and perhaps other wealthy members of OPEC.[10] Strategies designed to reduce Syria's consumption of arms must take each of these factors into account if they are to be successful. The same is true for each arms client in the Third World.

III.   Why the Third World needs arms control

Although the simple possession of weapons does not guarantee their use, governments that build up their armed forces and provide them with ample supplies of military equipment may be more inclined to seek to resolve conflicts by the use of force than through negotiated settlement. All Third World countries face serious development problems, and the resources available to help solve these problems are more often than not quite limited. It is clearly in the best interests of the general public in the Third World that outstanding conflicts be resolved peacefully and rapidly so that scarce resources can be devoted to the development process rather than to the security sector.

It was pointed out in the previous section that governments have frequently sought to purchase the loyalty of the armed forces by providing them with weapons. Such a strategy has not always succeeded, and the armed forces have become an increasingly important political force throughout Asia, Africa, the Middle East and Latin America, taking advantage of the absence of well-functioning democratic systems and of the gross political inequalities that characterize much of the Third World. Military *coups d'état* are frequently associated with an increase (most often temporary) in overall security expenditure. While salary rises awarded by new military rulers to themselves and their troops tend to absorb much of this money,[11] some of the additional funds can be allocated to the purchase of weapons.

It has been suggested that military governments, by embracing doctrines which exaggerate the role of force and military preparedness and equate national development with an expansion of national power, are likely to allocate larger sums to the armed forces than civilian-dominated governments.[12] Such an assertion needs to be examined on a case-by-case basis. It is none the less clear that, in view of the lack of serious external threats, the doctrine of national security which prevailed in Brazil, Peru, Argentina and Chile during much of the 1960s and 1970s enabled governments to maintain larger armed forces than would have been necessary had these forces been oriented solely towards external defence.[13]

In attempting to guarantee the loyalty of the armed forces, Third World governments (military as well as civilian) may be undermining their position. By purchasing more weapons than a balanced assessment of the threats faced by the country (not the government) warrants and acceding to demands for higher salaries and other benefits, governments may be demonstrating their lack of legitimacy and strengthening the armed forces at the expense of other groups and institutions. The participation of the armed forces in government has not proven to be a recipe for promoting Third World development. It is true, of course, that as a group civilian-led governments are no more successful in generating development than military-dominated ones. All too often economic and political development in the Third World is retarded as different groups of elites battle among themselves for control. The top priority for the resultant government is more often than not the retention of power—in order to guarantee the pre-eminent position of the elites—not the development of the country or its political and economic institutions.

Despite the less than satisfactory record of many civilian-led governments in the Third World, it is important for the armed forces to abstain from playing a political role. For development to occur, all societal groups must be able to participate in the decision-making process. Restricted participation, even for competing elites, is one of the hallmarks of a military regime. Many civilian-led governments in the Third World similarly restrict the involvement of the opposition. In countries governed by civilians where the security forces are effectively kept in the barracks, however, it is at least *possible* that the kinds of compromise that must be made among the different social groups if all segments of the population are to participate freely in the economic and political systems can be reached. This will not occur quickly or easily, but for it to occur at all the security forces must refrain from political activities.

Controlling the flow of weapons to the Third World is far from the only, or even the most important, factor in restraining the domestic power of the armed forces. Reducing the availability of weapons and seeking to resolve conflicts peacefully may, however, function as a signal to the armed forces that it is the civilians who control the political system and that political solutions to problems will be accorded higher priority than military ones. If one considers the events in the Philippines since February 1986, the importance of preventing the active involvement of the armed forces in the political process becomes clear.

The purchase of weapons also inhibits economic growth and development in more direct ways. Chief among these are by intensifying Third World indebtedness and by reducing the capital available for investment in productive undertakings. Despite the growth of the arms trade with the Third World and the decline in security-related grants which occurred during the 1970s, no detailed analysis has yet been made of the security sector's contribution to the very large debt problems confronting the Third World today. In 1985, SIPRI estimated that 'at least one-fifth of new borrowing [between 1972 and 1982] was directly or indirectly for weaponry'.[14] In the absence of reliable information on security-related loans, however, it is difficult to determine how accurate such estimates are.

Even if it were possible to state with relative certainty that a given percentage of total Third World debt were security-related, that would not provide much information on the proportion of individual countries' indebtedness derived from imports for the security forces. It cannot be assumed that because both Third World indebtedness and arms imports have risen sharply during the past 10–15 years all countries in Asia, Africa, the Middle East and Latin America owe a large share of their debt to security-related purchases. As noted in the previous section, some of the major Third World purchasers of major weapons have had sufficient income from sales of petroleum products to enable them not only to procure large amounts of weaponry for their own forces but also to subsidize the arms procurement of other countries. Others, such as Israel, Egypt and Viet Nam, have benefitted from the willingness of superpower patrons to write off all or a large portion of security-related debts. Still others, such as India, have reduced the size of their security-related debt by bartering weapons for domestically produced goods whenever possible.

Even a relatively small security-related debt may, however, pose problems for developing countries that face serious resource constraints, particularly a shortage of foreign exchange. When a government uses a certain amount of its income to purchase weapons, it decreases the resources available for investment in productive undertakings and for improvements in the health and education systems which can be expected to upgrade the quality of the workforce over the longer term and thus strengthen the development process. These problems are not removed, as it is sometimes suggested, when a country produces some proportion of the weapons it procures domestically. For one thing the foreign-exchange component of domestic arms production in all but the largest arms producing countries (essentially the USA and the USSR) is significant. For another, resources continue to be diverted from more productive investments. The benefits that may accrue in terms of manpower training, technology transfer and the construction of physical plant more often than not fail to justify the huge investments required in domestic arms production.[15]

Once again, pursuing arms control would not automatically create the conditions necessary for successful development in the Third World. Heavy expenditure on the security forces in general and on weapon procurement in particular does, however, complicate the task of setting Third World economies on the path of self-sustaining development. Third World governments would therefore be well-advised to make a realistic assessment of the threats facing them, to seek to resolve outstanding conflicts with both domestic and foreign groups in a peaceful manner, and to employ those resources at their disposal for the benefit of all groups in society.

IV.   How to promote Third World arms control

A review of past efforts to limit the supply of weapons to the Third World suggests that several conditions must be met if such initiatives are to succeed. To begin with, negotiations aimed at making a substantial dent in the arms trade with the Third World will probably fail without a 'tolerable level of co-operation between the United States and the Soviet Union'.[16] This would be true even if the negotiations were not bilateral (as with the CAT Talks during the Carter–Brezhnev period) but included other major suppliers. A second condition which must be met if arms control negotiations are to succeed is that governments must be aware of the objectives they seek to attain through such efforts and be able to minimize bureaucratic and political in-fighting which can all too easily undermine arms control negotiations. Former US Department of State officials have argued that the primary cause of the failure of the CAT Talks was the US Government's decision to pursue politically oriented negotiations aimed at reducing Soviet–US rivalry in the Third World when it was not prepared to discuss certain international political relations with the USSR that had to be addressed if the talks were to succeed.[17]

The thrust of this paper, however, is the need for recipient action, both independently and as participants in negotiations with suppliers. The involvement of Third World governments is important for at least two reasons. It has been suggested by former US State Department officials that 'arms transfer limitations would best be pursued in a multilateral context in which the influence and problems of recipient states could mitigate the superpower rivalry'.[18] Just as important, the participation of Third World recipients is necessary if they are not to argue that, once again, their interests have been disregarded. What is more, it is likely to be easier to negotiate reductions in arms transfers if both suppliers and recipients agree that some form of restriction is desirable. The problem will be to convince Third World governments that it is in their interest to negotiate on this issue.

Focusing on technical limitations might encourage Third World recipients to participate since the focus would be on specific categories of weapon that should be limited, rather than on specific regions. This could reduce the suspicions that might develop in the minds of some Third World leaders that the negotiations were directed specifically at them. The technical approach would be particularly non-threatening if the first weapons selected for limitations were of a category that was not widely deployed in the Third World. The purpose of agreeing to limit such weapons would be to build up acceptance of the notion that restrictions on arms transfers are possible and to construct a viable negotiating procedure in as uncontentious an atmosphere as possible.

Concentrating on technical issues might, however, produce resistance on the part of the recipients since some Third World governments might choose to argue that a major source of conflicts, and hence arms procurement, in the Third World is intervention by the major powers and that limitations on arms transfers can be discussed only when such activities cease. There can be no doubt that involvement in an ongoing conflict—generally but not exclusively external in nature—is a major source of demand for weapons in the Third World and that conflicts are frequently exacerbated, if not actually caused, by foreign intervention.[19] A very large portion of the responsibility for the existence of inter-state and domestic conflicts in the Third World rests none the less with Third World governments. To the extent that these conflicts are exacerbated by major-power intervention, it is up to Third World governments to demonstrate their genuine independence by refusing to be manipulated by outside powers. (Unfortunately, the manipulator is increasingly a Third World government, for example, Libya or South Africa.) Although international politics are unquestionably still dominated by the two superpowers and their relations with each other, the degree of control capable of being exercised by any of the major powers has declined over the past three decades. This means that Third World governments have a greater scope for independent action than they did 10 or 20 years ago. They would accordingly be wise to use this relative freedom of action constructively, to concentrate those resources to which they have access on development rather than conflict.

Since at present Third World conflicts would scarcely disappear in the absence of major-power intervention, a *quid pro quo* that recipient governments might offer to suppliers in return for non-intervention agreements would be to begin serious negotiations aimed at resolving outstanding conflicts peacefully. This change in attitude and behaviour among recipients is just as urgently needed as that among the suppliers. To put a genuine cap on arms transfers, it would be necessary to negotiate an end to the internal, as well as the external, disputes that give rise to the demand for weapons in the Third World. This is an extremely sensitive issue, since no government welcomes what it considers to be interference in its internal affairs or challenges to its sovereignty. Beginning with external conflicts of some magnitude would offer considerable scope for reducing the flow of arms to the Third World. Countries involved in no serious external disputes purchase significantly fewer weapons than those engaged in major conflicts, even if they have access to substantial amounts of foreign exchange.[20]

A second way in which the suppliers might induce Third World recipients to negotiate in good faith is by agreeing to discuss weapon production. The question of inequity—that is, of suppliers refusing to consider possible limitations on their production of weapons—was first raised 60 years ago.[21] However desirable reducing the flow of weapons to the Third World may be for the recipients themselves, some Third World governments are likely to be tempted to use as an excuse for their non-participation in negotiations the injustice of focusing solely on the transfer of weapons while leaving their production and deployment in the industrialized world essentially unregulated. Discussing production becomes increasingly important as a growing number of countries build up the capacity to produce at least some categories of weapon domestically. Although the possession of weapons does not automatically imply that military solutions to problems will take precedence over negotiations and compromise, it seems likely that as more and more Third World producers seek to emulate Brazil's success in the arms export market, the peaceful resolution of conflicts will suffer accordingly. It also must be recognized that, as the number of arms producers proliferates, it becomes correspondingly more difficult to restrain the trade in weapons.

Another method of acquiring Third World participation in arms control negotiations may be to build upon proposals put forward by Third World leaders. At the time of his inauguration on 28 July 1985, Peru's President Alan García made the following statement, which was reiterated in an address to the United Nations in September 1985:

I proclaim the need for a regional agreement to reduce expenditure on armaments and freeze the acquisition thereof, in conformity with the spirit of the Declaration of Ayacucho signed in 1974, believing, as in the case of indebtedness, that it is essential to proceed from words and good intentions to action and example. In keeping with this principle, I hereby announce to the people of the world our decision to reduce substantially all purchases of war material, beginning with a cut in the number of Mirage aircraft we are at present negotiating to purchase.[22]

On 29 July, a number of Latin American presidents who had attended the García inauguration signed the Declaration of Lima in which they stated that they would consider 'positive and convenient the balanced reduction of military expenditures and the assignment of major resources for confidence building measures in the region and particularly between neighboring countries'.[23] Similar proposals and undertakings have, of course, been made before by Latin American leaders and have come to nothing.[24] If, however, major suppliers were to work in concert with the signatories of the Declaration of Lima, it is possible that the chances for success might increase.

Despite the lack of interest in controlling the trade in weapons and weapon-production technology that has been exhibited since the end of World War II, there are two recent events that suggest that serious efforts in this direction could have a greater chance of success in the coming years than they have for some time. The first is that relations between the United States and the Soviet Union no longer appear to be locked in a downward spiral. If the Soviet Union were able to maintain its newly found interest in arms limitation until the end of the Reagan Administration and the latter's successor were less hard-line, it is possible that progress could be made on proposals for limiting the transfer of weapons to the Third World as well as on strategic issues.

The second potentially encouraging point is the decline in resource availability experienced by many Third World purchasers—including some of the major ones. Alan García's 1985 arms-limitation proposal in all likelihood owed a great deal to the size of Peru's external debt. The drop in the price of petroleum means not only that countries such as Saudi Arabia, Libya, Iran, Algeria and Venezuela cannot purchase as many weapons for their own use as they did during the mid- and late-1970s but also that countries such as Saudi Arabia and Kuwait will find it increasingly difficult to underwrite sizeable purchases by third parties. The major powers, particularly the United States and the Soviet Union, could do much to intensify this shortage of available resources by reducing the grant element in their military transfers and hardening credit terms.[25]

Reduced resource availability coupled with a genuine concern on the part of the major powers to decrease their intervention in the Third World and to support limitations on arms transfers to developing countries could do much to promote progress in limiting the transfer of arms to the Third World. Third World governments, however, have an equally large role to play. They must cease to portray themselves as nothing more than the victims of attempts by the great powers to dominate the global economic and political systems and begin to take advantage of the relative freedom of action they enjoy as leaders of independent states in a multi-polar world. They must make development, not the pursuit of narrow, individual gain, the centrepiece of their policies. By genuinely seeking to resolve outstanding disputes peacefully and by promoting the development of their societies, they would reduce their demand for weapons. By reducing their demand for weapons, Third World governments would expand their development options and increase the likelihood that what development does occur will be shared among all social groups in a more equitable manner than at present and not limited to a small group whose main interest is in protecting its gains from all other groups in society.

Notes and references

[1]   Unpublished arms trade and military expenditure statistics as of June 1986.

[2]   Beker, A., 'The arms–oil connection: fueling the arms race', *Armed Forces and Society*, vol. 8, no. 3 (Spring 1982), pp. 436–37. See also Luck, E. C., 'The arms trade', in ed. D. A. Kay, *The Changing United Nations: Options for the United States* (Academy of Political Science: New York, 1977), p. 177.

[3]   Non-producing nations have recognized this basic inequality for many years. During the drafting of the Geneva Convention in 1925, many governments complained that the measures under discussion for publicizing the arms trade were not to be extended to the production of weapons as well. See SIPRI, *The Arms Trade with the Third World* (Almqvist & Wiksell: Stockholm, 1971), pp. 95–97, 118–20. For information on the growth of the Third World's capacity to produce weapons, see Brzoska, M. and Ohlson, T. (eds), SIPRI, *Arms Production in the Third World* (Taylor & Francis: London, 1986); Katz, J. E. (ed.), *Arms Production in Developing Countries* (Lexington Books: Lexington, MA, 1984); and Ball, N., 'The growth of arms production in the Third World', *National Forum* (Special Issue on 'The Militarization of the Globe'), Fall 1986, pp. 24–27.

[4]   Ra'anan, U., *The USSR Arms the Third World: Case Studies in Soviet Foreign Policy* (MIT Press: Cambridge, MA, 1969), pp. 30, 69. On some of the reasons behind the USSR's cautious behaviour towards the Middle East in the decade following World War II, see Safran, N., *From War to War: The Arab–Israeli Confrontation, 1948–67* (Pegasus/Bobbs-Merrill: Indianapolis and New York, 1969), pp. 94–96.

[5]   SIPRI (note 3), p. 701, points out that, 'Argentina and Brazil, as the largest recipients, tend to compete with one another. Chile generally follows the Argentinian lead. Peru, which has always displayed special concern with Chile's military posture—a concern which dates back to the war in the 1870s when Chile annexed a large part of Peruvian territory—justifies rather large purchases in terms of Chile's acquisitions'. In addition, Peru and Ecuador react to each other's arms purchases. See Varas, A., *Militarization and the International Arms Race in Latin America* (Westview Press: Boulder and London, 1985), pp. 52–56; and Portales, C. and Varas, A., 'The role of military expenditure in the development process: Chile 1952–1973 and 1973–1980: two contrasting cases', *Ibero Americana* (Stockholm), vol. 12, no. 1–2 (1983), pp. 23–24, 42. On perceived threats, see Kolodziej, E. A. and Harkavy, R. E., 'Developing states and regional and global security', in eds E. A. Kolodziej and R. E. Harkavy, *Security Policies of Developing Countries* (Lexington Books: Lexington, MA, 1982), pp. 344–45.

[6]   Ostheimer, J. M. and Buckley, G. J., 'Nigeria' and Schultz, A. T., 'Iran', in Kolodziej and Harkavy (note 5), pp. 290, 253.

[7]   SIPRI (note 3), p. 50.

[8]   SIPRI (note 3), p. 56.

[9]   SIPRI (note 3), p. 46. There are numerous examples of governments acceding to demands of the armed forces for weapons in an attempt to remain in power or to reward them for their support in removing a previous government from power. In the 1950s and 1960s, for example, governments in Somalia, Liberia and Ethiopia sought to buy the loyalty of the armed forces with increased weapon imports. In the Philippines, the value of arms imports increased substantially following Marcos' imposition of martial rule in 1972.

[10]   On Syria, see Rabinovich, I., 'Syria', in Kolodziej and Harkavy (note 5), pp. 267–82.

[11]   The *coup d'état* in Liberia in 1980 was followed by a doubling of salaries for the armed forces.

Since personnel costs accounted for some 70 per cent of Liberian security expenditure at this time, the effect was a substantial increase in the total defence budget.

[12] Varas (note 5), pp. 56–57.

[13] Although the details of the national security doctrines adopted by these Latin American governments varied, the broad outlines were essentially the same. National security was seen to depend not only on the defence of a country from external attack but also on the existence of a strong economy and a unified society. The perception on the part of military officers that civilians could not produce the developed and ordered society that the former saw as necessary for the preservation of national security provided the justification for the military coups that occurred in these countries in the 1960s and the 1970s.

[14] SIPRI, *World Armaments and Disarmament: SIPRI Yearbook 1985* (Taylor & Francis: London, 1985), p. 448. Kitchenman, W. F., *Arms Transfers and the Indebtedness of Less Developed Countries*, N–2020–FF (Rand: Santa Monica, Dec. 1983), p. 14, estimates some 9 per cent of 'total average yearly debt service' between 1962 and 1982 derived from military purchases.

[15] For more details on this point, see Ball, N., *Security and Economy in the Third World* (Princeton University Press: Princeton, NJ, 1988).

[16] Blechman, B., Nolan, J. E. and Platt, A., 'Pushing arms', *Foreign Policy*, no. 46 (Spring 1982), p. 148, 149.

[17] The National Security Council, under the leadership of Zbigniew Brzezinski, argued that the USA should refuse to discuss potential limitations on exports to East Asia—where the USA was seeking to normalize relations with China—and West Asia—where the long-time ally of the United States, the Shah of Iran, was facing an increasingly difficult domestic situation in 1978. Brzezinski was able to have his view prevail, and the US delegation to the CAT Talks was instructed to inform the Soviet Union that if these regions were discussed, the USA would withdraw from the Talks. See note 16, p. 147 and chapter 7.

[18] See note 16.

[19] Leitenberg, M., 'The impact of the worldwide confrontation of the great powers: aspects of military intervention and the projection of military power', in ed. G. Fischer, *Armaments–Development–Human Rights–Disarmament* (Establissment Bruylant: Brussels, 1985). Internal conflicts can often be fought 'on the cheap' since sophisticated aircraft and naval vessels are less useful than small arms, artillery, lightly armoured vehicles and small aircraft against what are often rather poorly armed insurgent groups.

[20] Venezuela, which is a member of OPEC, imported on average $256 million in major weapons each year between 1970 and 1984, according to SIPRI statistics. Syria, Israel and Egypt—all of which are involved in one or more aspects of the Middle East conflict—imported, on average, $1310 million, $1019 million and $1413 million, respectively, each year during the same period.

[21] SIPRI (note 3), p. 97.

[22] 'Letter Dated 7 August 1985 Addressed to the President of the Conference on Disarmament from the Acting Charge d'Affaires of the Delegation of Peru, Transmitting the Proposal on Regional Disarmament Formulated by the Constitutional President of Peru, Dr Alan García Perez, in his Inaugural Message on Taking Office on 28 July 1985'. See also 'Address by H. E. Alan García, President of the Republic of Peru at the Fortieth Session of the General Assembly', 23 Sep. 1985.

[23] 'Peru at a final crossroads', *F.A.S. Public Interest Report* 39 (Apr. 1987), p. 4.

[24] Varas (note 5), pp. 92–97.

[25] The present reality is, of course, considerably different. The Soviet Union continues to provide Cuba and Viet Nam—two Third World interventionary powers—with military grants valued at $300–400 million per year. The United States recently softened the terms on which military credits are extended to many of its more important arms clients, ostensibly to avoid creating additional burdensome debt for these countries. See Library of Congress, Congressional Research Service, Report, *US Military Sales and Assistance Programs: Laws, Regulations, and Procedures*, prepared for the Subcommittee on Arms Control, International Security and Science of the Committee on Foreign Affairs, US House of Representatives, 99th Congress, 1st session (US Government Printing Office: Washington, DC, 23 July 1985), pp. 50, 53, 57; 'Statement by William Schneider, Jr., Under-Secretary of State for Security Assistance, Science and Technology, before the Senate Foreign Relations Committee', mimeo, 26 Sep. 1985, pp. 8–9; and *Congressional Presentation: Security Assistance Programs, FY 1986*, Washington, DC, pp. 15–18.

Paper 4. Third world arms control, military technology and alternative security

CHRIS SMITH

I. Introduction

Although the control of arms sales to the Third World seems as far away as ever, there are clear signs that this issue is moving closer to the central agenda of international politics. However, there are many obstacles to be overcome before it will be possible to construct a regime which is capable of guaranteeing the security of Third World states while at the same time reducing the demand for armament. In order to address this complex issue it is necessary to understand why previous initiatives have failed, what drives the systematic transfer of military technology to the Third World, what changes are occurring and, finally, how the present fluid period can be exploited to institute changes based upon an alternative security regime and the adoption of radically different defence policies by Third World countries.

Ever since World War I, when several nations faced hostile armies equipped with weapons and ammunition produced from within their own industrial base, the international community has periodically shown concern and interest in the international traffic in arms.[1] But the urgent need to quantify and control arms transfers has been unequivocally frustrated by the unco-operative attitude of both exporters and importers, *ergo* a large proportion of UN member states. The failure of both suppliers and recipients to control the flow of arms from North to South is rooted in the inescapable fact that restraint is generally seen to be against the interests of both. The several attempts at restraint have their time and place in the pattern of international relations since World War I. By and large they have been reactive measures animated by the effects rather than the causes of violent breakdowns in the international system. Thus, it was the inordinate bloodletting of World War I and the partial responsibility of the 'merchants of death' which prompted concern within the League of Nations. The embargoes enforced during the Indo-Pakistani War of 1965 and the Six-Day War of 1967 were reactive measures which followed the mutual recognition on the part of both superpowers and their allies that wars in sensitive geo-political areas of the Third World could ramify into direct superpower confrontation. The CAT Talks initiated by President Carter were a consequence of the new President's resolve to raise the moral standard of US foreign policy above the prevailing level of crude economic gain and political advantage. Carter himself was elected to office partly as a result of the USA's existential crisis following the Viet Nam War and the Watergate affair.

The lessons of the 1970s may have introduced more checks and controls into how and when the major suppliers sell arms to the Third World; witness the continuing tension between the US legislature and the executive over arms sales to the Middle East and Pakistan, and the retention of elements of restrictiveness in most national arms export policies. But at no point were the major exporters ever committed as a body to the negotiation of a policy of control or restraint. The reasons for this apathy are unequivocally the driving forces of the arms trade.

II.   The arms trade in the 1980s: an approaching crisis

Since World War II arms production has become a large and important industrial sector in most of the member countries of the two primary military blocs, NATO and the Warsaw Pact. Politically, for an individual country to maintain the potential for war preparedness it is considered by governments well worth the costs which such an activity incurs, although judgements about how great the costs are differ markedly.[2] The embodiment of increasingly sophisticated technology in weapon systems has created complex industrial requirements. The size and complexity of arms production spanning the complete cycle of invention, innovation and production involve hundreds of thousands of managers, bureaucrats, and skilled and semi-skilled workers. If such a capability is to be maintained, the arms industries must have orders. But, as governments become less able to allocate increasing resources to the military owing to poor growth rates and cyclical downturns, the full utilization of capacity becomes impossible. These problems are greatly compounded by the increasing cost of weapon systems, a function of increasing sophistication.

As such, the export market is a vital element which sustains production and prevents military spending from rising beyond acceptable political and fiscal levels. All countries must now consider the export market if national defence production capabilities are to be maintained. An optimal production run will be of sufficient duration to satisfy initial domestic demand and then for exports to continue through until a successor system is either ready or affordable. The Third World offers the most lucrative and straightforward export market.

On the demand side, arms imports are the result of several interlocking factors. The conventional wisdom which links the demand for arms to the turbulence of intra-Third World relations at the regional level and the slow and uneven progress of political development tells only half the story. The other view, which sees demand patterns as the orchestration of Third World leaders by the unscrupulous representatives of government and industry or as the irresponsible actions of authoritarian leaders, is equally selective.

In the Third World, decision making in relation to defence often seems misguided and unsympathetic to other, pressing national needs, particularly those relating to economic development. But this should not obscure the fact that defence policy is rarely if ever an issue that is treated lightly. The demand for military technology differs from country to country and from region to region. As in the North, the policy which defines defence needs is comprised of competing claims to scarce resources. As such the result is one of domestic political bargaining processes set in the context of available resources and foreign policy, of which threat perceptions are a sub-set. What obscures this process in the Third World is the fact that the outcome of bargaining is not necessarily compromise.

In reality, within Third World countries there exists an armament process that is significantly different from those within the advanced producer countries but present nevertheless. Thus, decisions on the how, why and wherefore of armament procurement can be explained to varying degrees by a mix of perceptions of external threat, differing professional responses to how threats should be countered or diminished and what military technology can be acquired from either external or indigenous sources. Certainly, while all these factors are present, their salience will differ according to the size, geo-political position, stage of political development, influence of the military, economic capacity and nature of threat perception.

The arms trade can be understood as a subsystem of the international system which has prevailed since the end of World War II. The system exists on two axes: North–South and East–West. The transfer and sale of armaments from North to South have performed several functions for both suppliers and recipients. Third World countries exploited the cold war to amass the maximum defence capability in the minimum time and at the lowest price. Arms transfers also permitted Third World countries to confront regional problems, to defend themselves against irredentist claims, insurgencies and great-power interventions and, above all, to consolidate and protect sovereign rights. But the economic and political conditions which facilitated the rapid accumulation of arms in the Third World no longer obtain. Already these changes are being reflected in the statistics on military expenditure in and arms sales to the Third World.[3] In effect, the systemic transfer of military technology from North to South is currently approaching a crisis owing to several factors.

All major arms producers face pressures to export; but at certain times the pressure to export is more intense, particularly for the major industrial exporters such as France, Britain and West Germany. Periodically, military expenditures in the West European countries enter into a period of structural crisis. This is due to combinations of poor overall economic performance, military inflation, higher inelastic costs (fuel and forces pay), and the prevailing procurement culture. As a result the pressures upon military budgets rise and opportunity costs become more difficult to endure. Arms exports are a means of alleviating many of the costs associated with military inflation and cushioning the effects of falling domestic demand.

The problem faced by the major arms suppliers is that the market for arms in the Third World does not exist as it did in the 1970s.[4] During the 1970s the increasing need on the part of all major arms suppliers to export arms coincided with the economic conditions which prevailed in the Third World. In 1973 oil prices rose by 400 per cent and doubled again in 1978–79. This rapid accumulation of wealth by the OPEC countries opened up a massive arms market for arms exporters in both East and West. Other Third World countries financed their arms imports through drawing on reserves or through a positive net flow of capital on their balance of payments. Thus, directly or indirectly, these arms imports were financed through borrowings from official bilateral and multilateral sources and the international capital market.[5] Furthermore, during this period the major arms importers found it necessary to replace equipment generally considered to be obsolete. One reason why arms imports in South Asia are still rising while elsewhere they are declining is because the modernization programmes in India and Pakistan started much later.

In recent years, Third World countries have found themselves less able than ever before to afford to import arms, which are themselves becoming more expensive. Declining terms of trade, debt crises, the reduction of oil prices and the global recession have severely reduced arms markets. Given the unique characteristics of the OPEC phenomenon, the conditions which prevailed during the late 1970s are unlikely to be repeated.

During a period when many modernization programmes are well advanced, there exists more potential for adjustment. Moreover, some of the stronger developing countries, such as Brazil, have become producers themselves, and with relatively low levels of domestic demand they are now aggressive exporters free of the restrictions imposed on many of the traditional suppliers. As a result, arms sales to the Third World are declining, and West European countries are either buying indigenous products or products from consortiums in which they are involved. At the 1986 Farnborough Air Show, the biggest military aircraft showcase, the US aerospace firm Grumman decided not to put in an appearance, and other US companies declined the option to display.[6]

Third World states have been prevented from raising or maintaining military expenditure because of pressing economic problems: there is no widespread intent to practise armament limitation and control. Looking ahead to the future suggests that the current period of restraint may not last until the end of the century. The debt crisis is unlikely to afford many options for certain countries. Continued uncertainty and disagreement among OPEC countries might also reduce defence and security options. However, over the next decade, defence decision makers will begin to request follow-on systems to replace those currently in use. Wars in the Third World will be followed by re-equipment programmes. Inelastic costs, such as those for maintenance, repair and spare parts, will increase. The current trend towards force multipliers, such as AWACS, will involve considerable extra costs. Head and shoulders above other claims, the military will continue to argue that national security considerations are paramount; the lessons of history suggest that they will succeed. Adjustment policies will continue to fight shy of issues pertaining to defence and national security. Legislatures and executives will continue to relinquish completely the task of translating defence policy into technological requirements. The armed forces will continue to be the hostages of the technology they require. It would seem that in both the present and the future the Third World will not be able to sustain its current level of defence. Financial resources are not available, and economic recovery is unlikely to be sufficiently dynamic to afford the military options of the future. Somehow, Third World countries must think themselves out of this dilemma and begin to break not just the link between armament and underdevelopment but also the monopoly of military institutions in this sphere.

III.   Common security, arms control and the Third World

The problem which must be faced by those who argue the need for arms control and disarmament in the Third World is that radical changes in defence policies are not yet considered to be commensurate with national interests. Security and defence tend to be seen as symbiotic; all countries, including those in the Third World, perceive a direct relationship between national security and advanced military technology.

Within the Third World, security considerations are both visible and paramount. While it may be argued that other countries place no less emphasis upon national and collective security arrangements, it is also the case that the emphasis and concern are less sharp. For the past four decades Europe has been able to avoid war, but during the same period the Third World has experienced over 63 conflicts involving the death of over 16 million people. US, Soviet, British and French forces have intervened in disputes and conflicts in the Third World as and when their interests appear sufficiently threatened. US forces alone were used in 262 incidents between 1946 and 1982, many of which were located in the Third World.[7] Unlike Europe, territorial disputes are common and widespread, ranging from frequent border skirmishes to irredentist claims and sub-imperialism. Third World states generally perceive themselves to be more vulnerable than their developed counterparts.

In their approach to external security issues, Third World states place great store on defence as a means of safeguarding political independence and territorial integrity. Often overlooked by contemporary historians is the magnitude of change which occurred in Africa and Asia between 1945 and 1960. No fewer than 40 countries and one-quarter of the world's population revolted against colonialism and won independence. The rapidity of change was unprecedented in human history.[8] Once change had been achieved, the problem of defending the new *status quo* became paramount. Given the degree of tension within the Third World, between North and South and East and West, and the interface between the three, defence became of paramount concern. Certainly, there were attempts to reduce the taxing demands of defence. Jawaharlal Nehru tried between 1947 and 1962 to construct a new foreign policy for India based upon non-alignment. He also attempted to design a defence policy commensurate with his ambitions for foreign policy.

Both failed, in part because of the Sino-Indian War but also because Nehru and his advisers could not translate their political ambitions into military strategy and doctrine.[9] Another casualty of the Sino-Indian War was the powerful spirit of Bandung. The ensuing loss of dynamism greatly affected the future of the non-aligned movement and the potential for a new form of collective security (see also paper 1).

The unavoidable fact of contemporary life in the Third World is that regional security moves and initiatives have largely failed to guarantee security. Instead, in the face of failures on the diplomatic and foreign policy fronts, states have relied upon gradually increasing defence expenditure and modernizing defence capabilities. Of late, there has been a refreshing acknowledgement of this dilemma in several quarters. While the arms race in the Third World is universally recognized as deleterious for development progress, equally, there is a growing acceptance that a new paradigm is required which would effectively redefine security and offer new alternatives to the defence–security dilemma in the Third World.

During the early 1980s, when East–West relations were at a low ebb and when deep-seated structural problems in the global system became evident, a series of reports from West European liberal opinion-shapers advocated far-reaching and wide-ranging reforms to the international system. The Report of the Independent Commission on Disarmament and Security Issues, the so-called Palme Commission Report, is one such example.[10] Although the bulk of intellectual effort was directed towards the pressing need for arms control and disarmament in Europe, the report also projected a particular perspective on the negative effects of armament and military expenditure in the Third World.

Where the report differed from previous initiatives was in its outspoken condemnation of the attainment of security through the pursuit of relative power. Instead, the Commission advocated an approach to security based upon co-operation, hence the development of the common security concept. Although the tenets of common security apply to countries in both North and South, the Commission saw an increase in collective security measures as particularly important. In addition to a proposal to increase the effectiveness of the United Nations, the Commission advocated other, specific proposals—nuclear weapon-free zones, conferences on security and co-operation, regional zones of peace, increased control over the nuclear fuel cycle, wider adherence to the Non-Proliferation Treaty and control over arms transfers.[11]

The report has been followed by several other attempts to broaden the parameters of the security debate pertaining to the Third World. Those who once advocated a linkage between disarmament and development now advocate a dynamic relationship between disarmament, development and security. Influential environmentalists have entered the debate, bringing with them a new perspective on the relationship between militarization and the environment. In a recent *Worldwatch Report*, Lester Brown argued that the extensive deterioration of natural support systems and the declining conditions evident in many parts of the Third World pose dire threats to national and international security that now rival the traditional military threats. Consequently, there is an urgent need to redefine national security to encompass economic and environmental factors.[12] The Socialist International has made a similar point, but in a different way, arguing that armament and conflict are inseparable from the battle against poverty and underdevelopment, which is rapidly being lost.[13]

The influential opinion-shapers have rendered both a service and a disservice to our understanding of armament and disarmament issues in the Third World. There are undeniable benefits in looking at the security problem through 'green tinted' spectacles. A broader perspective raises the highly relevant question of the relationship between national security and people's security.[14] It alerts decision makers and the public to the severity of environmental crisis and the impotence of the national security framework; common security offers a conceptual alternative to the prevailing international system. Of particular importance for the Third World, it highlights an essential paradox: arms imports and high levels of military expenditure are seen by states as fulfilling security demands and underpinning sovereignty, but in practice they do neither.

Obversely, the common/alternative security debate contains within it a degree of confusion which diminishes its appeal and credibility. At the prescriptive level, common security amounts to little more than a shopping list of global reforms, but it does nothing to suggest that, at present, an alternative (or much reformed) international security regime would appeal to the interests of Third World governments, which is an essential pre-condition for change. For example, a prevailing assumption is that the cold war has continued to the disadvantage of the Third World. High levels of military expenditure are often considered inappropriate and damaging for Third World countries, but elites often do not accept the linkage between armament and underdevelopment. Instead, defence is considered essential and a means of complimenting, stimulating and protecting development. Above all, those who advocate new security regimes often overlook just how popular advanced military technology is in the Third World, both in the policy-making and in the public domain.

The prospects for arms control in the Third World begin to appear very paradoxical. On the one hand, the spiralling price of arms and the declining fortunes of Third World countries, both inside and outside OPEC, suggest that any regional or global initiatives aimed at creating new security regimes and reducing the pressure on defence budgets would be welcomed as initial steps towards arms control. Recent developments in Latin America would seem to support this view. Initiatives from President Alan García of Peru and complimentary steps by the Contadora Group have been geared to the reduction of military expenditures and a freeze on conventional armament imports into the region. García's proposal may in the future be accepted by the Andean countries—Argentina, Bolivia, Chile, Ecuador and Peru—although the Brazilian claim that regional initiatives should be dependent upon positive moves by the superpowers is an obstacle.

There have been several other promising moves towards enhancing regional security. With the increasing possibility of political change in South Africa, there also exists the possibility of an African nuclear weapon-free zone; all countries but South Africa support such an initiative. In September 1985 the South Pacific Forum opened a treaty to establish the South Pacific as a nuclear free zone, and signatories by 1987 include Australia, New Zealand and Fiji. In early 1986 North Korea pledged to launch an anti-imperialist and anti-nuclear campaign to rid the Korean peninsular of nuclear weapons and thereby create a nuclear free zone. The USSR and Japan have started talks based upon Far East confidence-building measures (CBMs) aimed at the concern of the Soviet Union's eastern neighbours lest arms control measures in Europe take place at the expense of a Soviet nuclear buildup in the East. China, Taiwan, and North and South Korea are also involved. In December 1985 India and Pakistan reached agreement not to attack each other's nuclear facilities. In addition negotiations over a non-aggression pact or a treaty of friendship are ongoing, which keeps open the possibility of a South Asian nuclear weapon-free zone. In early 1986 the leaders of New Zealand and Indonesia met to discuss the possibility of pursuing a South Asian zone of peace.[15]

Yet, these initiatives should be taken for what they are and for what is excluded—they are both partial and cosmetic. The prospect of a Middle East nuclear weapon-free zone is nowhere near the agenda. Recent reports which suggest that Pakistan has edged closer to attaining a full nuclear capability have put on the back-burner any calls for a South Asian nuclear-free zone, and in India the option to deliver a pre-emptive strike on Pakistan's Kahuta plant is once again on the agenda. Negotiations over creating the Indian Ocean as a zone of peace have languished. Political change in South Africa would virtually obviate the need to create a nuclear weapon-free zone in Africa, temporarily at least, unless a successor regime discovers a bomb in the basement and equivocates over what to do with it. The García initiative in Latin America is hardly a departure. In 1974 the Declaration of Ayacucho committed the Andean Group plus Argentina and Panama to the creation of conditions permitting an effective limitation of armaments and an end to their acquisition for offensive purposes. In 1978 a conference was convened to consider exclusively the problem of conventional arms control in the region, followed in 1980 by the adoption of a Charter of Conduct on the peaceful settlement of disputes.[16] Significantly, none of these initiatives has included or received blessing from Brazil, the major power in the region. All in all, arms control has largely failed; in no shape or form does it really address the real security problems of Third World countries.

IV.   Military technology—an ally of arms limitation?

Seen from this perspective, the prospects for control and limitations of conventional weapons in the Third World seem remote, but there are changes occurring in a different dimension which suggest that a more positive defence and security system for the Third World is becoming more feasible. Arms control in the Third World has yet to be seen as in the interests of Third World governments. However, an alternative or much reformed security system based upon alternative defence strategies may come to be seen as one route out of the increasingly contradictory armament process in the Third World.

It has been argued that the rising cost of weapon systems coupled with the declining economic conditions in the Third World have created a crisis for the systematic transfer of military technology to the Third World. In addition, it is also becoming evident that the characteristics of advanced military technology are becoming less appropriate for Third World countries. On the one hand there is some evidence that the armed forces of many Third World countries are experiencing problems in their ability to exploit the technology upon which they rely so much. On the other hand, whether or not advanced military technology will function efficiently, both in time of conflict and in the often extreme geographic conditions which prevail in the Third World, is becoming an increasingly relevant question on the basis of a growing body of evidence on the shortcomings and limitations of advanced military technology.

The realization of the capabilities of a weapon system depends not only upon its import and deployment. It also requires the adoption by a military establishment and, further, its assimilation into tactics, doctrine and organization.[17] The act of import/procurement suggests that a weapon system has been adopted by the military establishment, although this might not always be the case.[18] In developed countries there is continuing tension between the invention and the adoption of weapons and a rich array of evidence which documents the lag between what industry can produce and what the military is prepared to accept and assimilate.

For Third World countries, the problem manifests itself in a different way. In 1965 the Pakistan tank crews were unable to operate the automatic fire controls on their Patton tanks.[19] This indicates graphically the adverse effects of importing and deploying sophisticated technology while neglecting or being unable to cope with aspects of training; in some instances technological advantage can be turned into military disadvantage. Lack of centralized command coupled with inherent confusion (fog or war) prevented a full application and exploitation of the Argentine Exocet option during the Falklands/Malvinas War.[20] In 1981 Iran had the ability to use tanks, artillery, air defence and close-support aircraft in concert to mount offensive and potentially decisive operations against Iraq. However, owing primarily to the internal, domestic chaos of the time, in particular Khomeini's brutal purge of the officer corps in 1980, Iran's offensive potential dissolved in a sea of logistical chaos resulting in the permanent loss of the requisite organizational framework.[21].

Much more suspect than the ability of Third World militaries to assimilate advanced military technology is the ability of the technology itself to survive in difficult conditions. Unfortunately, the successes and failures of military technology in the Third World are somewhat difficult to assess. Military success in conventional war tends to be explained by superior military technology coupled to effective organization and high morale. Failures are more often than not explained by poor tactics, misuse of resources, chaos and military incompetence. In some respects these views are valid. Wars in the Third World often take place during periods of political crisis and national disaffection, which inevitably ramifies into civil–military command problems and logistical shortcomings. Equally, the Third World invariably provides the theatre in which modern military technology is subjected to its only relevant test, that of performance under real rather than simulated conditions. Thus, the Yom Kippur War in the Middle East was seen as a triumph for Syrian and Egyptian air defences and anti-tank weapons. The potency and potential of precision-guided munitions were once again confirmed during the Falklands/Malvinas War when the Exocet became a 'combat proven' system. Israel's efficient destruction of Syrian air defences based in the Bekaa Valley in 1982 was closely analysed primarily for the military lessons contained therein, but the tendency, it seems, is for defence analysts to look closely at Third World conflicts for signs of technological success but to explain away failures in terms of human error.

The same cannot be said of the debate in the West, where there is considerable concern over the implications of the deployment of complex weapon systems which are becoming increasingly inefficient, particularly in the United States. The US multi-option defence posture, global role and enormous defence budget have maintained that country's position at the cutting edge of advanced military technology. The US perception of military strength is the unshakable belief in the formula of organization, morale and superior technology, all of which are given a forward momentum through an ideology of manifest destiny. Yet, this formula is being seriously compromised by an unforeseen and contradictory trajectory. As weapon systems become more complex, they also become less robust and more prone to failure. In addition, unit costs are escalating, as are the logistical problems in relation to service, repair and maintenance. Some of the more advanced systems bought by the US armed forces—such as the M-1 tank, the cancelled Sergeant York/Divad anti-aircraft gun, the Copperhead 'smart' missile and the Maverick air-to-ground missile—have proved to be either operationally flawed or only barely fit for service during peacetime. In time of conflict or when subject to adverse weather conditions, many advanced weapon systems may be serviceable for only a fraction of the time intended. Fractures in an ever increasing logistical chain involving disruptions to spare parts and maintenance facilities will render virtually useless large parts of NATO and US conventional defence capability.[22] In addition to the 'reformist' movement and the media, there are dissenting voices from within the US defence community. Franklin Spinney, a Pentagon systems analyst, has noted that while many of the technical failures can be ironed out with sufficient investment of resources and expertise, the root problem is a conceptual failure. The pursuit of technological complexity has become confused with capability, and the former is more a cost than a benefit.

Increasing complexity increases the number of parts, thereby decreasing the ability of an individual to comprehend the whole. Increasing complexity is a cost, because it decreases the ability to understand and consequently makes it more difficult to adjust to, or shape, internal and external change. Put another way, increasing complexity increases rigidity in a game in which flexibility is a paramount virtue.[23]

While Spinney argues that increased complexity at the sharp end of defence capability does little to improve overall defence efforts, he also raises concern over the secondary effects. Operating and support costs are difficult to determine once the opportunity costs *vis-à-vis* other areas of the defence budget increase. Reductions in training and supplies and maintenance short-cuts have eroded capability and weakened morale. Furthermore, increasing complexity requires a commensurate rise in skills for operation and repair, and entails costs which the military paymasters are viewing with concern.[24]

What are the implications for Third World countries which are wedded to this particular technique of force? At the conceptual level, and with few exceptions, the armed forces of the Third World have completely adopted the Western model of defence: technology embodied in weapon systems to afford firepower, mobility and protection and facilitated by an organizational struc-ture utilizing techniques of command, control and communication to ensure the optimum use of the technology available. But it is difficult to estimate to what extent Third World countries have absorbed the problems and contradic-tions inherent in Western defence capabilities. For political, strategic and morale reasons, few of the major exporters are willing to export state-of-the-art technology, although there are several examples where this has happened: witness the sale of the MiG-29 to India, Iraq and Syria, or the Tornado MRCA and AWACS to Saudi Arabia, or the F-16 to Thailand and Pakistan. Fur-thermore, although many developing countries may want this type of tech-nology, they must first be able to pay for it. China rejected the Harrier VSTOL on the basis of cost, not capability. But, eventually, most advanced weapon systems released on to the export market, both good and bad, appear to find their way into Third World inventories. For example, during the 1970s India agreed to procure the Jaguar Deep Strike Penetration Aircraft to be replaced in the 1980s by the Mirage 2000. Foreign exchange shortages during the 1970s prevented the immediate procurement of the Jaguar. As and when political and economic conditions permitted, India procured and deployed both the Jaguar and the Mirage simultaneously.

The mounting evidence regarding the adverse cost and utility of advanced military technology for Third World countries is a persuasive argument for radical changes in defence policy and the adoption of alternative defence policies. However, when seen through the eyes of those who define defence and security needs, the perspective is very different. For professional bodies noted for their conservatism, advanced military technology has much in its favour. World War II was an overwhelming victory for superior technology deployed on a wide scale. As and when structural problems occur, it is often less complicated to argue that increased resources will suffice. Indeed, considering the blinkered approach towards product improvement, is it fair to expect anything more than the improvement of the product through a constant process of 'debugging'? Moreover, alternative defence policies spanning the continuum from the present debate in Western Europe through to the more time-honoured approach to territorial defence and non-violent civil resistance have been neither tried nor tested at the state level. Also, these policies are essentially strategies for coping with defeat, and the political cost of implementation would be massive.[25]

Nevertheless, a situation is evolving whereby the tenacious retention of the *status quo* is no longer appropriate and may be impossible. Alternative defence policies will not appear overnight and, in the present environment, few analysts would advocate their adoption. However, the approaching watershed behoves those with a professional and political interest in security, defence, arms control/limitation and disarmament to design new vistas in this direction. This is particularly apposite given the polarization of the security debate which has stifled innovative thinking for so many years:

> ... because Realist policies require the arming of the state and a power-struggle analysis of the system, they naturally clash with idealist policies based on disarmament, international co-operation, and a harmony-of-interests model of the system. If that clash is seen as so basic that it precludes a meaningful mix between them, then each alternative must carry alone the whole burden of security. To do this the Realist policy must exaggerate the necessity for a powerful state, and the idealist one must leap all the way into utopias of general and complete disarmament and world government.[26]

The call for a more realistic approach to the problems of security and disarmament has been partially answered by the Palme Commission, but this shopping list of global reforms, though relevant, is clearly inadequate. Thus, the contemporary debate on common/alternative security should continue and become more orientated towards providing an environment conducive to unilateral initiatives.

Against the backdrop of an emerging new security paradigm, Third World states should open up their own debates on the future of defence. Small states, island states, land-locked states, NICs and OPEC countries all have very different defence problems, security threats and the economic capability to react; there is no one defence policy which will be appropriate for all Third World countries. However, in order to pursue alternative defence policies, there are some self-evident guidelines. First, states should attempt a broader debate than exists at present. If it is the military which continues to define exclusively the parameters of defence policy, it will be reluctant to compromise its professional integrity. It would be unrealistic for an institution not to defend its turf. Experts from both inside and outside the defence community must intervene and be heard. In addition, the way in which defence-related decisions are taken should be considered in the context of increased political and public accountability. Second, the nature of advanced military technology should be carefully studied. In mounting a critique on armament, care should be taken to

avoid throwing out the baby with the bathwater. Military technology, sophisticated and otherwise, may have a role to play in defence. Simple, uncompli-
cated weapon systems have yet to prove their value or their cost-effectiveness.
The 'reformist' arguments are based largely upon supposition. Third, in
pursuing alternative defence strategies states should seek guarantees from a
strengthened international system to reduce the political cost of their
implementation and their security threats thereafter. This suggests a more
effective international policy on the control of out-of-area roles and regional
power struggles. True, the United Nations may no longer be the appropriate
institution to act as the guarantor of a new security regime, but the type and
scale of arms limitation and disarmament which are required in the Third
World to avoid a much more serious causal relationship between armament
and underdevelopment require as a prerequisite a more stable and benign
international environment. The common security initiative is an adequate
starting-point. This concept now needs to be developed into a more policy-
oriented perspective which is capable of giving depth to the initiatives of García
and others and a practical hue to the deliberations of the Palme Commission.
Fourth, future strategy, tactics and doctrine should be discussed in relation to
the past. Alternative defence makes little sense if traditional patron–client/
supplier–recipient relations continue unchecked. Here the role of indigenous
defence production or consortiums requires thought. So, too, should indigenous production be considered in relation to comparative advantages.
Defence strategies which are subject to high cost and low efficiency should be
replaced by appropriate defence strategies which consider factor endowment,
physical environment, low cost and the accepted laws of war as their guiding
principles.

It is already possible to detect pockets of concern and innovative thinking
along the lines of alternative defence for Third World countries, but primarily
in quarters with no apparent axe to grind in the arms limitation/disarmament
debate. Technical/professional journals, defence analysts and the military are
occasionally given to measured critiques of the prevailing philosophy of
defence.[27] As economic conditions continue to afford fewer choices, more
questions will be asked. But the debate must go beyond defence alone in order
to add credibility and imagination to an alternative security regime. At present,
those with a professional or political axe to grind in this domain are stunted by
the conceptual shortcomings which have characterized the debate over disarmament in the Third World. In both the near and the distant future,
disarmament will be a vague and unobtainable goal. At a point between the
present system which guarantees neither defence or security and the vagaries of
general and complete disarmament or disarmament and development there
lies a host of policy options for developing countries which offer a new realism
and a means of overcoming the inertia of the past.

The maintenance of the *status quo* would be wrong. We have already seen
the horrific consequences of chemical weapons in the Gulf War—such scenes
could become more widespread if more states opt for the deployment of the

'poor man's deterrent' in the face of growing cost and operational problems at the conventional level. Despite a growing body of empirical evidence which testifies to the relationship between armament and underdevelopment, this has not effected a move towards arms limitation in the Third World. If the current system is not replaced by adequate alternatives, history may well repeat itself with dire consequences, and not just for the Third World. Finally, this type of armaments limitation in the Third World could significantly influence the situation in the rest of the world. Arms sales, it can be argued, have avoided the inevitable confrontation with structural crises in the defence sectors. By radically changing patterns of demand, the crisis would no longer be avoidable.

Notes and references

[1] Thayer, G., *The War Business: The International Trade in Armaments* (Weidenfeld and Nicolson: London, 1969), pp. 28–29.

[2] A most pessimistic view of how defence expenditure and production can seriously damage the economy is provided in Kaldor, M., *The Baroque Arsenal* (Andre Deutsch: London, 1980). A more benign view of the economic effects of military expenditure can be found in Kennedy, G., *The Economics of Defence* (Faber and Faber: London, 1975).

[3] These developments have been studied and discussed by the SIPRI arms trade and military expenditure team whose reports are to be found in the *SIPRI Yearbooks*. See also Brzoska, M. and Ohlson, T., SIPRI, *Arms Transfers to the Third World, 1971–85* (Oxford University Press: Oxford, 1987).

[4] See Brzoska and Ohlson (note 3), chapter 4.

[5] Kitchenman, W. F., *Arms Transfers and the Indebtedness of Less Developed Countries* (Rand Corporation N–2020–FF: Santa Monica, CA, Dec. 1983), p. 8.

[6] Bedard, P., 'Overseas markets drying up for US arms makers', *Defence Week*, vol. 7, no. 35 (8 Sep. 1986), pp. 1, 12.

[7] Blechman, B. M. and Kaplan, S. S., *Force Without War: U.S. Armed Forces as a Political Instrument* (Brookings Institution: Washington, DC, 1978).

[8] For an excellent appraisal of these events see Barraclough, G., *An Introduction to Contemporary History* (Penguin: Harmondsworth, 1967), chapter 6.

[9] Smith, C., *The Armament Process in the Third World: A Case Study of India* (United Nations University/Ford Foundation: Delhi, Feb. 1986), mimeo, chapter 2.

[10] *Common Security: A Programme for Disarmament: The Report of the Independent Commission on Disarmament and Security Issues* (Pan Books: London, 1982).

[11] Note 10, p. 157–72.

[12] Brown, L. R., 'Redefining national security', *State of the World—1986* (Worldwatch, Norton: New York, 1986), pp. 195–211.

[13] *Global Challenge: From Crisis to Co-operation, Breaking the North–South Stalemate: The Report of the Socialist International Committee on Economic Policy* (Pan: London, 1985), p. 196.

[14] Deshingkar, G., 'People's security versus national security', *Seminar*, no. 280 (Dec. 1982), pp. 28–30.

[15] Details of these and other arms control negotiations can be found in the authoritative *Arms Control Reporter* produced by the Institute for Defence and Disarmament Studies, Brookline, MA.

[16] For a discussion of the Latin America proposal which preceded the García initiative see, Goldblat, J. and Milan, V., 'Militarization and arms control in Latin America', in SIPRI, *World Armaments and Disarmament: SIPRI Yearbook 1982* (Taylor & Francis: London, 1982), pp. 393–416.

[17] Dupoy, T. N., *The Evolution of Weapons and Warfare* (Hero Books: Fairfax, VA, 1984), p. 301.

[18] In India there is a great deal of support for the development of nuclear weapons, but the armed forces are not in favour of taking the nuclear option, as they realize that it will reduce their power of decision-taking during time of crisis.

[19] Albrecht, U. and Kaldor, M., 'Introduction', in M. Kaldor and A. Eide, *The World Military Order: The Impact of Military Technology on the Third World* (Macmillan: London, 1979), p. 8.

[20] Ullman, H. K., 'Profound or perfunctory: observations on the South Atlantic conflict', in R. E. Harkavy and S. G. Neuman, *The Lessons of Recent Wars in the Third World: Approaches and Case Studies*, vol. I (Gower/Lexington: Aldershot, 1985), p. 250.

[21] Stuadenmaier, W. O., 'Iran–Iraq (1980–   )' in Harkavy and Neuman (note 20), pp. 214, 224.

[22] Rasor, D. (ed.), *More Bucks, Less Bang: How the Pentagon Buys Ineffective Weapons* (Fund for Constitutional Government/Project on Military Procurement: Washington, DC, 1983).

[23] Spinney, F. C., *Defense Facts of Life: The Plans/Reality Mismatch* (Westview Press: London, 1985), p. 6.

[24] Note 23, p. 39.

[25] Clark, M., 'The Alternative Defence Debate: Non-Nuclear Defence Policies for Europe', *ADIU Occasional Paper No. 3* (Armament and Disarmament Information Unit: Sussex, Aug. 1985), p. 9.

[26] Buzan, B., *People, States and Fear: The National Security Problem in International Relations* (Wheatsheaf: Brighton, 1983), p. 250.

[27] For example, Vlahos, M., 'Designing a Third World nave', *Journal of Defense and Diplomacy*, vol. 3, no. 3 (Mar. 1985), pp. 39–42, 62. Defence analysts include S. J. Deitchman and F. C. Spinney. Sources of military dissatisfaction include confidential conversations with the author.

Part II. Supplier control

Paper 5.   US policy on arms transfers to the Third World

MICHAEL T. KLARE

I.   Introduction

For the past 30 years, US Government policy on conventional arms transfers to the Third World has experienced sharp swings in direction, shifting from a posture of relative restraint to one of relative permissiveness, and then back and forth again, in response to changing political, economic and military priorities. This shifting stance on arms transfer policy is a consequence of the fact that arms transfers—and particularly arms transfers to the Third World—have long been viewed by the US Government as elastic tools of foreign policy, to be used in such fashion as the administration in power sees fit. Diminished arms transfers may, on occasion, be the proclaimed goal of US policy—but this generally reflects a belief that US foreign policy objectives will best be served thereby, not a belief that arms transfer restraint is an important goal in and of itself.[1]

While it is possible to identify periodic swings in US policy on arms transfers to the Third World, it is important to note that government policy is set within a context of supply and demand that has its own influence on the configuration of trade patterns. When US arms manufacturers face a shrinking domestic market (as occurred at the end of the Viet Nam War), they will invariably put pressure on the government to loosen the controls on export sales; when external demand is depressed (as occurred during the international 'debt crisis' of the mid-1980s), even the most enthusiastic proponents of arms transfers will have difficulty in boosting export sales.[2] Thus arms transfer agreements will sometimes rise in a period of announced 'restraint' and fall during a period of official permissiveness. None the less, US arms export patterns have been relatively responsive to fluctuations in government policy.

The interaction between policy shifts and market forces is clearly seen in figure 5.1, which charts the annual level of US arms export agreements with Third World countries. (Arms *agreements* are the most useful measure of arms transfer policy, since they represent the total of all new contracts signed by the government within that particular year; arms *deliveries*, on the other hand, may not occur until several years later, when a different set of policy guidelines has been put into effect.) Beginning in 1973, US sales experienced a pronounced upward turn, reflecting the Nixon Administration's efforts to arm friendly powers in the Third World (as mandated by the Nixon Doctrine) and to stem

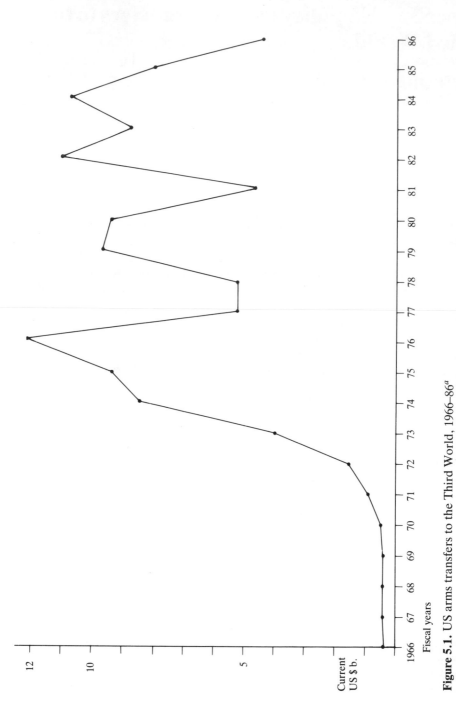

Figure 5.1. US arms transfers to the Third World, 1966–86[a]

[a] Orders placed under the Foreign Military Sales programme (incl. Foreign Military Construction Sales programme (incl. Foreign Military Construction Sales); excludes exports under the Commercial Sales programme.

Source: US Department of Defense.

the outflow of dollars caused by the sharp increase in oil prices. The 1973–75 upsurge was followed, in 1976, by a drop in US arms sales caused by the world-wide recession which followed the OPEC oil price rise. US arms sales rose again in 1978–79, following the Camp David accords and new US overtures to Saudi Arabia, Egypt and Israel. Another drop occurred in 1979, following the fall of the Shah of Iran, and another peak in 1981–82, with the Reagan Administration's drive to refurbish US military alliances with friendly Third World governments. Finally, in 1983–85, a sharp drop in new sales was produced by another global recession and the accompanying 'debt crisis'.

The evident *responsiveness* of US arms export patterns to changing policy priorities can be attributed to the effective control exercised by government officials over the volume and character of US military exports. Under US law—specifically, the Mutual Security Act of 1951, the Foreign Assistance Act of 1961 and the Arms Export Control Act of 1976—all exports of military goods are subject to government supervision and control.[3] US law also distinguishes between two categories of arms transfer: government-to-government transactions administered by the Defense Security Assistance Agency (DSAA) through the Foreign Military Sales (FMS) programme; and 'commercial sales' of military goods by private US firms to foreign governments, firms and individuals. FMS sales, which account for approximately 80–90 per cent of US military exports, are entirely controlled by the federal government. Commercial sales, which account for the remaining 10–20 per cent, are regulated through the licensing function of the State Department's Office of Munitions Control (OMC). By shifting the parameters and priorities of FMS transactions and commercial sales licensing, the federal government effectively determines the pace and character of US military exports.[4]

Presidential authority over the management of arms transfers is clearly stipulated by the Arms Export Control Act (AECA). 'In furtherance of world peace and the security and foreign policy of the United States', the Act states, 'the President is authorized to control the import and export defense articles and defense services and to provide guidance to persons of the United States involved in the export or import of such articles and services'. The AECA further invests the Secretary of State with direct responsibility for oversight of arms transfers: as stated in Section 2, 'the Secretary of State . . . shall be responsible for the continuous supervision and general direction of [military] sales and exports . . . to the end that . . . the foreign policy of the United States is best served thereby'.[5] Congress has from time to time banned the transfer of arms to certain countries which have been cited for persistent violations of human rights or has imposed limits on the sale of sophisticated weapons to particular Third World areas (see also below); for the most part, however, arms-sales decision making is the exclusive province of the Executive Branch.

US policy on arms sales is therefore Executive Branch policy—and thus, as in other areas of foreign policy, subject to the periodic shifts in direction triggered by the turnover in administrations. To be sure, certain impulses remain constant: the military services tend to favour export sales as a way of recouping their investment in research and development (R&D) and to reduce the unit costs they pay for their own supplies of new weapons; the Commerce Department generally seeks new opportunities to balance the nation's international trade accounts; and so forth. Moreover, prominent US defence contractors can be counted on to lobby vigorously on behalf of their pending export orders.[6] None the less, the President still enjoys considerable leeway with which to put his stamp on arms export policy if it is his desire to do so.

All recent US administrations have permitted major sales of conventional arms to favoured Third World recipients. For some, however, relative restraint in the export of munitions was an important foreign policy concern. President Kennedy sought to discourage costly high-technology arms purchases by impoverished Third World countries, and President Carter sought to diminish the intensity of regional arms races in volatile Third World areas. However, these impulses were motivated not so much by a belief in the importance of restraint *per se*, but rather by a belief that such restraint, under certain conditions, best served US foreign policy objectives. Thus, whether permissiveness or restraint was the avowed US policy at any given time, the management of arms transfers was still seen as an important tool in the conduct of US relations with Third World countries.

To fully appreciate the myriad ways in which arms transfer policy have been reconfigured in consonance with the changing goals of US foreign policy, it is necessary to examine the outlook of successive administrations—for it is in the White House that US arms export policy has largely been shaped. Accordingly, the evolution of US export policy is charted, from the Kennedy period to the Reagan era, paying special attention to Latin America (as that is a region in which the shifts in US arms export policy are often most pronounced).

II.   From 'containment' to 'counterinsurgency'

For the first full decade of the cold war (1950–60), US arms transfer policy was largely governed by the doctrine of 'containment'. Believing that the United States bore primary responsibility for the defence of the 'free world' against communist aggression, successive US administrations advocated the supply of arms and military equipment to friendly governments in the Third World. Most of these arms were provided *gratis* through the Military Assistance Program (MAP) of the Department of Defense, under procedures specified in the Mutual Security Act of 1951.

In line with the strategy of containment, which envisioned a global US military effort to prevent further conquests by the USSR, US arms aid in this period stressed the enhancement of allied defences against conventional military attack. Favoured US recipients, particularly the 'forward defense countries' on the borders of the Soviet Union and China (notably Greece, Turkey, Iran, Pakistan, Taiwan and South Korea), received billions of dollars worth of US tanks, aircraft, artillery pieces and other front-line combat systems. In Latin America, which is somewhat removed from what was then seen as the main arena of conflict, the emphasis was on anti-submarine warfare and the defence of coastal areas. The particular arms supplied to Third World nations in this period were not normally of the first quality—many were taken from surplus World War II and Korean War stockpiles—but nevertheless endowed these countries with a significant war-fighting capability.

With the triumph of the Cuban Revolution in 1959, the USA was forced to reconsider the basis for its arms export policy towards the Third World. By waging a successful guerrilla war against Batista's US-equipped army, Fidel Castro demonstrated that strategies emphasizing defence against conventional, external attack did not necessarily contribute to defence against unconventional, internal attack. The Cuban upheaval also occurred at a time when US policy-makers were beginning to accord the Third World increased geopolitical significance, reflecting growing US trade with these once-neglected areas. Together, these developments stimulated a new interest in guerrilla warfare and in strategies for combating what were called 'wars of national liberation' in the Third World. Out of this effort emerged the strategy of 'counterinsurgency', which was to dominate US military thinking throughout the 1960s.[7]

John F. Kennedy, who succeeded Dwight D. Eisenhower as President in 1961, placed special emphasis on the development and implementation of counterinsurgency doctrine. 'Subversive insurgency is another type of war, new in its intensity, ancient in its origins', he told US Army cadets in 1962. 'It requires in those situations where we must counter it . . . a whole new kind of strategy (and) a wholly different kind of force.'[8] In line with this outlook, Kennedy established a Special Group for Counterinsurgency at the sub-Cabinet level and ordered a thorough revision of US arms export programmes.[9] As a result, counterinsurgency became the principal objective of US aid to Latin America and other Third World areas, while external defence was relegated to a decidedly second place. As noted by Professor Edwin Lieuwen of the University of New Mexico in a 1969 Senate study, 'the basis for military aid to Latin America abruptly shifted from hemispheric defense to internal security, from the protection of coastlines and antisubmarine warfare to defense against Castro-communist guerrilla warfare'.[10]

Beginning with the fiscal year 1963 Military Assistance Program, Third World countries which had signed mutual security pacts with the United States became eligible for grants or credit-assisted sales of counterinsurgency hardware and training. The USA scaled back its deliveries of heavy combat gear but increased its transfers of small arms, trucks and utility vehicles, anti-riot gear, and other systems suitable to internal security and counter-guerrilla operations.

As viewed by strategists of the Kennedy and Johnson Administrations, counterinsurgency implied more than the transfer of military and paramilitary technology: it also implied a commitment to economic and social development on the part of recipient countries. Believing that revolution can only flourish in an environment of underdevelopment and stagnation, Secretary of Defense

Robert S. McNamara argued that the counterinsurgency effort must include a positive effort to advance development, in order that the impoverished masses might be won over to the government's side. The United States could facilitate development, McNamara suggested, by providing economic assistance through the Alliance for Progress, by promoting private investment, and by helping the military and the police to maintain the necessary environment of 'order and stability'.[11] At the same time, Third World armies were encouraged to promote development by lending their managerial and technical skills to civilian development projects, and by curbing their appetite for costly, high-technology weapons that would absorb funds needed for economic modernization.

In accordance with this outlook, arms transfer restraint—at least in so far as it pertained to sales of sophisticated front-line equipment—became an important objective of the Kennedy and Johnson Administrations. When Peru in 1965 asked for permission to purchase a squadron of supersonic F-5A Freedom Fighters, the USA denied the request on the grounds that it constituted 'a prime example of wasteful military expenditures for unnecessarily sophisticated equipment at a time when generous US credits were being extended for economic development'.[12] This decision was viewed by many in Washington as an important US move in promoting arms restraint by underdeveloped Third World countries; it is important to recognize, however, that the USA was not advocating restraint *as such* but rather was seeking to persuade Peru to concentrate on internal war rather than external defence.

The US refusal to sell the F-5A to Peru set off a chain of events whose consequences can still be felt today. When rebuffed by Washington, Peru turned to France, where an export-conscious government was all too eager to provide credits for the sale of the Dassault-Breguet Mirage-5 fighter. Other Latin American governments, in line with their traditional policy of matching the military acquisitions of their rivals, acquired Mirage fighters of their own. US resistance to these moves—at one point the USA threatened to suspend economic aid to Peru—prompted some countries to develop a policy of diversifying their sources of arms among several suppliers (in order to avoid becoming overly dependent on any single source), and also prompted Argentina and Brazil to step up efforts to establish indigenous arms industries. Despite this, the Johnson Administration continued to adhere to a developmentalist approach to arms sales; however, other constituencies in the United States began lobbying for a change in export policy. Aerospace executives launched a campaign for the repeal of all restrictions on military exports to the Third World, and many Pentagon officials—concerned that Latin America's turn toward Europe would undermine their ties with the area's military leadership—joined the lobbying effort.

III. The Nixon Doctrine

Ideologically opposed to restraints on arms sales, President Nixon quickly set out to discard the austere, developmentalist approach of the Kennedy and Johnson Administrations and to adopt a more permissive policy in its place. In doing so, Nixon was not so much repudiating the political intent of the Kennedy–Johnson policy (with its heavy emphasis on counterinsurgency) as he was attempting to advance another US goal—the maintenance of close ties between US and foreign military leaders. Because the developmentalist approach of Presidents Kennedy and Johnson had alienated some Third World military leaders who desired (often for nationalistic and symbolic reasons) modern military equipment, Nixon sought to placate these officers—many of whom wielded considerable political power—by lifting prior restraints and approving sales of high-performance US arms.

The new stance was most evident in Latin America, which had been the principal target of the Kennedy–Johnson approach. Soon after taking office, President Nixon asked Nelson Rockefeller—then Governor of New York State—to assess US arms policies during a 'presidential mission' to Latin America. Upon returning to the United States, Rockefeller proposed a less restrictive stance on arms sales. He argued that if the United States is to maintain cordial relations with the region's military leadership, it must drop its restrictions on the export of sophisticated armaments and permit sales of 'aircraft, ships and other major military equipment'.[13]

Although the White House immediately endorsed Rockefeller's recommendations, Congress was not so accommodating. Angered by the Mirage sales to Latin America (which seemed to nullify the intent of US economic aid programmes) and concerned by the growing unpopularity of the Viet Nam War, the legislature imposed several new restrictions on arms exports to the Third World. In 1968, a new Foreign Military Sales Act (FMSA) was adopted which prohibited sales of 'sophisticated weapons systems' to underdeveloped countries (except to the 'forward defense countries' on the border of China and the USSR) and imposed a limit of $100 million on military aid to Latin America (excluding training), with a presidential waiver of 50 per cent of that ceiling. At the same time, an amendment was added to the Foreign Assistance Act requiring that aid be cut to any country which diverted excessive funds to the acquisition of sophisticated military hardware.

To overcome these obstacles to a more flexible export programme, Nixon Administration officials conducted a vigorous campaign for the repeal of statutory restraints on arms transfers, particularly the ban on exports of high-technology weaponry to Third World countries. In pursuing their case, administration officials charged that such restrictions undermined US national security by weakening long-established ties between US and Third World military officials. This argument was given special emphasis in 1973, after the maverick military regime in Peru placed an order for 200 Soviet T-55 tanks—this being the first major purchase of Soviet arms by any South American country. Because arms transfers are believed to foster a close working relationship between supplier and recipient (through the supply of training, maintenance, services, spare parts, and so forth), Latin America's shift to European and Soviet weapons was thought to weaken US ties while enhancing the influence of other powers.

Although sympathetic to these arguments, Congress was still disinclined to promote expanded US ties with Third World military regimes and thus resisted any changes in its stance on arms transfers. As is so often the case, however, Congress had left the President a loophole—and in 1973 President Nixon decided to forgo further pleading and to take matters into his own hands. On 5 June 1973, he invoked Section 4 of the FMSA—which allowed the President to waive congressional restrictions on the transfer of sophisticated items when he determined that such sales were important to the national security of the United States—in order to permit sales of the Northrop F-5E supersonic fighter to Argentina, Brazil, Chile, Colombia and Venezuela. (Brazil eventually bought 42 F-5Es, and Chile bought 18.) Nixon subsequently invoked Section 4 to permit sales of other sophisticated arms to Latin America, thus producing a sharp rise in US military exports to the region. Total FMS sales to Latin America. rose to $48 million in FY 1971, $104 million in 1972, $105 million in 1973 and $206 million in 1974 (all figures in current dollars).[14]

As the 1970s proceeded, two crucial events occurred which irrevocably altered the political-economic context within which US arms export policy was shaped. The first was the US defeat in Viet Nam, which produced a fundamental shift in the domestic political environment, and the second was the OPEC oil price increase of 1974, which produced a fundamental change in the world economic environment. In response to the first event, Nixon attempted to shift some US global defence responsibilities to 'surrogate gendarmes' in the Third World (a policy which came to be known as the Nixon Doctrine); in response to the second, he launched a major drive to increase US military sales to the oil-exporting nations.

Both of these steps generated enormous upward pressure on US military *sales* (as distinct from grants) to the Third World. Under the Nixon Doctrine, Washington sought to enhance the military capabilities of selected Third World powers through accelerated arms transfers; and because, in light of the Viet Nam fiasco, Congress was reluctant to increase grant spending on the MAP programme (which was perceived as a possible precursor to direct US military involvement in overseas conflicts), this inevitably led to increased military sales. Similarly, in attempting to improve the US trade balance *vis-à-vis* the oil-producing nations of the Middle East, the USA was forced to sell what the Arab countries and Iran seemed to want the most—namely, sophisticated weaponry. Impelled by these pressures, President Nixon further loosened US restraints on sales of sophisticated munitions to Third World countries and encouraged US firms to solicit new military orders from the oil-producing nations.[15] When Nixon was replaced as President by Gerald Ford in 1975, these policies were continued under the leadership of Secretary of State Henry Kissinger.

Kissinger's approach to arms transfers is perhaps most evident in the 'shuttle diplomacy' he conducted between Israel and Egypt in the mid-1970s. In order to woo Cairo from the Soviet orbit and reduce tensions in the Middle East, Kissinger held out the promise of extensive US arms aid as the reward for progress on new peace agreements between the two long-time adversaries.[16] The apparent success of this effort led many in Washington to view arms transfers as a valuable instrument of political and diplomatic leverage—a perception that was to haunt Jimmy Carter later in the decade, when he set out to restrain US arms transfers to the Third World.

Nixon's decisions, combined with the sudden affluence of the Persian Gulf nations, resulted in a dramatic rise in US military sales to Third World countries (and particularly to the oil-exporting nations of the Middle East). Total Third World orders under the FMS Program rose from $0.9 billion in FY 1971 to $1.6 billion in 1972, $4.1 billion in 1973, $8.5 billion in 1974, $9.4 billion in 1975, and a record $12.6 billion in 1976[17] (see table 5.1). Sales to the Persian Gulf countries posted an even more spectacular rise: from $410 million in FY 1970 to $11.3 billion in 1976, a five-year increase of 2500 per cent. These

Table 5.1. US arms transfers, 1968–86

By fiscal year; current US $b.

Year	Foreign Military Sales Programme[a]			Commercial sales programme: licensed exports
	Third World orders	World-wide orders	World-wide deliveries	
1968	0.46	1.18	0.99	n.a.
1969	0.44	1.18	1.28	n.a.
1970	0.53	1.13	1.34	n.a.
1971	0.87	1.39	1.35	0.43
1972	1.60	2.91	1.46	0.49
1973	4.08	4.85	1.51	0.36
1974	8.46	9.23	3.18	0.50
1975	9.42	15.76	3.50	0.55
1976	12.11	13.95	5.78	1.40
1977	5.26	6.31	7.03	1.52
1978	5.26	7.45	7.56	1.68
1979	9.66	12.39	8.04	1.53
1980	9.39	14.70	7.23	1.97
1981	4.57	7.64	9.20	2.20
1982	11.05	20.29	10.60	1.80
1983	8.78	16.62	13.16	4.01
1984	10.72	14.35	9.82	3.82
1985	8.04	12.47	9.57	2.28
1986	4.44	7.13	7.74	2.01

[a] Includes Foreign Military Construction Sales.

Source: US Department of Defense, *Foreign Military Sales, Foreign Military Construction Sales and Military Assistance Facts*, as of September 30, 1986 (and earlier editions).

increases in the dollar value of US arms exports were accompanied, moreover, by increases in the *sophistication* of US weapons sold to Third World countries. Most notable in this regard was the 1972 decision to sell to Iran—then viewed as Washington's principal 'surrogate' in the Persian Gulf area—virtually any non-nuclear weapon sought by Shah Mohammed Reza Pahlavi. By 1976, the Shah had ordered 80 Grumman F-14 Tomcat fighters (the most advanced combat aircraft in the US Navy inventory), 209 McDonnell-Douglas F-4 Phantom fighter-bombers, 202 Bell AH-1J Cobra helicopter gunships, 25 000 TOW and Dragon anti-tank missiles, and 4 Spruance Class missile destroyers.[18]

Despite the sharp increases in US arms exports to the Middle East and the growing trend toward the sale of high-performance weaponry, no fundamental changes were made in the legislative basis for the US arms export programme. As the sales tallies began to mount, therefore, many US lawmakers concluded that the arms programme was 'out of control', and in need of serious revision. The first step towards a revised arms sales policy was taken by the legislature in 1974, through the adoption of the Nelson Amendment to the Foreign Military Sales Act, giving Congress a limited veto over major FMS transactions. This amendment was subsequently incorporated into the International Security Assistance and Arms Export Control Act (AECA) of 1976, which superseded the FMSA and constituted the first comprehensive piece of legislation to establish formal policy guidelines for the military sales programme. Besides the veto measure, the 1976 act contained restrictions on the 're-transfer' of US-supplied arms from one recipient to another and established review procedures for licensing and co-production programmes. In these years, Congress also imposed restrictions on arms transfers to a number of Latin American countries charged with flagrant human rights violations, including Argentina, Brazil, Chile, El Salvador, Guatemala and Uruguay.[19]

Following the passage of the AECA, the momentum in the reform of US export policies shifted to the Executive Branch. Following his election to the presidency in 1976, Jimmy Carter promised to make arms export control a top priority of his administration. In his first White House interview, on 24 January 1977, he told reporters that the National Security Council (NSC) had already discussed the issue and had reached a consensus on 'the necessity for reducing arms sales' and for placing 'very tight restraints on future commitments' to US arms producers and their overseas customers.[20] To convert this outlook into formal government policy, Carter ordered his Secretary of State, Cyrus Vance, to develop a set of recommendations for a new arms export policy.

IV.   The Carter 'policy of arms restraint'

After several months of internal debate, a new set of arms export guidelines were adopted by President Carter on 13 May 1977, with the signing of Presidential Directive No. 13 (PD-13). The new policy was made public on 19 May 1977, with the release of a presidential statement on conventional arms transfers.

In the introduction to the 19 May statement, President Carter notes that his new policy was based on two fundamental assumptions: first, that the unrestrained spread of conventional weaponry 'threatens stability in every region of the world'; and second, that as the world's leading exporter of arms, the United States bears 'special responsibilities' to take the lead in restraining its military sales. On this basis, Carter enunciated a new principle to govern US arms-export decision making: rather than view military exports as a normal instrument of US policy, 'the United States will henceforth view arms transfers as an *exceptional foreign implement*, to be used *only* in instances where it can be clearly demonstrated that the transfer contributes to our national security interests' (emphasis added).[21]

To implement this 'policy of arms restraint', as he called it, Carter imposed several specific controls. These constraints were not, however, to be universal in their application: they did not apply to countries with which the United States had 'major defense treaties' (specifically, the NATO countries and Australia, Japan and New Zealand), and would not be allowed to conflict with Washington's 'historic responsibilities to assure the defense of Israel'. They did not, moreover, apply to military services (training, technical assistance and construction work), which account for as much as 40 per cent of US military sales. Finally, they could be waived by the President in response to 'extra-ordinary circumstances' or when he determined that 'countries friendly to the United States must depend on advanced weaponry to offset qualitative and other disadvantages in order to maintain a regional balance'. These exceptions having been established, Carter imposed the following controls.

Ceiling: The total dollar value (in constant 1976 dollars) of US arms transfers to non-exempt countries in fiscal year 1978 would not exceed the FY 1977 level and would be diminished in subsequent years.

Sophistication: The United States would not be the first supplier to introduce into Third World areas 'newly developed, advanced weapons systems which could create a new or significantly higher combat capability'.

Modification: The development or 'significant modification' of advanced combat systems 'solely for export' was prohibited.

Promotion: US Government personnel assigned to embassies and military missions abroad would no longer be permitted to help representatives of US arms firms to market their products to foreign governments.

Human rights: In deciding on proposed arms transfers, the United States would attempt to 'promote and advance respect for human rights in recipient countries'.

Multilateral negotiations: Because 'actual reductions in the worldwide traffic in arms will require multilateral co-operation', the United States would initiate negotiations with other major suppliers—including the Soviet Union—to develop 'possible measures for multilateral action'. (Carter subsequently initiated a series of Conventional Arms Transfer (CAT) Talks with the Soviet Union, which were held between December 1977 and December 1978.)

When first announced in May 1977, these guidelines were the subject of considerable criticism, both from representatives of the arms industry—who thought they were too restrictive—and from arms control and disarmament experts—who considered them too weak. The arms producers, and their allies in Congress and the military, argued that the Carter guidelines unfairly penalized the US companies by permitting firms in other major supplying countries (none of which appeared likely to adopt similar restrictions of their own) to pursue sales that would otherwise have gone to US producers. The arms controllers, on the other hand, argued that the guidelines were of dubious value because of all the waivers and exceptions described above.

Even with the waivers, both camps anticipated major changes in the way the Executive Branch conducted its arms export operations.[22] As the administration began to process actual arms transactions, however, it behaved more or less as its predecessors had—turning down some of the more dubious orders from abroad, but approving most of the requests submitted by principal US customers. By October 1977, only a few months after the Carter policy had been formally announced, analysts at the Congressional Research Service (CRS) of the Library of Congress found that there had been no fundamental shift in US arms export policy. 'Rather than being used as an "exceptional foreign policy implement"', the CRS team observed, 'arms transfers continue to occur on a rather routine basis'.[23]

Despite such criticism, President Carter continued to insist upon the efficacy of his policy, contending that the export ceiling—however imperfect—had produced a slowdown in the level of arms sales. 'While high', he observed, the level was 'considerably less than it would have been in the absence of new restraints we introduced, particularly in sales commitments to the developing countries'.[24]

Unfortunately for Carter's credibility, the increase in sales to the exempt countries exceeded the decrease in sales to the non-exempt countries, and thus the overall level of US exports continued to rise. (Total FMS orders rose from $8.8 billion in FY 1977 to $11.7 billion in 1978.) As these figures became known, Carter's export policy was scathingly described as 'doublethink' by critics in both parties.

Despite the criticism, President Carter reaffirmed his commitment to arms restraint and in December 1978 announced yet another reduction (the first was announced in February 1978) in sales to the non-exempt countries—from $8.55 billion in FY 1978 to $8.43 billion in FY 1979 (a reduction of 8 per cent when adjusted for inflation). However, Carter left himself room for a retreat in the future, saying that any further reductions would depend 'on the degree of cooperation we receive in the coming year from other nations' in restraining their own exports.[25]

Indeed, by this point, Carter had already begun to alter his stance on the arms issue, approving several controversial sales to the Middle East and loosening restraints on sales to other regions. In February 1978, he authorized the sale of 200 modern combat aircraft to three Middle Eastern countries (60

F-15s to Saudi Arabia, 50 F-5Es to Egypt, and 15 F-15s and 75 F-16s to Israel) in a move that aroused strong congressional opposition. Then, in August of that year, he gave preliminary approval to the Shah of Iran's request for another $12 billion worth of sophisticated US weaponry, including some 200 F-16 fighters and 7 super-sophisticated AWACS radar surveillance aeroplanes. At about the same time, Carter terminated the CAT Talks with the USSR.

Although President Carter never formally rescinded the guidelines announced on 19 May 1977, his 'arms restraint' policy was effectively abandoned in March 1980 when he barred any further reductions in sales to the non-exempt countries.[26] In the remaining months of his administration, President Carter announced major new sales to Egypt and Israel (in accordance with the Camp David accords) and began the series of negotiations with Saudi Arabia that eventually led to the AWACS sale of 1981. While the total level of FMS sales actually dropped during this period (because so many of the orders placed by the Shah of Iran in the late 1970s were cancelled by his successors), the pendulum had clearly swung away from a pro-restraint position back in the direction of increased exports.

In attempting to account for this turnaround, most analysts pointed to specific foreign policy constraints—the need to 'sweeten' the Camp David accords, the need to tighten US ties with Saudi Arabia following the fall of the Shah, the need to resist Soviet adventurism in Africa and the Middle East, and so forth. Some observers also noted that Carter was a victim of his own overblown promises. In the final analysis, it was not any of these specific factors that led to the demise of the Carter policy, but rather his failure to seriously challenge the belief that arms transfers represent a flexible tool for the advancement of US foreign policy objectives. So long as Carter adhered to the Kissinger view that arms transfers could serve as an instrument of diplomacy and influence, he was not able to overrule those of his advisers who urged him to approve various major sales in the interest of improved US relations with various friendly governments. This belief had become deeply embedded in the US national security bureaucracy, acting as a constant check on any presidential inclination to reduce the level of military sales.

V. The Reagan reaction

With the election of Ronald Reagan, the pendulum completed its swing back toward a policy of permissiveness in the export of arms. As a candidate, Reagan had expressed his opposition to the Carter restrictions; upon taking office, he ordered the State Department to devise an alternative policy. Even while this process was under way, however, Reagan approved several major transfers that had been held up by the Carter Administration. These transactions—notably the $8.5 billion sale of AWACS patrol aircraft and other high-technology gear to Saudi Arabia—represented a dramatic introduction to the administration's approach toward arms transfers.

Although many components of this approach were fully visible from the very onset of the new administration, the Reagan policy was not formally unveiled until 21 May 1981, when Under Secretary Buckley addressed a meeting of the Aerospace Industries Association in Williamsburg, Virginia. Flatly rejecting the notion that military sales are 'inherently evil or morally reprehensible', Buckley affirmed that 'this Administration believes that arms transfers, judiciously applied, can complement and supplement our own defense efforts and serve as a vital and constructive instrument of our foreign policy'. Contending that the Carter restrictions had undermined the defences of nations whose support was vital to US national security, he argued that the USA should lift those restraints in order to strengthen the common defence. We must, Buckley declared, substitute 'a healthy sense of self-preservation' for the 'theology' of the Carter period.[27]

This outlook was subsequently incorporated into a new presidential directive signed by President Reagan on 8 July 1981 and released to the public one day later. This directive formally rescinded the Carter guidelines and established new precepts for the conduct of arms transfers.[28]

The Reagan directive, like Carter's, rested on two fundamental propositions: first, that the greatest threat to world stability is the growing military assertiveness of the Soviet Union; and second, that the United States cannot defend the free world against this threat by itself, but must 'be prepared to help its friends and allies strengthen their [defenses] through the transfer of conventional arms'.[29] From this perspective, arms sales were seen not as an independent foreign policy concern but rather as a vital adjunct to the USA's own military modernization effort. As Buckley explained on 21 May, 'We are faced not only with the need to rebuild and modernize our own military forces, but to help other nations in the free world rebuild theirs'.[30]

Consistent with this outlook, Buckley enunciated a new governing principle: instead of viewing arms transfers as an 'exceptional foreign policy implement', as decreed by Carter, they were to be considered as 'a vital and constructive instrument' of US foreign policy. The administration would continue to weigh the merits and hazards of pending transactions on a case-by-case basis, but favourable consideration would normally be given to transfers which would help enhance 'the state of preparedness of our friends and allies'.[31]

Turning now to the seven specific measures originally introduced by President Carter, the Reagan policy substituted the following.

Ceiling: The ceiling on arms exports to non-exempt countries was abolished. Pending arms transactions were to be judged on their own merits, irrespective of their effect on the total dollar values of such exports.

Sophistication: The United States would take care not to overburden the defence capabilities of less-developed nations, but transfer of high-technology arms would be governed more by 'their net contribution to enhanced deterrence and defense', rather than by any fears of a local arms race.

Modification: In place of the ban on such programmes, this administration would actively 'encourage' US firms to 'produce equipment which, in terms of cost, complexity, and sophistication, is more appropriate to the needs of non-industrialized nations'.

Promotion: US embassy and consular officials were ordered 'to provide the same courtesies and assistance' to firms selling arms as to other US companies seeking business abroad.

Human rights: The United States would no longer withhold essential security support from friendly nations solely because of a poor record on human rights. As President Reagan explained shortly after his election, 'I don't think that you can turn away from some country because here and there they do not agree with our concept of human rights'.[32] This outlook was reflected in the administration's efforts to repeal the embargo on arms transfers to Argentina and Chile, and to resume military aid to Guatemala.

Multilateral negotiations: While the United States would retain 'a genuine interest in arms transfer restraint', no major effort would be undertaken by the United States to solicit co-operation from the USSR or the other major suppliers.

All of these considerations suggest that, at the very least, the Reagan policy represented a sharp break with the restrictive approach of the Carter Administration and a return to the more permissive approach of the Nixon and Ford administrations. But Reagan went beyond this, introducing several initiatives designed further to enhance the utility of arms sales as instrument of US foreign policy. These initiatives included the following.

Liberalized credits: In order to facilitate arms purchases by credit-starved Third World nations, the administration offered FMS credits to several favoured regimes on a special basis—a 10-year grace period followed by a 20-year repayment period (instead of the usual one- to three-year grace period and 9- to 12-year repayment span). In FY 1982, such terms were offered to Egypt, Greece, Somalia, Sudan and Turkey.

Special Defense Acquisition Fund: Arguing that previous US efforts to assist allies in times of crisis had been hampered by the time-consuming FMS procurement process, the Reagan Administration created a Special Defense Acquisition Fund (SDAF) to stockpile arms in anticipation of future requests. The stockpile, financed by monies received from previous FMS sales, consisted of basic combat gear (tanks, anti-tank missiles, artillery pieces, etc.) commonly used by Third World forces.

Spurred by these initiatives and the adoption of a generally permissive approach toward arms transfers, US sales under the Foreign Military Sales programme soared to new heights. Total FMS orders rose from $7.6 billion in FY 1981 to $20.3 billion in FY 1982—a one-year increase of 150 per cent. If those transfers approved by the Administration in FY 1982 but not yet formally accepted by the recipients were added, the year's total would have been $30 billion—more than twice the amount for any previous year.

Accompanying this surge in the volume of US sales, moreover, was a striking increase in the sophistication of the arms sold to Third World buyers. In his first two years in office, President Reagan approved the sale of AWACS patrol aircraft to Saudi Arabia, F-16 fighter aircraft to Pakistan, South Korea and Venezuela, AH-1 Cobra helicopter gunships to Jordan and E-2C Hawkeye radar patrol aircraft to Singapore. These sales, coming one after another in rapid succession, led critics to charge that the administration had no real export policy other than a generalized impulse to sell.

To some degree, President Reagan's permissive stance on arms exports was motivated by a desire to reduce the USA's overseas trade imbalance. However, an analysis of White House statements suggests political and military rather than economic motives predominated. Indeed, the Reagan Administration clearly saw arms transfers as a powerful tool in its drive to restore US influence in the Third World. 'We intend to employ [arms transfers] as an instrument that can and should be used flexibly and carefully to serve our interest', Buckley testified in 1981. 'We believe that with effective US Government control and direction, but without the arbitrary prohibitions and annual ceilings of the past, arms transfers can help enhance the state of readiness of friends and allies, to demonstrate US determination to respond to threats to our interests . . . [and] to revitalize our alliances and co-operative security relationships and develop new ones . . .'[33]

Although President Reagan has remained steadfast in his commitment to arms transfers as an instrument of US foreign policy, economic conditions have not been such as to sustain high levels of exports. With many Third World nations staggering under mountainous levels of debt and the oil-exporting countries suffering from vastly diminished revenues, the overseas market for costly arms has been severely constricted. As a result, US sales under the FMS programme dropped from $20.3 billion in FY 1982, to $16.6 billion in FY 1983, $14.4 billion in FY 1984, $12.5 billion in FY 1985, and $7.13 billion in FY 1986.

Aside from market conditions, there is another factor that could operate to discourage major increases in US arms exports to the Third World: congressional indignation over the Reagan Administration's secret arms sales to Iran. The sales produced an immediate storm of protest when disclosed in late 1986.[35] Further adding to congressional ire was the fact that proceeds from the sale were reportedly used to finance arms purchases by the Nicaraguan anti-Sandinista contras (*contra-revolucionarios*) in violation of US law.[36] In response to these dramatic disclosures, many lawmakers proposed significant alterations to existing legislation.[37] Because the next shift in US policy on arms transfers is likely to occur on Capitol Hill, it is appropriate to turn now to a brief look at the congressional input into export policy.

VI.   The role of Congress

After the Secretary of State (or the President) has given formal approval to a particular arms transaction, the Department of Defense prepares a Letter of Offer specifying the item(s) to be sold, the buyer, the estimated cost, delivery dates, and so on; once this form is completed—and only then—Congress enters the decision-making process. Under Section 36(b) of the AECA, all applicable Letters of Offer for major combat systems worth $14 million or more, or for complete arms packages worth $50 million or more, must be submitted to Congress for examination and review. (Pending sales to the NATO countries and to Australia, Japan and New Zealand are exempted from this reporting requirement.) At this point in the proceedings, Congress can block the sale by adopting a joint resolution of disapproval; such a resolution, which requires a majority vote in both Houses, can be overturned by a presidential veto (which would then require a two-thirds majority vote by Congress to override). Through the years, Congress has used the threat of such action to force the President to withdraw a proposed sale or to scale back its size; as of January 1987, however, it had succeeded only once in voting such a joint resolution (involving the sale of Sidewinder and Harpoon missiles to Saudi Arabia), and that vote was subsequently invalidated by a presidential veto.[38]

Although US lawmakers have occasionally objected to particular arms sales with considerable vigour—the 1978 Mideast jet fighter package to Israel, Egypt and Saudi Arabia, and the 1981 AWACS sale to Saudi Arabia are notable examples—the present decision-making process does not allow for extensive congressional involvement. Not only are such transactions submitted to Congress only after the Executive Branch has already decided on a particular outcome, but also most proposed transfers are presented to Congress only after years of negotiation have produced a *de facto* commitment to the buyer involved—a commitment that Congress can reverse only at some cost to US relations with that country. To complicate matters further, Congress is rarely united in its position on foreign policy issues, with many lawmakers predisposed by party loyalty or constitutional interpretation to accept the president's leadership in such matters. Although Congress has adopted amendments to the AECA requiring Executive Branch consultation with the legislative on pending sales, these measures have not fundamentally diminished the president's control over arms sales decision making.

In light of the Iran–contra arms scandal of 1986, however, concerned lawmakers may be able to garner sufficient votes to provide Congress with greater control over US arms exports. This being the case, it is likely that the Executive will lose some of its authority over arms-export decision making to the Legislative Branch—and thus, in time, we may see some moderation in the policy swings that have tended in the past to accompany changes in administration.

VII. The prospects for restraint

Successive US administrations have periodically altered the stated intent of US policy on arms transfers to the Third World. Thus President Carter sought to diminish the intensity of regional arms races, while President Reagan sought to bolster the defences of friendly Third World countries. Consistent throughout this period, however, is a belief in the efficacy of arms transfers as a means of advancing one or another US objective.

Given this perception, true restraint in arms transfers has, until now, been at best a secondary objective of US policy. Although some presidents have called for a reduction in transfers of high-technology arms to Third World areas, they have always made exceptions in order to satisfy favoured clients or have expressed a preference for exports of other, less sophisticated arms. This was especially evident during the Carter period, when the White House approved major new sales of sophisticated arms to Egypt, Iran, Israel and Saudi Arabia, despite an official policy of arms restraint. It is not that Carter was hypocritical in his statements on arms sales, but rather that his belief in the diplomatic utility of arms transfers outweighed his commitment to restraint. So long as this outlook prevails, restraint will always be a subordinate goal.

Clearly, belief in the diplomatic efficacy of arms transfers remains strong in Washington, particularly in the Executive Branch. However, it is evident that a growing number of US lawmakers have become sceptical about the utility of arms transfers. These critics charge that abundant US sales to the Shah of Iran did not prevent his collapse in 1978–79 and that equally extensive sales to Saudi Arabia have not prompted Saudi acceptance of the Camp David accords. 'We kidded ourselves [in Iran], and we allowed the Shah to kid himself', Senator Joseph R. Biden observed in 1982. 'We had $30 billion of the most sophisticated arms in the world in Iran, [and] without a shot being fired, the Shah was marched out of the country'.[39] Similar comments have been made by other influential members of Congress, thus setting the stage for reform of the Arms Export Control Act along the lines noted above.

Even with tough new restrictions in the AECA, however, future presidents will still be able to wield considerable influence over the pace and direction of US arms exports. Any meaningful commitment to restraint will, therefore, have to be made by the Executive and not the Legislative Branch. Clearly, the institutional pressures *against* such a commitment remain strong and are not likely to abate even if a Democrat occupies the White House in 1989 and beyond. But the embarrassment produced by the Iran–contra affair, and the growing disillusionment with arms transfers as an instrument of policy, could create the space for an energetic and determined president to make real progress in this area—especially if Soviet leaders prove amenable to new multilateral restraints.

Notes and references

[1] This chapter draws on the analysis developed in Klare, M., *American Arms Supermarket* (University of Texas Press: Austin, 1984).

[2] For a discussion of market forces and their impact on arms transfer patterns, see Brzoska, M. and Ohlson, T., 'The future of arms transfers', *Bulletin of Peace Proposals*, vol. 16, no. 2 (1985), pp. 129–37; and Klare, M., 'The state of the trade: global arms transfer patterns in the 1980s', *Journal of International Affairs*, vol. 40, no. 1 (1986), pp. 1–21. See also Pierre, A., *The Global Politics of Arms Sales* (Princeton University Press: Princeton, NJ, 1982).

[3] For the text of these statutes, see US Congress, *Legislation on Foreign Relations Through 1985*, Joint Committee Print (US Government Printing Office: Washington, DC, 1986).

[4] For a discussion of US arms export regulations and procedures, see Klare (note 1), chap. 4; and Farley, P. J., Kaplan, S. S. and Lewis, W. H., *Arms Across the Sea* (Brookings Institution: Washington, DC, 1978), chaps 2–5. See also US Department of Defense, Defense Security Assistance Agency, *Military Assistance and Sales Manual* (Department of Defense: Washington, DC, 1978).

[5] International Security Assistance and Arms Export Control Act of 1976 (P   .:c Law 94–329; 90 Stat. 734), Sect. 2, 38.

[6] For a discussion of the motivational pressures behind US arms exports, see Klare (note 1), chap. 2.

[7] For background on the strategy of counterinsurgency, see Barber, W. F. and Ronning, C. N., *Internal Security and Military Power* (Ohio State University Press: Columbus, 1966); Blaufarb, D., *The Counterinsurgency Era* (The Free Press: New York, 1977); and Klare, M., *War Without End: American Planning for the Next Vietnams* (Knopf: New York, 1972).

[8] Quoted in Hilsman, R., *To Move a Nation* (Doubleday: Garden City, NY, 1967), p. 415.

[9] See Klare (note 7), pp. 31–55, 270–310.

[10] Lieuwen, E., 'The Latin American Military', in US Congress, Senate, Committee on Foreign Relations, Subcommittee on American Republics Affairs, *Survey of the Alliance for Progress*, Compilation of Studies and Hearings (US Government Printing Office: Washington, DC, 1969), p. 115.

[11] McNamara, R. S., *The Essence of Security* (Harper & Row: New York, 1968), p. 149.

[12] Einaudi, L., Heymann, H. Jr., Ronfeldt, D. and Sereseres, C., *Arms Transfers to Latin America: Toward a Policy of Mutual Respect* (RAND Corp.: Santa Monica, CA, 1973), p. 2.

[13] Rockefeller, N. A., 'Quality of life in the Americas', Report on a Presidential Mission for the Western Hemisphere, *Department of State Bulletin* (8 Dec. 1969), pp. 516–18.

[14] US Department of Defense, Defense Security Assistance Agency, *Foreign Military Sales and Military Assistance Facts*, 1979 edn, p. 3 (hereinafter cited as: DSAA, *FMS Facts*). On the Nixon veto, see *New York Times*, 6 June 1973.

[15] For discussion, see Karnow, S., 'Weapons for sale', *New Republic* (23 Mar. 1974), pp. 21–23; and 'US accelerates aerospace export drive', *Aviation Week & Space Technology* (2 June 1975), pp. 47–53.

[16] For discussion, see Pierre (note 2), pp. 137–38, 159–60; and Sheehan, E. R., *The Arabs, Israelis, and Kissinger: A Secret History of American Diplomacy* (Reader's Digest Press: New York, 1976).

[17] DSAA, *FMS Facts*, 1979 and earlier edns.

[18] See US Congress, Senate, Committee on Foreign Relations, *US Military Sales to Iran*, Staff Report, 94th Congress, 2nd Session, 1976 (hereinafter cited as SFRC, *Sales to Iran*). For discussion of the US arms-supply relationship with Iran, see Klare (note 1), chap. 6.

[19] For background on these congressional initiatives, see US Congress, House, Committee on Foreign Affairs, *Executive–Legislative Consultation on US Arms Sales* (US Government Printing Office: Washington, DC, 1982), pp. 5–9 (hereinafter cited as HCFA, *Executive–Legislative Consultation*). The comment 'out of control' appears in SFRC, *Sales to Iran*, p. xiii.

[20] Quoted in *New York Times*, 25 Jan. 1977.

[21] For the text of the Carter statement, see US Congress, House, Committee on Foreign Affairs, *Changing Perspectives on US Arms Transfer Policy*, Report by the Congressional Research Service (US Government Printing Office: Washington, DC, 1981), pp. 122–23 (hereinafter cited as: HCFA, *Changing Perspectives*).

[22] For discussion, see Benson, L. W., 'Turning the supertanker: arms transfer restraint', *International Security*, vol. 3, no. 4 (1979), pp. 3–17.

[23] Quoted in *New York Times*, 11 Oct. 1977.

[24] *Munitions Control Newsletter*, no. 50 (Feb. 1978), p. 1.

[25] Quoted in *Washington Post*, 5 Dec. 1979.

[26] See *Washington Post*, 29 Mar. 1980.

[27] For text of Buckley's Williamsburg address, see HCFA, *Changing Perspectives* (note 21), pp. 124–26.

[28] For text of the Reagan Directive, see HCFA, *Changing Perspectives* (note 21), pp. 127–28.

[29] Note 21, p. 127.

[30] Note 21, p. 125.

[31] Note 21, p. 125.

[32] Quoted in *Newsweek* (15 Dec. 1980), p. 53.

[33] Buckley, J. L., Statement to the Senate Foreign Relations Committee, July 28, 1981, as cited in HCFA, *Changing Perspectives* (note 21), pp. 129–32.

[34] DSAA, *FMS Facts*, 1986, p. 3.

[35] See *The Tower Commission Report*, The Full Text of the President's Special Review Board (*Times* Books and Bantam Books: New York, 1987), esp. pp. 18–51, 148–337. See also 'From many strands, a tangled web,' *Time* (8 Dec. 1986), pp. 28–31; and *New York Times*, 22 Nov., 8 and 15 Dec. 1986, and 19 Jan. 1987.

[36] See *Tower Commission Report* (note 35), esp. pp. 51–55, 450–75.

[37] See Morrison, D. C., 'Congress up in arms over Iran', *National Journal*, 3 Jan. 1987, pp. 27–28.

[38] See Morrison (note 37) and *New York Times*, 28 Jan. 1987.

[39] Quoted in *Arms Sales: A Useful Foreign Policy Tool?*, An AEI Forum, John Charles Daly, moderator (American Enterprise Institute: Washington, DC, 1982), p. 6.

Paper 6. Soviet arms transfer restraint

JOACHIM KRAUSE

I. Introduction

There are two very different but equally wrong opinions in the West with respect to restraints on Soviet exports of conventional arms to the Third World. According to one view, there are no substantial restrictions, and the USSR delivers weapons to anyone who can pay for them or whose strengthening lies in the interest of the Kremlin. This view is wrong: Soviet arms export policy towards the Third World contains important restraints, both declared and factual. But the opposite view, that Soviet arms transfer restrictions are similar to or might be harmonized with those of Western countries in order to form an international control regime, is also erroneous. Soviet arms export restraints are different from those of other countries—especially the United States—and offer hardly any basis for joint control agreements. Yet there is a common interest in avoiding the escalation of Third World crises into a nuclear war that provides for limited tacit or open co-operation between Moscow and Washington; but beyond that, there are few similarities between the Soviet and the US approaches to arms transfer restraint. While for the USA and other Western countries arms export restrictions are the results of *foreign policy* as well as *arms control* considerations, the latter play no important role in Soviet policy. Up to now, the Soviet leadership has put limits and restrictions on arms transfers only in the pursuit of various short- and medium-term foreign policy motives.

This paper investigates those differences by describing the features of Soviet arms export restraints and examining the reasoning behind them. This is done in three sections: first, declaratory and legal limitations of arms export in theory and practice are analysed. In the second section, the factual restraints that can be regularly observed in Soviet arms export policy are discussed. Third, the Soviet position with respect to international agreements on arms transfer restraints is addressed.

II. Declaratory and legal restrictions

In Soviet press and political publications, arms exports to developing countries are seldom mentioned. Articles and speeches criticizing arms exports by Western countries are more frequent. Whenever mention is made of Soviet arms exports or military aid, then—as a rule—certain restrictions are claimed which are said to contribute to basic differences between Soviet and Western arms export policies.[1] In dealing with these claims, one must distinguish between those restrictions which are implicit in general foreign policy doctrines and those which explicitly pertain to the transfer of arms to the Third World.

Probably the most important declaratory restraint of Soviet arms export policy is only an implicit one and is contained in the very notion of *peaceful coexistence*, the declared Soviet foreign policy doctrine since the late 1950s. The basic idea of that concept is that, while the struggle between socialism and capitalism continues unabated, the outbreak of nuclear war must be avoided. Statements on the theory of peaceful coexistence do not exclude the possibility of local conventional wars and usually advocate the supply of weapons to progressive and national forces in the Third World. The prevention of nuclear war is, however, paramount.[2] As a consequence, the Soviet leadership has time and again exercised restraints with respect to arms sales to the Third World when there was a danger of a direct US–Soviet confrontation. The actual features of that restraint are discussed below.

Another impression is given if one scrutinizes those restrictions which pertain directly to Third World arms sales. The first one concerns the recipients of Soviet weapons. As a rule, Soviet publications point out that the Soviet Union and its allies do not deliver weapons to every nation in the Third World. Only states that defend their independence against Western or Western-supported aggression are eligible for Soviet arms aid, or, as one Soviet author puts it, 'the military aid the USSR renders to other countries pursues the aim only of ensuring the defense of these countries against forces of aggression and arbitrariness'.[3] The basically defensive character of Soviet arms deliveries to the Third World is also stressed by the *Soviet Military Encyclopedia*:

The military aid of the Soviet Union and the other socialist countries was one of the most important factors underlying the failure of imperialist aggression in Korea and Indo-China. The military aid of the socialist countries played a decisive role in the struggle of Arab peoples against international imperialism and zionism. Thanks to Soviet aircraft, tanks and other weapons, Egypt and Syria could resist Israeli aggression in 1956, 1967 and 1973. The military aid of the socialist countries has been of great importance to the peoples of Asia, Africa and Latin America in their fight for and defence of national independence.[4] *(Unofficial translation)*

This declared restraint is, however, hardly more than a propaganda plea. The wording of the *Soviet Military Encyclopedia* is so vague that it gives the political and military leadership of the Soviet Union enough leeway to categorize any country as a 'victim of imperialist aggression' or at least of a 'conspiracy'. Even if one were prepared to take the Soviet criteria seriously, the record of Soviet arms transfers is full of contradictions and exemptions. In the past 20 years the Soviet Union delivered conventional arms and related materials to more than 40 states in the Third World. Among them were a number of states that could hardly be categorized as 'victims of imperialist aggression or conspiracy'. It is hard to see to which imperialist aggression India, Iran, Jordan, Kuwait, Morocco, Peru or Pakistan were subjected at the time they received Soviet arms. Rather, the Soviet Union was often helpful in bringing about those 'imperialistic menaces' by delivering weapons to rival states. The most conspicuous case was Ethiopia which received huge Soviet arms deliveries in 1977. The Soviet Union actually helped Ethiopia to fend off Somalian aggression, but Somalia's attack was anything but an imperialistic plot, since it was the Soviet Union which had enabled Somalia to launch that attack. The country was Moscow's closest ally in Africa until 1977, and the Somalian Government, notwithstanding its well-known territorial claims, received generous arms aid from the Soviet Union in the years before.

Another restraint that is stressed time and again in Soviet statements also belongs to the sphere of propaganda. The Soviet Union, it is said, would deliver weapons to the Third World only in exceptional cases. In the main, the support would be of the civilian or peaceful kind: 'In keeping with the principles of proletarian internationalism the Socialist states lend victims of aggression comprehensive assistance that may, if need be, include arms deliveries'.[5] One author even goes further by contending that the major Western powers recklessly aggravate the economic predicament of Third World states by pumping in huge amounts of arms, while the Soviet Union is carefully taking into consideration the requirements for socio-economic development of those states to which it grants military assistance.[6] At the heart of these assumptions lies the Soviet theory of imperialism, according to which the historic decline of Western societies is linked to their growing militarization. This trend is said to find its expression in the increased use of military means in foreign policy.[7] The Soviet Union claims to be fundamentally different in that it relies primarily on political and peaceful foreign policy instruments.

However, this declaratory restraint is in sharp contrast to the practice of Soviet arms export policy. Especially in the 1970s, arms exports and military aid have become the most important instruments of Soviet foreign policy vis-à-vis the Third World. The Soviet Union is still the largest single arms supplier to the Third World; and in recent decades the value of arms deliveries amounted to between six and eight times the value of economic and relief aid. This can be compared to a ratio of roughly 1:1 for the USA or 1:3.5 for FR Germany in favour of development aid.[8] For a few years, the Soviet Union has increased the level of its economic aid programmes, but most of that money goes to a few, mostly communist countries such as Afghanistan, Cuba, Kampuchea, Laos and Viet Nam. For the other developing countries that have ties to Moscow, there is an often substantial imbalance between military supplies and development and relief aid. The Soviet Union is also economically more dependent on arms exports than are Western countries. In the past decade, the share of arms exports in total exports fluctuated between 12 and 17 per cent. The same share for the USA oscillated at that time between 3 and 5 per cent. Only the corresponding share for Israel was higher, at times up to 25 per cent of all exports.[9] In the late 1970s and early 1980s it can be assumed that more than one-half of Soviet exports to developing countries were actually arms or otherwise military exports.[10]

In summary, the declaratory restraints on Soviet arms export policy are not practised in reality. Only where the aim of avoiding a nuclear war is concerned should these declarations be taken literally. It is also difficult to find restrictions on arms exports in Soviet foreign trade legislation. Owing to the unique structure of Soviet arms production and the foreign trade monopoly, the situation is completely different from that in a Western country, where arms production is mostly in private hands and where norms for the regulation of arms exports can be found in foreign trade acts and special ammunition control acts. Soviet trade regulations have a different function and are thus irrelevant to an analysis of Soviet arms transfer restrictions.

However, there are restrictions which are codified, but these are internal understandings between concerned agencies within the Soviet state apparatus. Owing to the lack of openness, such understandings cannot easily be reconstructed from an outside perspective. There are, however, end-user and non-transfer clauses as well as general clauses on secrecy. Article 7 of an agreement between the Soviet Union and Grenada of July 1982 on the delivery of weapons gives an impression of how such clauses might look:

The Government of Grenada shall not without the consent of the Government of the Union of Soviet Socialist Republics sell or transfer, formally or actually, the special equipment, delivered under the present Agreement, the relevant documentation and information or give permission to use the equipment and documentation by a third party or any physical or legal persons but the officials and specialists of the citizenship of Grenada being in the service with the Government of Grenada.

The Government of the Union of SSR and the Government of Grenada shall take all the necessary measures to ensure keeping in secret the terms and conditions of the deliveries, all the correspondence and information connected with the implementation of the present Agreement.[11]

It is also known that Soviet weapons and other military goods (e.g., jet engines, components and spare parts) produced under licence in Third World countries are not allowed to be exported without permission from Moscow.[12] However, the Soviet Union seems to exercise this veto sparingly. There are few reports of Soviet denials of applications for the export of Soviet-designed weapons by a Third World country.

III.   Factual restraints

The more important restrictions in Soviet arms export policy are those which cannot be derived from publicized norms or laws but stem from foreign policy considerations. They reflect the existence of competing priorities in Soviet foreign and military policy towards the Third World and lessons learned from often painful experiences in the past. It is impossible to analyse and categorize all elements of restraint, but an attempt might be made to identify and exemplify some major features. In the past, there were three principal reasons for the Soviet leadership to attach limitations and restrictions to their arms exports to Third World countries: mistrust in the reliability and the political intentions of their recipients; apprehensions concerning uncontrollable military consequences of deliveries (especially the danger of US–Soviet clashes); and, finally, the determination to limit the transfer of military technology and arms production technology as much as possible. As a consequence, three different types of restraint are salient: those restraints that occur in the *bilateral relationships* between the Soviet Union and its arms customers; those that relate to *global strategic considerations*; and, finally, those aimed at *preventing the diffusion of Soviet military technology*.

Bilateral restraints

In the nearly 40 years in which the Soviet Union has delivered weapons to the Third World, it has often had negative experiences with most of its arms customers. As a consequence, the Kremlin has become more prudent and usually links arms deliveries with a number of political measures and restrictions that are designed to prevent the loss of political control and not to be an economic detriment to the USSR. The Soviet Union had, for instance, a host of problems with Third World governments that assumed a communist, socialist or otherwise progressive image in order to elicit favourable conditions for arms deliveries. Many of these governments then used Soviet support to pursue national goals or even changed sides (e.g., Indonesia, Egypt, Somalia). In other cases the Soviet Union had to deal with Third World politicians who, on the one hand, were charismatic and powerful but, on the other hand, led their respective countries into economic and political difficulties through military adventures, thus eventually adversely affecting Soviet interests. The Soviet Union also had difficulties with states, such as China or India, that had great-power ambitions and were demanding weapons in quantities and with qualities much beyond what Soviet politicians judged to be prudent.

In order to cope with these problems, the Soviet leadership usually looks first and foremost for a political solution that allows it to steer demand for and use of weapons. Direct restrictions on arms exports are secondary and only imposed reluctantly, obviously because their low efficiency is well known. The political strategies that the Soviet leadership is pursuing in that respect differ with respect to the country the USSR is dealing with. As a rule, the Soviet assessment of the relative proximity of these countries to the Soviet system plays an important role in determining the political strategy.

From a Soviet perspective, the most trustworthy state in the Third World is one in which the following conditions are fulfilled: political power is in the hands of a Marxist–Leninist vanguard party that copies the Soviet political and economic system; the political leadership accepts that its foreign policy is oriented towards the Soviet Union and would never come into conflict with Soviet policy (internationalist orientation); the state is dependent on Soviet military and economic aid; and it is susceptible to other—even military—

measures to enforce Soviet control over them if necessary. Only a few countries come close to these requirements: Cuba, Kampuchea, Laos, Mongolia and Viet Nam. They are all part of the so-called socialist community of states and are thus entitled to receive massive arms deliveries at low cost.[13] The degree of control over these countries is obviously deemed tight enough to prevent undesired military activities by the respective governments. But up to now, only a few Third World states were prepared to accept such tight control of domestic and foreign policy, and it seems that not too many others will follow suit. Besides that, the Soviet Union could afford to support only a few such states, since this has placed a heavy economic burden on the Soviet Union.

With respect to other Third World states, the Soviet Union relies on other methods. Again, the relative proximity to the Soviet system is a decisive but not exclusive factor. In the Soviet perspective the other countries of the Third World are divided into three categories: first, states with a socialist orientation, that is, countries which call themselves 'socialist' without necessarily copying the Soviet model (e.g., Algeria, Libya and Syria); second, states with a socialist orientation, in the Kremlin's view on the way towards a genuine communist model of 'real socialism' (e.g., Angola, Ethiopia and South Yemen); and non-socialist or feudal countries (e.g., India, Jordan and Kuwait). With respect to all these states the Soviet Union uses two alternative strategies in order to avoid negative political consequences of arms deliveries: either an effort is made to win a maximum of influence through a network of political and military co-operation; or arms transfers are made as informal as possible in order to give the Soviet Union a face-saving retreat at any time.

Especially with respect to states in the first two categories, the strategy of tying recipients by establishing a network of military and political bonds is followed by the Soviet Union. As a rule, the USSR directs its efforts towards those countries which are considered important in terms of either regional or global political considerations. The main instrument is the conclusion of treaties of friendship and co-operation, entailing clauses that require—often mandatory—consultations with the Soviet leadership in cases of major international or regional crises. In addition, military co-operation is often broadened to a degree where (a) large number of officers and non-commissioned officers are trained by Soviet or East European military personnel; (b) Soviet or East European military advisers, instructors or other military experts are active on all levels of the military apparatus of the Third World country; and (c) closer and more profound forms of co-operation (military bases, joint exercises, possibly joint military operations) become feasible. Financial modalities of arms transfers are also sometimes used in order to create subtle forms of dependence to strengthen these ties.

The effectiveness of this strategy is difficult to assess. On the one hand, the Soviet Union has obviously gained some kind of leverage with most of its arms customers. On the other hand, the Kremlin was in some instances unable to prevent arms clients that were hitherto bound relatively strongly to the Soviet bloc from initiating military campaigns that were undesirable in Soviet eyes, for example, Egypt, Iraq, Somalia or Syria.

Concerning states in the third category, the main emphasis is on avoiding dependencies that might result from previous arms deliveries and on keeping some kind of visible distance to the arms client. As a consequence, countries like Jordan, Kuwait, Peru and previously also Iran and Pakistan receive or have received only limited numbers of selected categories of weapons, but never in volumes that would force the Soviet leadership to make difficult decisions in crisis situations.

In addition to these cases some Soviet weapon customers are not prepared to accept the level of ties wanted by the Soviet Union but are so important to the USSR that deliveries of weapons cannot be reduced to a minimum level. Here the Soviet Union is left only with instruments to directly limit arms transfers. Such instruments are: the 'creation' of bottlenecks or short-term stops in the supply of small arms, spare parts, ammunition and fuels or the postponement of negotiations about further deliveries. However, these instruments have proved to be ineffective in the past: either they were of little relevance for the military decisions of the recipients or they led to secured political relations. It can therefore be assumed that the Soviet leadership attaches little weight to such limitations and uses them only as an emergency brake.

Global strategy-motivated restraints

The Soviet leadership is aware of the danger of confrontation with the USA as a consequence of regional crises and conflicts in the Third World. The USSR is also aware of the limits of its military power in regions far away from the Soviet Union or where the United States traditionally has a strong military presence. Thus, whenever the Soviet Union delivered weapons to crises areas in which the US stakes were high, like the Middle East or South-East Asia as well as the Western hemisphere, it took care to connect the transfer of arms with certain limitations in order to avoid unwanted and uncontrollable developments.

Such limitations were felt in the 1960s and 1970s by Egypt and Syria. Despite extensive fulfilment of Arab demands for weapons, the Soviet Union saw to it that Egypt and Syria were not able to conduct fast and sweeping offensive operations. Thus, only few fighter-bombers for close support and battlefield interdiction were delivered in the 1960s. In addition, Soviet training activities in Egypt and Syria were not helpful in the preparation of fast offensive operations. In the 1970s—up to the October War in 1973—the USSR denied Syria and Egypt modern fighter aircraft and mobile air defence systems. The results were the same in both cases: Egyptian and Syrian armed forces could only conduct limited offensive operations and were better prepared for a long-drawn-out war of attrition.[14] Only when Egypt left the joint Arab military front against Israel, after breaking with Syria and most other Arab states in 1977, was the Soviet Union freed from the necessity of such limitations.

North Viet Nam had similar experiences in the 1960s when it demanded arms from the Soviet Union. Up to the end of the 1960s Moscow was prepared to deliver weapons only for the defence of North Viet Nam but not for the intensification of the communist insurgency in South Viet Nam. This approach was visible in the types of weapon supplied, namely, mainly air defence equipment, coastal artillery and fast attack craft for coastal defence, but— except for small arms—hardly any weapons useful for the war in South Viet Nam. Only when it became clear in 1967 that the USA would wind down its military engagement for political reasons were these restrictions removed step by step.[15] There are also indications of Soviet restraint with respect to weapon deliveries to Central and South America. Military aid to Peru was from the beginning handled by Moscow with great caution and thus never reached a level that could be considered as threatening by the USA. In Cuba and Nicaragua, communist or leftist political forces came to power which were judged by the US Government as a potential threat. Accordingly, for the USA, Soviet arms deliveries to these countries have become a very sensitive matter. Not surprisingly, the Soviet Union has reacted with substantial restraints in its arms supplies to Cuba and Nicaragua.

1. Although Cuba has been propped up to a major military power by the Soviet Union, Cuba can hardly attack neighbouring countries directly, since it does not dispose of those weapons and equipment which are necessary to successfully pursue landing operations and invasions.

2. Up to the end of the 1970s, the Soviet Union virtually denied Cuba the right to re-transfer Soviet weapons to South and Central American guerrilla movements.

3. Nicaragua mainly received weapons suitable for fighting the internal resistance movement (contras). Heavy ordnance, tanks or jet fighters which could present a threat to neighbouring countries were not delivered.

In the Cuban case, however, it can be demonstrated that such restraints are not meant to last forever. Although the Soviet Union agreed in the McCloy– Kusnezov agreement of 1962 not to station offensive weapons of strategic importance on Cuba,[16] in 1978 the USSR for the first time delivered nuclear-capable MiG-23 Flogger fighter-bombers which can reach US territory. Since the beginning of the 1980s the Cuban Air Force and Navy have received further weapon systems enabling them to heavily disturb NATO's transatlantic re-supply in the case of an East–West war.[17] The Soviet Union has also delivered amphibious landing craft and transport aircraft to Cuba in the past few years, thus increasing the hitherto small Cuban intervention capabilities. The restrictions concerning the re-transfer of Soviet weapons to liberation movements in Central and South America were also removed in the early 1980s.[18]

Restraints on export of technologies and production equipment

As a rule, the Soviet Union is much more restrictive in assisting developing countries to build up arms industries than are Western industrial states. During the previous two decades, the USA, France, the UK and FR Germany have exported equipment for the production of weapons—including licences—and components for domestic arms production to a great number of developing countries.[19] The Soviet Union, however, confined its assistance to two Third World countries, India and North Korea, as well as to China. Arms production equipment and licences were not exported in significant quantities to any state.

Nevertheless, Soviet support for arms industries in these countries was quantitatively substantial. According to its own figures, Moscow delivered about 100 military factories to China between 1950 and 1960.[20] The level of support to India is also remarkable. Since 1965 three major factories have been constructed with Soviet aid in Hyderabad, Koraput and Nasik; among other things, they have produced MiG-21 fighter aircraft since 1967.[21] At the same time, Indian licensed production of the Atoll air-to-air missile began, although manufacture is mainly limited to the integration of prefabricated components. Later, improved versions of the MiG-21 followed as well as licensed production of the Czechoslovakian OT-62 armoured vehicle, a copy of the Soviet BTR-50. In 1980 the Soviet Union granted India the licence for the manufacture of MiG-27 fighter-bombers and promised support in the construction of the production line.

Soviet assistance for North Korean arms production, especially naval construction, was and still is extensive. Soviet warship designs were often copied and changed in North Korea. This must have been regularly approved by Moscow. Such a contention is supported by the fact that the Soviet Union delivered engines, electronics and other components for the Korean projects. It is also likely that Soviet technicians and engineers assisted in modifying the design of Soviet naval vessels at North Korean shipyards. In the mid-1970s assistance was extended to the construction of missile-armed fast attack craft of the Komar Class and perhaps for MiG-21 fighter aircraft. There is also Soviet support for the construction of ordnance: North Korea produces—sometimes modified—versions of Soviet ground forces equipment. On the other hand, countries such as Algeria, Egypt, Iraq and Syria tried in vain to get Soviet support in the buildup of their own arms industries. The Soviet reluctance also included the licensed production of small arms and ammunition. It is only known that the PPSh 41 machine pistol is produced in Viet Nam and Iran as well as in North Korea, whereas it is doubtful whether or not the Soviet Union granted licences for those endeavours.

There are three possible and plausible explanations for this Soviet restraint: (a) India and North Korea are the only Soviet arms customers with an adequate industrial and technological capability to produce modern weapon systems; (b) the Soviet Union is usually careful not to loose its arms supply monopoly (the Soviet Union supports the creation of indigenous arms production in the Third

World only if special political circumstances are present); and (c) the Soviet Union has had negative political (China) and economic (India) experiences.

All three explanations may be partially correct, but none of them alone is sufficient to explain Soviet behaviour. Rather, all three explanations might be combined: India and North Korea have the best industrial bases for the buildup of domestic arms production. But Algeria, Egypt, Iraq or Syria could also have been supported—at least in the manufacture of technologically less advanced weapons. Here the second explanation comes into play as the exceptions seem to corroborate the basic assumption. In the case of India, the USSR had to compete with France and Britain, and a rejection of Indian demands for assistance in the development of its own arms production would have seriously weakened the Soviet stand in India. In the North Korean case, competition with China might have been the decisive factor, since China was also offering support for warship construction and the building of small arms factories. The third explanation may be helpful in finding out why the USSR changed its less restrictive attitude of the 1950s.

From a Soviet point of view, the extensive support for China's defence industry in the 1950s was recklessly misused by Beijing in order not only to lessen its dependence on Moscow but also to build up a new military threat to the Soviet Union and its East Asian allies. In the Indian case, the licensed production of Soviet weapon systems proved to be more expensive than direct imports owing to a number of technical, economical and structural problems.[22]

IV.   The Soviet attitude towards arms transfer control

The Soviet position on conventional arms transfer control has little in common with Western arms control thinking. The latter is concerned with the general decrease of the importance of military forces in order to reduce political and military risks associated with either the buildup, the presence or the further development of military forces, thus paving the way for a general improvement of East–West relations. Typical Western approaches to conventional arms transfer control have been: general renunciation of the delivery of certain specified qualities or quantities of weaponry to either all Third World states or all states within a given region; avoidance of regional arms races by agreement between possible arms suppliers not to transfer certain arms to any countries; understanding between the major arms-producing countries not to transfer arms production technology to the Third World, and so on.[23] The Soviet position, however, is based on the notion that arrangements between major arms suppliers on arms transfer limitations have to build upon judgement of who is fighting a defensive and thus just war and who is not. This approach is predicated upon the UN Charter, and in 1959 the USSR and its allies proposed an agreement between NATO and the WTO on not extending military or economic aid to an aggressor.[24] The Soviet Union in 1977 responded positively to an initiative of the Carter Administration to start talks on conventional arms transfers. The Soviet position at the so-called CAT Talks was a continuation of the 1959 proposal, albeit more elaborate and explicit (see also paper 7). During these talks the Soviet side suggested that 'reasonable and precise international criteria' are to be agreed upon, 'which would establish in what situation and in regard to what recipients arms transfers are justified and permissible and when they must be prohibited or drastically limited'.[25] Criteria for the determination of what is permissible should be taken from the UN Charter, the UN definition of aggression and UN resolutions about 'the material and moral support of peoples that struggle for their liberation from colonial and racist oppression'.[26] As a later publication by a high-ranking Soviet diplomat emphasized, the whole concept was based on the notion that the best way to curb the international arms trade was to agree on measures that would simultaneously dry up the arms supply of the aggressor and enhance the arms supply of the defender:

The recognition as a universal criterion of satisfying the needs of a state that is a victim of aggression, in order to give a speedy and effective rebuff to the attacking side, would significantly complement the criterion of the impermissibility of delivering arms to the aggressor and serve to weaken a local arms race, lessening the striving of states to stockpile arms.[27]

It is hard to believe that such criteria would work. The determination of who is the aggressor and who deserves support is, as a rule, moot between East and West. Thus, the prevailing interpretation at that time concerning the Soviet intentions was that the Soviet Government did not want to forgo any option to deliver arms to allied or friendly countries in the Third World but was trying to impose some restriction on US policy or—at least—make it more difficult for the US Government to supply weapons to their allies and friends in the Third World.[28]

This position remains by and large unchanged. There have been changes, but they were mostly incremental, such as the omission of the above-mentioned UN resolutions on support of peoples that struggle for their liberation as a criterion to determine whether or not a certain state or political force is eligible for foreign arms aid.[29] This is no surprise, since the Soviet Union and its Third World allies (e.g., Afghanistan and Viet Nam) have meanwhile themselves become the subjects of UN resolutions that call either for the retreat of Soviet or Vietnamese troops or for the support of liberation movements that fight Soviet or Soviet-supported forces.

The basic thrust of Soviet policy with respect to conventional arms transfer control, however, remains the same. Even under the new political leadership of Mikhail Gorbachev and the concomitant initiation of new thinking in Soviet foreign policy, the basic interest of the Soviet leadership remains not to give away any option of military support for Third World states. As V. Afanasyev, the chief editor of *Pravda*, recently put it, the overall foreign policy approach of the Soviet Union is still totally different from the Western approach:

In giving priority to common human values and human life and advocating a nonviolent world, the CPSU in no way renounces the party and class approach to social processes and wars. The CPSU's main aim has been and remains the ultimate aim of the working class—the building of communism. The CPSU supports the international workers, communists, and national liberation movements and wages an uncompromising ideological struggle against its class enemies. Marxists are not pacifists; they regard just—defensive and liberation—wars as natural and normal.[30]

Besides that general line, the Soviet leadership was in a few cases pragmatic enough to co-operate with the United States and other countries in order to impose arms embargoes or to stop arms deliveries as part of a larger regional peace effort. The Soviet Union was prepared to do so only in cases of extraordinary political circumstances.

1. During the Geneva Conference on Peace in Indo-China in 1954, the Soviet Union co-operated to achieve an agreement to stop hostilities between France and the Democratic Republic of Viet Nam. The agreement prohibited the transfer of foreign troops, military personnel and arms or ammunition to Viet Nam (articles 16 and 17). The Soviet leadership at that time was very keen on such an agreement since it not only legitimized the national and communist resistance against France but also provided some lever to further those forces in France which were opposed to the pending ratification of the treaty on the creation of a European Defence Union.

2. During the Middle East War in June 1967 the Soviet Union ceased to deliver weapons to the Arabs and co-operated with the USA in order to put a fast end to the war. A major reason for the Soviet Union was to avoid any possibility of a direct clash with the USA as a consequence of a prolonged war. But, besides that, the co-operation was also important from a political viewpoint, since it was the first time that Washington was prepared to deal with Moscow on an equal footing. Finally, the outcome of the war was virtually clear after a few hours, and the Soviet Union used the interest of the US Government to seek some kind of superpower co-operation to avoid its Arab arms clients being pushed further.

3. The Paris agreement to end the war and restore peace in South Viet Nam from January 1973 between the USA, North Viet Nam, South Viet Nam and the South Viet Nam Liberation Front contained articles designed to limit the transfer of arms to South Viet Nam. Although the Soviet Union was not a participant in those negotiations, the Soviet leadership exerted massive pressure on North Viet Nam to conclude an agreement. The Soviet policy was guided by the paramount interest not to jeopardize the seminal bilateral relationship with Washington at that time.

4. During the negotiations on a political solution to the Afghanistan War, led by delegations of the Afghan and the Pakistani governments under the supervision of the UN, the Soviet Union—as the mastermind behind the Afghan Government—demanded a binding obligation of the United States and other countries to terminate arms supplies to the Afghan resistance fighters as a pre-condition for a withdrawal of Soviet troops. Whether or not this indicates an honest attempt by the Soviet leadership to end their invasion

of Afghanistan on face-saving terms is still unclear. Interestingly enough, the Soviet Union sets store by arms transfer regulations that, however, should be applied only to the Afghan resistance.

5. Like most countries of the world, the Soviet Union has adhered to the UN arms embargo against South Africa from 1977.

There are no further instances of Soviet interest in international arms transfer regulations. Some authors, however, contend that the Soviet Union has tacitly joined unilateral US arms transfer restraints. One example mentioned is that neither Moscow nor Washington delivered modern tactical aircraft to the two Korean states during the 1970s. There were in fact no deliveries of such aircraft at the time, but a tacit agreement is hard to prove. While it is well known that the USA withheld modern aircraft from South Korea until 1981, it is not certain whether North Korea had requested such Soviet fighter aircraft during the 1970s. Political relations between North Korea and the Soviet Union had reached a bottom level in the second half of the 1970s, and the fact of no supplies could have other reasons. On the other hand, there are numerous examples where the Soviet Union did not honour unilateral supply restraints by the USA or Western countries: Afghanistan, Egypt, India, Indonesia, Nigeria, North Yemen, Peru and Somalia are examples of countries that became Soviet customers only because the USA or other Western suppliers were not prepared to meet their demands for arms.

The tendency not to be bound by arms transfer limitations and to keep all options open is also noticeable in the Soviet reaction to the creation of the committee of liberation movements within the Organization of African Unity (OAU). This committee was founded in the 1960s in order to channel the support—civilian as well as military—for liberation movements that fought against colonialism. The aim was to funnel aid only to those liberation movements that were accepted and legitimized by the OAU and to prevent foreign powers—especially China and the Soviet Union—from supporting liberation movements at their own discretion, thus making them pawns in their global competition. The Soviet Union never showed any interest in channelling its military supplies through this committee, but delivered weapons directly or via allied or friendly states to various liberation movements.

V. Conclusions

In summary there are four pertinent points. First, there is a big difference between Soviet declaratory policy on the one hand and the actual performance on the other hand with respect to conventional arms transfer control. Also, the actual content of its policy in that area is far from any Western type of arms control thinking. Second, the existing restraints in Soviet arms transfer policy mainly result from foreign political and strategic considerations, like the wish to keep as much control as possible over the whereabouts and use of previously delivered weapons and to avoid clashes with the USA. The wish to retain its weapon monopoly as far as possible is also a very strong motivation. Third, the reasoning behind Soviet arms transfer restraint is not to contribute to any East–West co-operation in order to overcome basic mistrust and misunderstanding over Third World crises but to head off detriments or repercussions for Soviet foreign policy. A basis for co-operation between both superpowers is thus given only in two cases: where a danger of escalation towards a nuclear war is looming ahead, or where a communality of political interests concerning a regional conflict already exists. The fourth point is that, with respect to the general Soviet line on international negotiations on conventional arms transfer limitations, there is a consistency in the basic view that goes back to the 1950s and is still predominant, notwithstanding the advent of 'new political thinking' in the Soviet capital.

Notes and references

[1] 'Pomoshch' Voennaia' ('Military aid') in *Sovetskaia Voennaia Entsiklopediia* (*Soviet Military Encyclopedia*), band 6 (Defence Ministry Publishing House: Moscow, 1978).

[2] Sanakoev, S. P. and Katchenko, N. I., *O Teorii Vneshnei Politiki Sotsializma* (*Theory of the Foreign Policy of Socialism*) (Moscow, 1977), chapter 4.

[3] Kozyrev, A. *The Arms Trade—A New Level of Danger* (Progress: Moscow, 1985), p. 179.

[4] 'Military aid' (note 1), p. 447.

[5] Andropov, I. and Savinov, K., 'Das Ringen um Abrüstung geht weiter', *Deutsche Aussenpolitik* (Berlin-East), vol. 25, no. 1 (Jan. 1980), p. 40.

[6] Kozyrev (note 3), p. 180.

[7] Cf. Charisius, A. and Engelhardt, K., 'Militarismus heute—Hauptfeind von Entspannung und Sicherheit', *Einheit* (Berlin-East), vol. 23, no. 6 (1977), pp. 729–36; and note 2.

[8] Deutscher Bundestag, Hearing on 'Development and Armaments', *Stenographisches Protokoll*, Bonn, 22 Feb. 1984, p. 138.

[9] Krause, J., *Der internationale Handel mit konventionellen Waffen und Rüstungsgütern*, Ebenhausen (SWP-AZ 2437), Aug. 1985, p. 54.

[10] Krause, J., *Sowjetische Militärhilfepolitik gegenüber Entwicklungsländern* (Baden-Baden, 1985), p. 442.

[11] This agreement is reprinted in US Department of Defense, *Soviet Military Power 1984* (Washington, DC, 1984), p. 130.

[12] In 1976 India turned down a request by Egypt for the delivery of licence-built Soviet aircraft engines, since the USSR had objected to the sale.

[13] See Brezhnev's report to the 26th party rally of the CPSU in 1981, *New Times* (Moscow), no. 9 (1981), pp. 14ff.

[14] Glassman, J. D., *Arms for the Arabs: The Soviet Union and the War in the Middle East* (Baltimore, 1975), pp. 32ff.

[15] Krause (note 10), pp. 92–100.

[16] The McCloy/Kusnezov agreement terminated the Cuban Missile Crisis in fall 1962. It is no formal treaty, but an understanding which is recorded in protocols. It says that the USA refrains from military actions against Cuba if the Soviet Union obliges not to deploy offensive strategic systems on Cuba.

[17] In 1984 SACLANT Admiral Wesley McDonald was referred to this issue, saying that about two-thirds of US supply ships in times of war would have to pass sea areas near Cuba; *Süddeutsche Zeitung*, 1 Aug. 1984.

[18] 'U.S. asserts Cuba has tried to trigger armed revolt in 13 nations since 78', *Wall Street Journal*, 15 Dec. 1981; Lindner, R., 'Castros zweite Offensive—Die Kommunisten und der Guerilla-Krieg in Latinamerika', *Osteuropa*, vol. 32, no. 3 (1982), pp. 226–37.

[19] Brzoska, M. and Ohlson, T., 'Arms production in the Third World: an overview', in Brzoska, M. and Ohlson, T. (eds), SIPRI, *Arms Production in the Third World* (Taylor & Francis: London, 1986), pp. 22–27.

[20] See *Europäische Wehrkunde*, vol. 29, no. 6 (June 1980), p. 314, where various Soviet sources are quoted.

[21] SIPRI, *The Arms Trade With The Third World* (Almqvist & Wiksell: Stockholm, 1971), pp. 741–53.

[22] SIPRI (note 21), pp. 737–407.

[23] For an overview of various Western approaches and ideas see Krause, J., 'Conventional arms transfers to the Third World', *Aussenpolitik-German Foreign Affairs Review*, vol. 29, no. 4 (1979), pp. 396–410; Binnedijk, H. *et al.*, *Prospects for Multilateral Arms Export Restraint*, Staff Report Prep. for the Use of the Committee on Foreign Relations, US Senate, Washington, DC, Apr. 1979.

[24] Kozyrev (note 3), p. 190.

[25] Soviet Paper on 'Practical Ways toward a Cessation of the Arms Race', *UN Do*, A/S–10/AC.1/4, (1978), p. 10.

[26] See note 25.

[27] Kozyrev (note 3), p. 192.

[28] Betts, R. K., 'The tragicomedy of arms trade control', *International Security*, vol. 5, no. 1 (Summer 1980), pp. 80–110; Krause, J., 'Amerikanisch-sowjetische Gespräche über Begrenzung und Kontrolle des internationalen Rüstungstransfers', *Europa-Archiv*, vol. 34, no. 15 (1979), pp. 473–82.

[29] Compare Kozyrev's criteria (note 3, p. 190) with those of the above-mentioned Soviet UN papers of 1978 (see note 25 and 26).

[30] Afanasyev, V., 'The new political thinking', *Pravda*, 5 Dec. 1986, p. 4, quoted here after FBIS-Soviet Union from 17 Dec. 1986, p. CC 3.

Paper 7. The Conventional Arms Transfers Talks: an experiment in mutual arms trade restraint

JO L. HUSBANDS and ANNE HESSING CAHN[1]

I. The policy problem

In the early 1970s, as sales of sophisticated weaponry to the Third World increased dramatically, arms sales became a significant issue for US foreign policy. Congress was concerned with losing its oversight function as arms exports changed from grants, subject to congressional authorization and appropriation, to sales, where there was no formal congressional role.[2] The rise of Middle Eastern countries such as Israel, Iran and Saudi Arabia as the primary recipients of US arms made significant portions of the public uneasy about the role of arms transfers as a major tool of foreign policy. Beyond questions of whether arms were appropriate policy implements, in the wake of the Viet Nam War both the public and Congress worried that military assistance, including arms sales, might be the first step to entanglement in Third World conflicts. When President Carter announced his programme of restraint in May 1977, he was thus building upon substantial congressional and public sentiment that arms sales reform was badly needed. The Carter policy was intended to restrain the sale of sophisticated weapons to countries outside the primary US alliance network (for details of Carter's arms export policy, see paper 5).

The President stressed the responsibility of the USA to put its own house in order first, but he warned that the USA would not pursue reform alone for long. It was acknowledged that, 'if we do not begin to enlist the co-operation of other suppliers and recipients, it will be difficult to sustain unilateral US restraint over the longer term'.[3] At a conference for arms industry executives in December 1978, Under Secretary of State Lucy Wilson Benson made the connection explicit: '. . . the President made clear beyond the possible doubt in anybody's mind that what we do in the future will depend upon what kind of cooperation we get from other arms exporters. So there is no question but that we will not keep on with reductions in arms sales unless we get coopera- tion . . .'[4] This link gave the Carter Administration, or at least the advocates of arms sales restraint within it, a tremendous stake in the success of the diplomatic effort.

The search for this co-operation soon became centred on the Conventional

Arms Transfers Talks (CATT) with the Soviet Union. Before examining the talks themselves, the next section briefly outlines the multitude of players and issues involved in the arms trade in the mid-1970s that played a role in efforts for arms transfers restraint.

II.   The cast of characters

The United States

The postwar US arms transfer programme had undergone an almost complete transformation by the mid-1970s. During 1950–67, grants had accounted for three-quarters of all US arms exports.[5] By the time the Carter Administration took office, however, well over 90 per cent were being paid for by foreign customers, either in cash or with some form of credit.[6] The huge stocks of surplus equipment that had made grants possible were exhausted by the late 1960s, but the shift to sales was more than just the natural consequence of emptying warehouses. For over 15 years, successive US administrations actively promoted the commercialization of the arms trade. In his survey of postwar policy, David Louscher cites three primary reasons: (a) the 'search for an inexpensive economic and military assistance instrument'; (b) efforts to redress the increasingly adverse US balance of payments; and (c) attempts to foster greater standardization of NATO weaponry.[7] The sudden increase in oil prices after the OPEC boycott in 1974 merely reinforced the balance-of-payments pressures and added the incentive to 'soak up' the flood of 'petro-dollars' with sales of expensive military hardware.

The shift to sales was accompanied by a change in customers, essentially parallel to changing US foreign policy preoccupations. Before the mid-1960s, Western Europe, Japan, Canada, Australia and New Zealand received 80 per cent of US exports. As the war in Indo-China consumed US attention, that region became the primary recipient of US arms transfers. When the conflict faded, a new focus—the Middle East—emerged. From fiscal years 1974–78, over 60 per cent of total sales went to Iran, Saudi Arabia and Israel.[8] As one US official commented: 'We would not need a policy if we were not selling arms to those three countries'.[9]

The third major change concerned the level of technology being sent abroad. With the supply of surplus equipment depleted, the USA no longer had hand-me-down hardware available for export. Moreover, customers paying cash could demand better than the second-hand weaponry for which grant recipients could be made to settle. As a result, the bulk of US exports became essentially equivalent to the weapons being supplied to its own forces.[10]

By the mid-1970s, therefore, the United States faced a new situation, only partly of its own making or under its control. As long as the arms exported to foreign governments came from surplus military stocks, US decision makers could choose their destination, while availability acted to limit both the volume of grants and the number of recipients. With the switch to sales, the government was attempting to manage a buyer–seller relationship, not its own actions.

Political incentives nevertheless remained the primary force behind US exports. Over the years, the USA had found arms transfers consistently attractive as a policy tool, in spite of periodic setbacks when regimes changed and former friends rejected US ties. There seemed to be little disposition within the US Government to examine closely the usefulness or long-term impact of arms transfers. Ironically, given public unease over arms sales as a back door to involvement in Third World conflicts, many policy makers, including those in the Carter Administration, saw arms sales as a means of avoiding direct intervention without having to abandon any commitments. As one US official explained in 1978:

Even before the announcement of the Guam (Nixon) doctrine we had begun gradually to reduce our forces abroad—a process that continues to this day. But to make it work, we had to insure that our allies had access to those American weapons necessary to fill in behind our departing forces and to carry out their enlarged self-defense responsibility. For this the foreign military sales program has been the primary instrument.[11]

The Carter Administration's efforts to reduce the importance of arms transfers to US foreign policy were thus controversial from their inception. Many argued that the risks were either exaggerated or well worth taking, and that the USA could not afford to surrender so valuable a tool in the competition with the Soviet Union in the Third World.[12] Without real progress in gaining Soviet co-operation, therefore, the restraints would almost inevitably crumble.

The Soviet Union

Arms exports had been a major instrument of the Soviet search for influence abroad since the mid-1950s, especially in the Third World. The gift or sale of arms always seemed welcome, whereas Soviet economic assistance proved far less popular. Arms thus frequently offered the best means of securing and keeping friends and allies.[13]

The character of the Soviet programme had also changed by the mid-1970s, in ways similar to what happened in the United States. Gifts of military hardware were generally replaced by sales. Generous credit terms and repayments in commodities gave way to demands for payment in hard currency when the weapons arrived. This insistence on cash extended even to the massive airlift to re-supply the Arab states during the 1973 Middle East War. Without an emergency bail-out by other Arab states, Egypt could not have paid for its equipment. Resentment of such tough treatment for an ally in wartime was another nail in the coffin of Soviet–Egyptian relations.[14]

The shifts in Soviet arms exports appeared driven by a number of factors. Unlike the changes in the US programme, economics appeared to play a significant role. Above all, arms export offered the USSR an important source of foreign exchange earnings. The US Central Intelligence Agency estimated that weapon sales accounted for just over 10 per cent of overall Soviet exports to the Third World in the mid-1970s, and that without those exports the USSR would have run a substantial trade deficit with those countries.[15]

The change to sales apparently also forced the Soviet Union to increase the sophistication of its exports. It still exported from its huge stocks of surplus hardware, but more first-quality Soviet equipment began appearing in the arsenals of important friends. The USSR might simply have been striving to match the qualty of US exports, but they probably also had found that customers paying cash demanded more for their money. Arms sales would never be a purely economic venture for the Soviet Union, but foreign policy interests and political advantages were no longer the sole determinants of where its arms supplies would go.

Given its powerful incentives for weapon exports, the prospects for Soviet interest in restraints on their trade appeared rather limited. CATT advocates were counting in large measure on the fact that the USSR had found arms transfers to be a mixed blessing. Over the years the Soviet Union had suffered numerous setbacks in its use of arms to pursue influence. The 'loss' of China was the most spectacular blow, but there had been a number of other painful reverses, including Egypt, Indonesia and Somalia. CATT supporters hoped that the USSR might be willing to recognize the limits of arms transfers and see a greater foreign policy advantage in limiting competition with the USA. Leslie Gelb, Director of the State Department's Bureau of Politico-Military Affairs and head of the CATT delegation, offered four reasons why he thought an agreement might be possible.

1. Probable Soviet realization that arms transfers beyond a certain point can complicate and can cause serious problems in their relations with the United States.

2. Recognition that they, like us, have had some bad experiences as a supplier . . . that they have not always achieved what they hoped for politically through arms transfers; and their arms have been used in ways that were not intended.

3. Calculations that, in the absence of some basis for international restraint, the United States has a far greater capability than the Soviet Union to increase arms transfers.

4. And, as in any arms control negotiation, a search for ways to promote difficulties between us and our allies.[16]

Western Europe

If one looked only at each nation's share of the Third World market, the European suppliers appeared to be very junior partners in the arms trade. For example, the US Arms Control and Disarmament Agency estimated that between 1972 and 1976 the USA provided 52 per cent of the arms delivered to 'developing' countries, while the Soviet Union provided another 27 per cent. By contrast, France delivered about 5 per cent, the UK just over 3 per cent and FR Germany just over 2 per cent.[17] West European sales were expanding rapidly during this period, however, so if one counted agreements rather than deliveries, by the mid-1970s the West European share of the market almost matched that of the Soviet Union.[18]

More important than aggregate totals was the impact on West European sales in various regional markets. In Latin America, for example, France and Britain outstripped the superpowers.[19] Many of their arms supply relationships reflected continuing political ties with former colonies or spheres of influence, such as French exports to Sub-Saharan Africa or British exports to the small states of the Persian Gulf. Economics and politics mixed in European arms exports to the Middle East, for their heavy dependence on foreign oil made good relations with the oil-producing nations essential.

Overall, the primary pressure for exports was economic, arising from the basic character of their arms industries. The USA had actively encouraged a robust European arms industry to strengthen NATO, and most nations felt strong nationalistic pressures for independent industries. Unlike the superpowers, however, whose vast internal requirements consumed most of their domestic production, Europe's own forces could not absorb enough to keep their arms industries cost effective. These nations wished to maintain national arms production capabilities for a variety of political and psychological reasons, but to do so they had to export a substantial percentage of the arms they produced. The export dependence varied from industry to industry, and among the different countries, but none escaped the problem.[20]

West European countries had reputations as aggressive marketeers, and US arms manufacturers complained bitterly about the support their governments supplied. Given the political dimension of their exports, the USA and the USSR were seldom in direct competition, but US and West European companies often met head-on. The huge intra-NATO market, dominated by the United States, was a continuing source of tension among the allies.

This was the central dilemma and irony of CATT and the Carter policy for Europe. The Carter policy was supposed to limit the US arms sales to unstable regions. Long-time allies in NATO, ANZUS and Japan were specifically exempted since these were certainly not exports that the USA viewed as inappropriate or dangerous. Yet setting up the policy in this way invited US companies denied sales in the Third World to turn their attention to the developed countries, while 'Buy America' restrictions and the general reluctance of the US military to rely on foreign suppliers kept the US market essentially closed.[21] If Europe was to restrain its trade to the Third World and face increased US competition on their home ground, then co-operating with the Carter policy would force them to accept a reduced market share. The potential damage to defence industries that the USA had encouraged for over 20 years was apparently never considered when the Carter policy was designed.

There was widespread recognition that Western Europe would be largely unenthusiastic about arms sales restraint. The Carter Administration seemed to believe that, if talks with the USSR were successful, Europe would be unable to hold out against a supplier regime composed of the two superpowers.

New producers, new problems

Beginning in the late 1960s, the ranks of arms suppliers expanded steadily. New producers included both smaller West European states such as Austria and Spain, and a number of developing nations. Keeping those fledgling industries economically viable generally demanded production levels beyond the requirements of each nation's military. As with the major European suppliers, arms exports presented the logical solution.

The new producers included a number of nations with ambitions for major-power status, for whom a domestic arms industry offered significant prestige. Some new producers faced severe security problems, including obtaining a reliable flow of arms from the traditional suppliers. Brazil fell into the former category, Israel into the latter. Other new producers attracting attention during this period were South Korea, Taiwan, South Africa, Argentina and India.[22]

The appearance of these new suppliers clearly complicated the task of seeking meaningful controls on arms transfers. The developing nations in particular were unlikely to show much sympathy for joining a supplier regime that sought to restrict their freedom of action and that of their peers. A staff report for the US Senate Foreign Relations Committee concluded that: 'These new producers have already begun to export arms, and soon they would need to become part of any supplier's effort to reduce worldwide arms traffic. The longer the delay in talks, the more complex the issue will become'.[23]

The recipients

The arms-supplying nations represent only one side of the arms transfers issue, for would-be exporters must have customers. Almost every country and many subnational groups import arms, presenting a dizzying array of individual motives and practices. In spite of the shadow cast by the Middle Eastern market, other regions had substantial arms import races of their own in the mid-1970s. Sub-Saharan Africa was the most recent, fuelled primarily by huge Soviet shipments to such new friends as Angola and Ethiopia, and the civil war over Zimbabwe-Rhodesia.[24] Appreciating the variety of reasons for importing arms is essential to understanding the range of issues any comprehensive approach to controlling conventional arms traffic would have to address.

The purchasers' motivations also demand attention, for these countries were seldom the hapless victims of slick arms salesmen. For some nations, arms served important domestic political purposes, providing valuable symbols of prestige and control. More important from a negotiating perspective were the national security concerns of the recipients, for if one granted each nation a legitimate right to self-defence, how did one measure the capabilities a nation needed? Who could do so in a disinterested fashion? No state appreciated being told by another what its 'proper' requirements were, and developing nations, where arms sales controls appeared most urgently needed, were especially sensitive. Moreover, a suppliers' agreement would inevitably resemble a consortium of old colonial and imperial powers, which further coloured the issue. The overall prospects for recipient restraints, except as part of broader regional political arrangements, appeared to most observers to be very slight.

The arms trade in the mid-1970s thus displayed a complex mix of policy issues and participants. As an arms control issue, arms transfers were inescapably multilateral and multi-dimensional. Against this background and with very little time if its unilateral restraints were to survive, the Carter Administration sought to foster the growth of an international restraint regime.

III.   A CATT chronology

The first steps

The Carter Administration quickly launched its efforts to foster arms transfer control. In his first foreign policy press conference, the President announced that Vice President Mondale would broach the subject during his visit to the major European allies and that Secretary of State Vance would approach the major purchasing nations.[25] During January and February 1977, Vance suggested several initiatives, such as a pilot ban on arms transfers to Africa or a mutual ban with the Soviet Union on arms transfers to the Middle East. The latter would be 'very constructive', but Vance conceded that it was probably 'unrealistic' until a political settlement had been achieved.[26]

Soviet participation was clearly central to the success of the Carter Administration's efforts. As the other major supplier, Soviet restraint would have the most immediate impact. The political significance was even greater. Unless the Soviet Union could be induced to curtail its use of arms transfers, domestic resistance to abandoning such a valuable policy tool would eventually triumph over unilateral restraints.

Initial contacts with the West European suppliers made it clear that they also regarded the Soviet Union as crucial. Reactions ranged from mild interest to polite scepticism to frank dismissal, but all made it clear that Soviet participation would be essential for any genuine multilateral efforts.[27] Aware of the fundamentally political character of US arms transfers and heavily dependent on their exports, these suppliers understandably preferred to assess the staying power of US restraints before contemplating any of their own.

France rejected any bilateral arrangements, arguing that only a genuine multilateral forum could properly address the issue. Britain and FR Germany took their cues from France, stressing that the USA needed to demonstrate the sincerity of its commitment and to enlist Soviet co-operation before expecting the Europeans to respond. As then British Ambassador Peter Jay explained to a conference of US arms industry executives:

We share with the United States the view that global expenditure on armaments is too high. My government believes that attempts to limit arms exports must be on a multi-lateral basis if they're to be effective. We are prepared to play our part in the international discussions amongst arms suppliers, but we feel, as the United States is the world's largest exporter of arms, it is appropriate as President Carter himself has acknowledged that She, the United States, should take the lead. For any arms sales policy to be effective, we also note that the co-operation of the Soviet Union will of course be necessary.[28]

As Leslie Gelb summed up the European reaction: 'They said "why should we participate in this kind of exercise if the Soviets aren't going to co-operate? Go get the Soviets to co-operate first"'.[29]

Focus on the USSR

Multilateral efforts thus quickly focused on co-operation with the USSR, which in the past had refused to accept arms transfers as a legitimate arms control issue. At the 16th Congress of Trade Unions in March 1977, however, Leonid Brezhnev hinted at a change in the Soviet position: 'In general the problem of international arms trade seems to merit an exchange of views'.[30] Although buried by the vehement Soviet rejection of the US proposals for SALT, Secretary Vance's visit to Moscow in March 1977 did result in the formation of several working groups on arms control issues. One of these concerned arms transfers.[31]

The Carter Administration continued to suggest potentially negotiable elements of the arms transfer problem, presenting the USSR with a number of options for defining the eventual negotiating agenda. In June 1977, for example, Lucy Wilson Benson outlined several alternatives in a speech to the National Women's Democratic Club in Washington. She emphasized US hopes that its own restraint would, over time, attract other arms buyers and sellers to develop a 'code of behaviour' based on their 'mutual interests' and proposed four areas for initial emphasis: (a) arms transfers to unstable regions; (b) sensitive weapons and technology; (c) equipment especially appealing to terrorists; and (d) highly and indiscriminately lethal weapons.[32]

The talks begin

The first formal meeting to discuss arms transfers with the Soviet Union finally took place in Washington in December 1977, several months behind the original schedule. The first round of CATT was conducted behind a thick wall of secrecy intended to encourage more frank and forthcoming discussion from the Soviets. Apparently very little common ground emerged from the exchange, which served primarily to give the United States a chance to lay out its position. US officials later stressed that no one had had high expectations for the meeting so they gave it relatively limited attention.[33] Sceptics contended that the Soviet Union would always be willing to talk and would gladly enmesh the Carter Administration in interminable conversations while continuing to expand its exports. CATT advocates countered that it was a considerable feat even to coax the Soviet Union to the conference table.[34]

The hopes of CATT advocates received a boost when the second round of meetings took place in Helsinki in May 1978. The Soviet Union was now willing to declare that arms transfers represented an 'urgent' problem and agreed that a basis existed for regular talks. A final communiqué was released, which CATT supporters had regarded as essential to demonstrate the seriousness of the enterprise.[35] The document stressed respect for the legitimate defence needs of the recipient countries, and the two nations' 'mutual desire' to assist other international efforts such as the UN Special Session on Disarmament taking place during that period. Regional arrangements and the need to find ways to engage other suppliers in restraint efforts received special mention.[36] Both sides appeared to be developing the perception that arms transfers could be a negotiable issue.

This encouraging session was followed by a new round of public position taking, especially by the Soviet Union. They repeated during the UN Special Session that progress was possible in CATT. They emphasized the need for political and international legal criteria to provide standards for arms transfers. They also stressed their determination, however, to continue supporting 'liberation groups' and 'victims of aggression'.[37]

The USA did not take particular advantage of the Special Session forum, but during congressional testimony Leslie Gelb expressed hope that the two countries would develop common 'norms of supplier restraint', which might include such elements as: (a) no-first-introduction of advanced weapon systems into a region which creates a new or significantly higher combat capability in the area; (b) restrictions on co-production and re-transfers; (c) development of norms for recipient restraint; (d) establishment of consultative mechanisms to enhance the exercise of restraint; (e) the integration of restraint efforts with diplomatic efforts to resolve regional disputes; and (f) reduction of possibilities for substitution by suppliers where others have exercised restraint.[38]

The third round of talks, in Helsinki in July 1978, produced more positive signs but no concrete achievements. Press accounts reported that the USA and the USSR were within 'hailing distance' of a set of principles to limit sales.[39]

By the end of July both sides had agreed on a three-part arms transfer restraint framework. It included political–legal criteria to determine recipient eligibility, military–technical criteria to govern types and quantities of arms that could be transferred, and arrangements to implement these principles and guidelines in specific regional situations.[40]

By now, most US officials acknowledged that the Soviet Union appeared more forthcoming than originally expected and far more co-operative than the European suppliers. The time between the third round and the fourth, scheduled for December, was to be used for informal contacts to clarify the emerging negotiating agenda. The question of how to define a 'region', for example, would require considerable work. The USSR wanted to include individual countries, such as China, while the USA held out for traditional Western geographical definitions.[41]

Both the USSR and the USA continued to put forth positions and suggest areas for possible agreement. In August, a Soviet article suggested the areas of restraint they preferred to explore, including limits on sales to: (a) racist regimes (especially those singled out for sanctions by the UN); (b) countries considered aggressors; (c) countries with militaristic policies; (d) countries that have unjust territorial claims on other states; and (e) states that reject disarmament efforts. Iran, South Korea, Israel and the People's Republic of China would all have been included in these categories according to Soviet definitions.[42] In congressional testimony in October, Leslie Gelb suggested that 'harmonized national guidelines' analogous to those of the London Suppliers' Group for nuclear exports and the development of regional and subregional restraint regimes appeared to be 'realistic possibilities'.[43] Press accounts during the fall reported that the most likely site for an initial effort was Latin America, where a precedent for restraint existed under the 1974 Declaration of Ayacucho.[44] Not even the observation that neither the USA nor the USSR were major suppliers to the region dimmed the precedent that such co-operation could establish. The fourth round, appropriately to be held in Mexico City, was expected to see the beginning of real negotiations.

Falling apart

The modest optimism built up through 1978 evaporated in a 'savage bureaucratic struggle'.[45] The primary protagonists in the internal bureaucratic struggle were Leslie Gelb, head of the CATT delegation and its chief advocate, and National Security Advisor Zbigniew Brzezinski, a belated but forceful opponent. The source of the confrontation was which 'regions' would be on the table for discussion in Mexico City. The Soviet Union, although willing to discuss Latin America and Africa, insisted that sales to China, South Korea and Iran be included in the talks. Permitting the USSR to single out these US friends and allies was completely unacceptable to Brzezinski. Gelb and the other CATT advocates, while not wishing to see these countries awarded special and unwelcome status, did not want to risk the prospect for genuine negotiation which this round appeared to offer.

The issue was eventually raised with President Carter, where Brzezinski won the confrontation. The President reversed the decision he had made before the July round of talks to permit discussion of regions other than those the USA suggested. Gelb was forced to go to Mexico City with instructions to inform the Soviets that the US delegation would walk out if China, Iran or South Korea were even mentioned.[46]

The Soviets responded angrily, and the talks deadlocked over the US refusal to discuss their proposals. In a rare interview, Soviet Ambassador Liev Mendelvich told a Mexican journalist: 'We have never aspired to match the United States, the most important supplier in the international market'.

Mendelvich stressed the essentially multilateral and political character of the arms trade: 'The question of limiting sales as well as the legitimate interest on the part of peoples fighting against aggression will be subject not only to decisions made by the world powers, but also to agreements they may reach with other nations, the suppliers of all types of weapons'.[47]

The battle between Gelb and Brzezinski revealed the limited support CATT actually enjoyed within the US Executive Branch. As long as CATT had been a relatively low-level discussion with little apparent prospect of success, it was able to proceed unmolested. Once it appeared that an agreement might actually be possible, the stakes and the number of interested parties within the US Government quickly expanded. Few of these new players turned out to be CATT enthusiasts.

Beyond this, CATT's supporters were divided. The essential disagreement was whether to view the negotiations as an 'arms control' problem to be solved with restraints on the weapons themselves, or whether to view the weapons as essentially symptoms and seek regional restraints as the cure. The Arms Control and Disarmament Agency (ACDA) favoured the first approach, while the State Department, led by Leslie Gelb, favoured the latter. The State Department had won President Carter's support for a regional approach just prior to the July round of talks, which some CATT supporters regarded as a fatal mistake.[48]

Finally, CATT was a victim of deteriorating US–Soviet relations and of competing foreign policy goals. In the end, CATT simply turned out to be a relatively low priority for the Carter Administration. The energy necessary to forge and sustain a bureaucratic consensus through the negotiations was not there. SALT was a far higher arms control priority. The Middle East peace process was consuming tremendous resources. Moreover, the USA had cut the Soviet Union out of those negotiations, and most officials had little wish to see them return through the back door of CATT.[49] And, unbeknownst to many in the bureaucracy, the USA was in the final stages of secret negotiations to normalize relations with China. CATT was not sufficiently important to place this breakthrough at risk.[50]

Although CATT received vague mention in the final communiqué of the Carter–Brezhnev summit in June 1979, the Mexico City debacle was the final round of actual discussions. As US–Soviet relations foundered in 1979, there was little interest in further exploration of joint restraints. Unilateral US restraints ended soon thereafter. The fall of the Shah of Iran and the subsequent cancellation of over \$12 billion in arms orders made the export ceiling, which had become the cornerstone of the restraints, essentially meaningless. The Soviet invasion of Afghanistan was the final blow.

In the renewed climate of intensified US–Soviet competition, arms transfers began to be regarded once again as a vital tool to counter Soviet gains. The Reagan Administration's basic statement on arms transfer policy declared that henceforth the United States would 'deal with the world as it is, rather than as we would like it to be'. The statement went on to note that since there had been 'little or no interest in arms transfer limitations manifested by the Soviet Union or the majority of other arms producing nations, . . . the United States will not jeopardize its own security needs through a program of unilateral restraint'.[51]

IV.   After the debacle: lessons and prospects

The prospect for an international effort by the major arms suppliers to limit their exports have been dim throughout the 1980s. Above all, the grim state of US–Soviet relations makes it difficult to imagine any common ground for restraining such a valid tool in their competition for influence. Nevertheless, there might have been opportunities had that fundamental base of decent superpower relations existed. For one, Argentina's use of imported French jets and missiles to sink a British guided-missile destroyer during the Falklands/Malvinas War brought one of the consequences of their exports home painfully and dramatically to the European suppliers.[52] For another, the massive increases in defence spending in the United States during the first Reagan term might have decreased US arms manufacturers' interest in pursuing overseas sales and hence eased domestic political pressures against restraining exports.

On the other hand, the collapse of the arms market in the Third World in the early 1980s created a number of contradictory pressures. The burgeoning debt crisis in many developing countries and the dramatic drop in oil prices forced many prospective importers to scale back their plans. This eased some of the regional arms races that had created interest in restraints in the 1970s. Yet brutal conflicts nevertheless continued in the Middle East and elsewhere. The shrinking market also increased pressures on those suppliers which depend on exports to sustain their domestic industries, with the Europeans and the new producers enjoying considerable success in increasing their sales. These contradictory pressures seem likely to remain into the early 1990s.

Over the years, many proposals have been put forward for controlling the international trade in conventional arms. Most fall into one of two broad categories: (a) attempts to control the weapons being exported, or (b) attempts to deal with the political situation that create motives for the trade. In making any assessment of strategies to control the arms trade, one first has to address the obvious question of *why* restraints would be desirable. Is the primary concern the flow of sophisticated weapons to more countries, and the effects this might have on future conflicts, including the prospects for major power intervention? Is it concern with the level of defence spending in developing countries, and a belief that, however difficult supplier restraints might be to achieve, they would still be less arduous a task than recipient restraints? Is it a belief that the major suppliers are exploiting and exacerbating conflicts in the Third World in order to satisfy economic motives for sales? Is it a hope that controlling weapon imports might be a path to resolving the national or regional conflicts that fuel them? Is it a concern that the arms a supplier provides might be used in ways it would not approve? Is it fear that a supplier might become embroiled in a local conflict because of the ties that arms sales create with friends and clients overseas? In particular, is it a concern that the USA and the USSR might become embroiled in a crisis with the potential to escalate to nuclear war through their arms supply relationships?

A restraint regime that satisfied any of these concerns might also satisfy others or even all of them, but the choice of approaches and priorities would be very different. Comments are confined to the risk of supplier entanglements and the spread of sophisticated weaponry, where the CATT experience appears most directly relevant.

If the concern is avoiding supplier involvement in its allies' or customers' conflicts, then unilateral restraints might suffice. This would be especially true if those restraints served to give the supplier a greater sense of control over its export policy. Certainly the Carter Administration was motivated in part by a concern that arms transfers were playing too prominent a role in US foreign policy, potentially with unintended consequences. In that case, tying unilateral restraints to the success of a broader international effort was probably a mistake, even if there were powerful political pressures to do so. The ties tended to minimize the direct benefits the Carter Administration believed the USA would derive from restraints. They also gave opponents of restraining arms transfers extra incentive to find ways to ensure that CATT failed. Public opinion polls consistently show that a majority of Americans are uncomfortable with the US role as a major arms supplier, but, as Jimmy Carter discovered, moral uneasiness is not enough to build and defend a policy of restraint within the US Government.[53]

Today, the most powerful motive for US interest in restraining arms exports is probably concern for potential superpower crises over Third World conflicts. US restraint thus appears most likely to come about as part of some broader political *rapprochement* with the Soviet Union. The Reagan Administration has held a series of meetings with the USSR on regional issues and interests, and if relations improved these could become the basis for revived negotiations on limiting arms transfers. The presumed general benefits of improved superpower relations would also provide a basis for resisting domestic political pressures in the United States against forgoing exports. If the concern is avoiding crises between the superpowers over Third World conflicts, then the most likely regime could begin by being, and for a considerable period remain, composed of the USA and the USSR. Regional arrangements, which might or might not include limits on particular weapons, would be the most likely means of applying the restraints.

One advantage of treating arms transfer restraint as an *arms control* problem and focusing on the types of weapon being exported is that there are numerous precedents and models for this type of enterprise. A focus on the spread of sophisticated weaponry, whether because of its potential impact on conflicts or its drain on developing countries' treasuries, would demand, however, that the regime's membership be expanded beyond the superpowers. How far to expand would depend primarily on how narrowly one defined 'sophisticated'.

At a minimum, the major European suppliers would have to be included and perhaps some of the new producers as well.

The CATT experience offers some lessons for this approach. In essence, the design of the overall Carter policy doomed CATT for the West European countries. The policy applied to all 'weapons and weapons-related items', rather than particular technologies or types of weapon system.[54] Exempting NATO countries from the world-wide ceiling simply encouraged US arms exporters to push sales to Europe to offset their losses in the non-exempt countries. Refusing to open the US market to West European arms suppliers, despite pious lip-service to making NATO weapon standardization a 'two-way street', forced Europe to choose between a reduced share of the world market and increasing sales to the Third World. Given the enormous consequences for their domestic military industries, Europe, not surprisingly, turned to the Third World.

West European resistance also played into the hands of those in the Carter Administration who opposed arms sales restraints, whether for economic, strategic or ideological reasons. It is not certain that universal application of the ceiling would have ensured the success of the Carter policy, but exempting the NATO countries without compensation condemned it to failure. More broadly, any serious attempt to limit the flow of modern weaponry would force the USA and its West European allies to confront a range of intra-NATO political issues almost as difficult as creating US–Soviet regional arrangements. Solutions to these dilemmas can be envisioned, but the primary point is that treating arms transfer restraint as an arms control problem does not offer a genuine escape from tough political issues.

In sum, any realistic strategy for achieving restraints on international arms transfers has to begin with a clear definition of the purposes these restraints are to serve. The Carter Administration apparently never resolved that fundamental question or never amassed sufficient support for one definition to give the policy a strong chance to survive. Second, the creation of all but the most limited regimes will demand a willingness to confront immense political problems with implications for other relationships and policy priorities. When a confrontation came, CATT could not prevail over these other pressures. The Carter policy and the CATT negotiations thus offer a valuable cautionary tale for anyone interested in seeking restraints on conventional arms transfers.

Notes and references

[1] The authors would like to thank Jonathan Kaplan of Stanford University for his valuable research assistance.

[2] Congress began to assert a role in arms sales in 1974 with the Nelson Amendment to the annual foreign aid bill. This was followed in 1976 by the Arms Export Control Act, a comprehensive overhaul of the US 'arms transfers' (sales and military assistance) programme.

[3] *Arms Transfer Policy*, Report to Congress for use of Committee on Foreign Relations, US Senate, 95th Congress, 2nd Session (US Government Printing Office: Washington, DC, 1977), p. 14.

[4] Johnsen, K., 'Review on arms restraint set', *Aviation Week & Space Technology*, 11 Dec. 1978, p. 14.

[5] *US Overseas Loans and Grants, July 1, 1945–September 30, 1977*, US Agency for International Development (US Government Printing Office: Washington, DC, 1978), p. 6. Authors' calculations.

[6] *Foreign Military Sales and Military Assistance Facts*, Defense Security Assistance Agency, US Department of Defense (US Government Printing Office: Washington, DC, 1978), p. 6. Authors' calculations.

[7] Louscher, D., 'The rise of military sales as a US foreign assistance instrument', *Orbis* (Winter 1977), p. 936.

[8] *Conventional Arms Transfers: Background Information*, Report to Committee on International Relations, US House of Representatives, 95th Congress, 2nd Session (US Government Printing Office: Washington, DC, 1985), p. 158.

[9] *Middle East Arms Sales Proposals*, Hearings before Committee on Foreign Relations, US Senate, 95th Congress, 2nd Session (US Government Printing Office: Washington, DC, 1978), p. 44.

[10] Cahn, A. and Kruzel, J., 'Arms trade in the 1980s', *Controlling Future Arms Trade*, ed. A. Cahn, J. Kruzel, P. Dawkins and J. Huntzinger (McGraw-Hill Book Company: New York, 1977), pp. 30–31.

[11] See *Middle East* (note 7), p. 4.

[12] For example, see Betts, R., 'The tragicomedy of arms trade control', *International Security* (Fall 1980).

[13] Pajak, R., 'Soviet arms transfers as an instrument of influence', *Survival* (July/Aug. 1981), p. 165.

[14] Pajak, R., 'Soviet arms and Egypt', *Survival* (July/Aug. 1975), p. 170.

[15] *Communist Aid Activities in Non-Communist Less Developed Countries of the Free World*, US Central Intelligence Agency (US Government Printing Office: Washington, DC, 1979), p. 3.

[16] *Indian Ocean Arms Limitations and Multilateral Cooperation on Restraining Conventional Arms Transfers*, Hearings before Committee on Armed Services, US House of Representatives, 95th Congress, 2nd Session (US Government Printing Office: Washington, DC, 1978), p. 17.

[17] US Arms Control and Disarmament Agency, *World Military Expenditures and Arms Transfers, 1967–76* (US Government Printing Office: Washington, DC, 1978), p. 10.

[18] *Prospects for Multilateral Arms Export Restraints*, Staff Report of Committee on Foreign Relations, US Senate, 96th Congress, 1st Session (US Government Printing Office: Washington, DC, 1979), p. 25.

[19] See *World Military Expenditures* (note 15), pp. 155–58. Authors' calculations.

[20] Franko, L., 'Restraining arms exports to the Third World: Will Europe go along?' *Survival* (Jan./Feb. 1979).

[21] See *Prospects* (note 16), pp. 31–32. US exports to non-NATO developed countries did increase in the late 1970s. See *Foreign Military Sales and Military Assistance Facts*, Defense Security Assistance Agency, US Department of Defense (US Government Printing Office: Washington, DC, 1985). Authors' calculations.

[22] See Brzoska, M. and Ohlson, T. (eds), SIPRI, *Arms Production in the Third World* (Taylor & Francis: London, 1986), *passim*.

[23] See *Prospects* (note 16), p. 41. The debate on the impact of the new producers continues. For two quite different assessments, see Neuman, S., 'International stratification and Third World military industries', *International Organization* (Winter 1984); and Klare, M., 'The unnoticed arms trade', *International Security* (Fall 1983).

[24] Hudson, G., 'Soviet–black African relations', *The Gun Merchants: Politics and Policies of the Major Arms Suppliers*, ed. C. Cannizzo (Pergamon Press: Elmsford, NY, 1980).

[25] 'President's press conference, February 14, 1977', *Department of State Bulletin* (Feb. 1977).

[26] Secretary's press conference', and 'Interview with the Secretary, February 21, 1977', *Department of State Bulletin* (Feb. 1977).

[27] Hammond, P., Louscher, D., Salomone, M. and Grahm, N., *The Reluctant Supplier: US Decisionmaking for Arms Sales* (Oelgeschlager, Gunn & Hain: Cambridge, MA, 1983), p. 173. This is the most complete published account to date of the internal US politics of CATT.

[28] American Defense Preparedness Association, *Third Annual Executive Seminar on Foreign Military Sales: Meeting Report* (ADPA: Washington, DC, 1977).

[29] Quoted in Hammond (note 25), p. 173. See *Indian Ocean* (note 14), p. 13.

[30] Quoted in Pierre, A., *The Global Politics of Arms Sales* (Princeton University Press: Princeton, 1982), p. 286.

[31] Blechman, B., Nolan, J. and Platt, A., 'Pushing arms', *Foreign Policy* (Spring 1982), pp. 142–43.

[32] 'Undersecretary's address to the National Womens Democratic Club, August 1, 1977', *Department of State Bulletin* (Aug. 1977).

[33] Bradsher, H., 'No common ground for US, Soviets in arms sales, *Washington Star*, 21 Dec. 1977.

[34] See Hammond (note 25), pp. 178–81, for a catalogue of the bureaucratic actors and coalitions involved in US decision making on CATT.

[35] See Blechman (note 29), p. 143.

[36] The communiqué is reprinted in *Department of State Bulletin*, July 1978.

[37] See *Prospects* (note 16), pp. 21–22.

[38] See *Middle East* (note 7), p. 10.

[39] Gwertzman, B., 'US and Soviets in arms progress', *New York Times*, 2 Aug. 1978.

[40] See Blechman (note 29), p. 146.

[41] See Hammond (note 25), pp. 175–76.

[42] See *Prospects* (note 16), p. 22.

[43] See *Indian Ocean* (note 14), p. 17.

[44] Oberdorfer, D., 'US, Soviet seek common rules to limit arms in Latin America', *Washington Post*, 26 Oct. 1978. In the 1974 Declaration, eight Latin American nations—Argentina, Bolivia, Columbia, Chile, Ecuador, Panama, Peru and Venezuela—pledged to work to 'create conditions which will allow an effective limitation on weapons'. See *Prospects* (note 16), p. 45.

[45] Oberdorfer, D., 'Policy shift puts arms sales talks in doubt', *Washington Post*, 19 Dec. 1978.

[46] See Oberdorfer (note 43).

[47] Becerra Acosta, J., 'Avances sin acuerdos en las platicas desarme URSS–US', *Unomasuno*, 14 Dec. 1978.

[48] See Blechman (note 29), pp. 144–45.

[49] See Hammond (note 25), pp. 181–85.

[50] See Pierre (note 28), p. 289.

[51] 'Conventional arms transfer policy', The White House, 9 July 1981.

[52] Ullman, H., 'Profound or perfunctory: observations on the South Atlantic conflict', *The Lessons of Recent Wars in the Third World*, vol. 1, eds R. Harkavy and S. Neuman (D.C. Heath and Company: Lexington, MA, 1985), p. 242.

[53] For polling data, see Pierre (note 28), pp. 71–72. For an evaluation of the Carter policy, see Husbands, J., 'The arms connection: Jimmy Carter and the politics of military exports', in Cannizzo (note 22).

[54] See *Arms Transfers Policy* (note 1), pp. 1–2.

Paper 8.   Problems and prospects of arms transfer limitations among second-tier suppliers: the cases of France, the United Kingdom and the Federal Republic of Germany

FREDERICK S. PEARSON[1]

I.   Introduction

The question of controlling the arms trade to the Third World is complicated by the quantity and hierarchy of suppliers, the mix of motives in selling and buying armaments, and the variety of restrictions that could be applied. Aside from their sales to industrialized states, Britain, France and FR Germany—the so-called 'second-tier' suppliers—compete and sometimes co-operate for a niche in a recently shrinking Third World market. In the process they contend with first-tier, that is, superpower suppliers, and with the emergent third tier of Third World arms manufacturers and exporters.

As a group, European exporters have recently outstripped the superpowers in Third World arms sales, with 31 per cent of the market in 1985.[2] Thus, despite hard economic times, second-tier suppliers have captured a larger share of the Third World market, based mainly on Middle Eastern sales. Heavy supplier competition and the resultant 'buyer's market' of recent years tend to worsen the prospect for future sales on the one hand; but the proliferation of civil and international violence in the Third World, the prominence of the military in Third World governments, and the continued availability of financing, in one form or another, for arms acquisition tend, despite mounting international debts, to buoy the market and encourage exporters.[3]

Second-tier suppliers are also strongly affected by the prevailing climate of superpower agreement or disagreement on international arms control questions. British, French and West German leaders found it convenient to put off confronting the question of stringent limits on Third World arms transfers while the superpowers haggled over the terms of the Conventional Arms Transfer (CAT) Talks during the late 1970s. If Washington and Moscow had been able to agree on principles of restraint in various regions, however, and were prepared to enforce them jointly, it would have been very difficult for London, Paris and Bonn to continue business as usual in those regions. By the same token, to speak of anything beyond the most minimal second-tier restraints without including at least one superpower and arms purchasers in a larger international agreement is probably fanciful.[4]

It is commonly agreed that second-tier exporters dispatch arms and related military equipment to the Third World for both economic and military/strategic reasons, that is, to sustain domestic military production and employment, improve trade balances, retain at least some autonomous arms manufacturing capabilities, and curry favour with influential Third World regimes.[5] Although such benefits appear to be overrated, any agreements to limit arms exports must provide alternative ways of satisfying these interests, or be part of a redefinition of such interests involving, for example, economic reconversion or changed security doctrines.

In addition, while it is convenient to speak generally of 'restraints' or 'limitations' on the arms trade, a wide variety of limits are conceivable, each with varying consequences for international economics or security. Clearly, some arms trade controls would result in a diminished flow to the Third World, while others would merely underwrite, identify or regulate the continued or even increased flow of weapons. Each of these forms of control would have certain consequences for supplier and recipient states, only some of which might be beneficial, depending on the criteria for arms control success employed, for example, reducing war frequency or damage, enhancing deterrence or predictability, and reducing defence budgets, international tension or militarism.

The twin issues of political feasibility and desirability complicate the prospect for export control, including that by second-tier suppliers. Deep cuts in Third World arms supplies might reduce the scale of Third World warfare but might not reduce the frequency of war nor increase spending on economic development.[6] Since the UN Charter recognized an inherent right of national self-defence, controls which build in regional force balances would be more feasible but also might not reduce warfare without measures to settle disputes.[7] Qualitative restrictions on high-technology weapon exports could result in more money being spent on less costly and advanced conventional armaments (e.g., automatic rifles, rockets and tanks) which, as the Lebanon and the Gulf wars have shown, ultimately could kill more people than a few expensive and sophisticated fighter aircraft. In short, any imposition of or agreement on export controls must be viewed in terms of its security consequences.[8]

In this paper the record of British, French and West German attitudes regarding arms export limitations will be reviewed in an effort to identify the type of control most feasible and desirable from the viewpoint of or in relation to second-tier suppliers. These states, of course, display a variety of opinion on these matters, both in contrasting foreign policies and among diverse domestic interest groups. Therefore, this paper describes the differences as well as common interests among second-tier suppliers, and the domestic forces which make arms trade controls more or less likely or comprehensive. It deals with both existing and potential controls.

II. Perspectives of second-tier suppliers

Arms transfer controls could stem from concerns about both national welfare and security, as well as about morality and peace.[9] In terms of welfare and national prosperity, arms manufacturers and government officials could conceivably become disillusioned about the viability of the Third World weapon market, especially given increased Third World debt and demands for 'offsets' or 'counter-trade'. In addition, changed market conditions, such as expanded US, NATO or European Community (EC) procurement of British, West German or French arms, and easier availability of oil and other natural resources, could obviate the need for and interest in Third World sales. On the other hand, increased standardization of sytems in NATO and continued US dominance of the NATO market might increase the perceived need for compensatory European exports to the Third World or compensatory US subsidies to Europe. Arms sales in general continue to be regarded as a 'quick fix' for trade imbalances, in spite of the fact that they do little to remedy the structural causes of those imbalances.[10]

Economic motives for limiting arms trade have so far been mainly hypothetical, but second-tier suppliers have demonstrated real security restraints for a number of years. Most of these reflect worries about arms falling into the 'wrong hands'. Embarrassing wartime experiences, such as West German arms cropping up in Algeria for use against the French in the 1960s, French and British arms being used to sink British warships in the Falklands/ Malvinas War, and Iraq's use of French arms to attack oil tankers bound for Western Europe, all raise West European concerns about the screening of arms recipients. Concerns about better end-use controls also stem from the possibility that lethal weapons, acquired by terrorist organizations, would be used against British, French or West German state interests. Qualitative controls on weapon transfers to Third World countries, including the modification and downgrading of systems or outright bans on some exports, are largely a product of military concern about the release of sensitive technologies. Indeed, such concern has proved to be a primary export licensing criterion in the UK, and of at least some concern in France and FR Germany.[11]

Export restrictions which would result in a sharp decline of second-tier supplies depend generally on a diminished government and economic stake in military production and therefore on a redefinition of national security which downplays weapon production autonomy. The French push for arms exports began with the view that, along with nuclear weapons, a vital conventional arms capability would ensure French sovereignty in the post-colonial era. This original aim expanded into a self-sustained economic interest in weapon production and trade.[12] The UK has also clung, with increasing difficulty, to a traditional capability for production in all three weapon categories: land, sea and air; and FR Germany has also gradually renewed at least partial capabilities in all three areas. Therefore, the influence of and support for 'military–industrial complexes' would have to diminish or be routed in new directions to ease the way for major restrictions on Third World arms sales.

Second-tier or mid-sized suppliers have retained selective interests as well in Third World political influence, and arms transfer controls have been and increasingly could be related to such interests. Regional instability and violence beyond certain limits become difficult for mid-sized European powers to tolerate, especially if the region in question supplies vitally needed resources. Concerns about human rights and the level of carnage in civil or international disputes or wars enter here as well. Yet while one option to regulate Third World warfare would be to reduce or ban arms shipments to combatants, and while at one time or another Britain, France and FR Germany all have articulated intentions to do so, other more appealing options also exist. The Iran–Iraq fighting illustrates European willingness to choose sides and/or seize the moment to take commercial advantage through continued or increased arms or spare parts shipments.[13]

Since second-tier suppliers generally are parliamentary democracies, domestic politics play a role in limiting the arms trade. However, traditions of secrecy and governmental privilege surrounding defence matters plus the strong momentum of military–industrial interests make it difficult for arms trade opponents to gain a share of decision making on specific sales, even to the extent possible in the relatively more open US system. Opponents are most vocal and effective in FR Germany, where they can point to constitutional and legal provisions limiting FR Germany's role in fuelling foreign wars. As a result, Bonn has adopted a more anonymous arms supplier role than other second-tier suppliers, relying on co-production and overseas licensed production arrangements.[14] In Britain a combination of interests, including a Campaign Against the Arms Trade by church groups and peace activists, together with political parties' human rights concerns, governmental fears about advanced equipment reaching Soviet allies, and military suspicions about arms export commercialism all contribute to a watchfulness concerning specific sales. Such interests and constraints, while present to an extent, are weakest in France.[15]

Based on these general perspectives, second-tier suppliers have formulated both unilateral and multilateral positions on the management, restriction or reduction of Third World arms transfers. These are examined separately in order to assess the restraints most likely to be adopted in the future. Arms trade *management*, whether unilateral or multilateral, implies rules for reporting or licensing sales in specific circumstances, as well as potential market sharing arrangements. *Restriction* of sales entails disapproval, banning or embargoes to specific states or classes of states or of specific types of weapon. *Reduction* of transfers includes more sweeping measures, such as qualitative or quantitative limits or ceilings, and deliberate government policies or international agreements designed to curtail weapon exports. In the process of devising restraints, there can be trade-offs, such as restraints on transferring arms versus the technology or equipment to make or use them, on naval versus air versus land systems, or on weapon deliveries versus new sales agreements.

Recent trends in second-tier arms supplies

Before delving into unilateral and multilateral British, French and West German arms transfer limitations, it would be well to examine these states' recent record of arms transfers to the Third World. Periods and locations of increasing or declining supplies can provide clues about existing or potential future arms transfer restraints.

As seen in table 8.1, and allowing for the inherent uncertainties of arms transfer data, only France has had consistent major increases of Third World arms transfers since 1973, although FR Germany has doubled its share of *major* weapon transfers. Therefore, France would appear to be the most invested of the three in the Third World arms market. This goes along with France's comparatively limited inroads into the NATO market since its withdrawal from the operational command structure in the 1960s. According to US estimates, which are higher than those reported elsewhere, nearly 100 per cent of recent French arms exports have been directed at developing countries. Of course, FR Germany also is linked to France in many joint projects stemming from the 1960s and 1970s, which may be underreported in the West German Third World totals. All three suppliers are generally over 80 per cent dependent upon Third World sales, although West German agreements have declined in the 1980s while Britain's have increased. Aggregate figures can be misleading, of course, as both British and French sales have in recent years tended to concentrate among certain states and regions, as seen below, and most recently France has been more successful in selling to the USA.

As to regional concentration of sales (table 8.2), not surprisingly all three suppliers are heavily oriented to the Middle East. Note, though, that when Italy is included, the second-tier group jointly are the dominant Latin American suppliers. It has been argued that recipients of European arms tend to be either former colonies with which close ties have been maintained, or assertive non-aligned states looking for an alternative to superpower dependencies. While not exactly non-aligned, Latin American states have sought to break away from US dependency status and were interested in the products in which European exporters have tended to specialize: light surface ships, diesel-powered submarines, light strike aircraft and trainers, helicopters and light armoured vehicles—many of which could be produced locally under licence and re-exported. European suppliers also took advantage of relative US sales restraint during the Carter years to build up their clientele.

France remains the least successful in breaking into new Third World markets in recent years, although French weapons still take a comparatively large share of the African and Latin American markets. In 1985, Paris launched a reorganized and stepped-up marketing approach to various Third World regions. Even France's sales to its former African strongholds have

Table 8.1. Percentage shares of French, British and West German arms transfers to the Third World, 1973–84[a]

| | % of Third World arms imports | | | % of own total arms exports going to Third World | | | % of major weapon exports only[b] | | |
| | | | | | | | Third World total | | Own total |
	1973–76	1977–80	1981–84	1973–76	1977–80	1981–84	1975–79	1980–84	1980–84
France deliveries	6.4	8.9	12.9	71.1	96.1	98.1	10.6	11.1	80.6
Agreements	11.0	14.3	14.9	95.9	98.9	99.1			
UK deliveries	4.5	5.6	5.3	76.0	85.2	81.8	6.1	4.8	73.5
Agreements	4.4	6.1	3.0	84.8	81.3	86.0			
FRG deliveries	3.1	4.4	4.6	86.7	80.0	87.3	1.5	3.1	61.0
Agreements	4.4	4.9	3.1	77.8	88.2	60.3			

[a] Based on calculations in billions of current US dollars. Data include conventional weapons, parts, ammunition, support equipment and services, and other militarily designed commodities. 'Third World' consists of ACDA's 'Developing' category. Source: *World Military Expenditures and Arms Transfers, 1985* (US Arms Control and Disarmament Agency: Washington, DC, 1985), table B, p. 45.
[b] From SIPRI, *World Armaments and Disarmament: SIPRI Yearbook 1985* (Taylor & Francis: London, 1985), table 11.1, p. 346.

Table 8.2. Percentages of the value of French, British and West German arms transfers to Third World regions, 1976–85

	East Asia/Pacific			Near East/South Asia			Latin America			Sub-Saharan Africa		
	1976–79	1980–83	1982–85	1976–79	1980–83	1982–85	1976–79	1980–83	1982–85	1976–79	1980–83	1982–85
France												
% own deliveries	2.0	2.7	1.7	72.0	80.0	87.9	13.0	11.2	4.8	12.9	6.2	5.6
% own agreements	2.1	1.9	1.8	70.4	89.5	88.8	16.7	5.5	6.0	10.9	3.0	3.4
% regional deliveries	1.5	2.7	2.3	7.1	12.3	14.1	12.6	14.6	6.4	9.9	10.2	8.7
% regional agreements[a]	2.1	2.4	2.1	9.9	15.3	15.4	21.6	11.0	11.5	12.0	7.1	6.6
UK												
% own deliveries	10.0	7.3	7.2	67.3	79.4	77.6	18.0	5.8	3.0	4.7	7.5	12.2
% own agreements	4.1	15.8	7.3	89.4	64.4	85.5	1.5	5.2	1.4	4.9	14.7	5.8
% regional deliveries	5.0	3.6	2.9	4.4	5.9	3.8	11.5	3.7	1.3	2.4	6.0	5.9
% regional agreements	2.4	6.1	4.3	7.1	3.5	7.6	1.1	3.3	1.4	3.0	10.9	5.8
FRG												
% own deliveries	5.0	6.7	9.0	62.3	48.1	35.7	14.5	30.2	51.9	18.2	15.0	3.5
% own agreements	4.3	22.1	18.2	39.7	52.3	48.9	39.9	20.8	14.3	16.0	4.9	18.7
% regional deliveries	1.9	1.8	3.6	3.0	2.0	1.8	6.9	10.4	21.3	6.9	6.5	1.7
% regional agreements	2.3	4.4	2.3	2.9	1.5	0.9	27.4	6.8	3.0	9.2	1.9	4.0

[a] Indicates supplier's percentage of regional total.

Source: Grimmett, R., *Trends in Conventional Arms Transfers to the Third World by Major Supplier, 1976–1983* (Congressional Research Service, Library of Congress: Washington, DC, May 1984); and *Trends in Conventional Arms Transfers to the Third World by Major Supplier, 1978–1985* (May 1986). Data include the value of weapons, spare parts, construction, associated services, military assistance and training programmes.

declined proportionately, as a result of sanctions against South Africa, growing French economic interests in Middle Eastern sales and the poverty of traditional Francophone Africa. French troop contingents in Africa partly obviate the need for much rearmament by France's African client states, which of course could not in any case afford or absorb much. In this way Paris maintains influence over former colonies, unthreatened by major inroads of other arms suppliers. By contrast, the presence of British forces in rich Middle Eastern client states, such as Oman, has not notably diminished Omani and Gulf states' tendencies to buy British arms and to diversify arms sources as well.

This pattern of second-tier supplier transfers has ramifications for Third World arms control prospects. With British and West German transfers spread more widely among regions, London and Bonn would be more affected than France by the prospect of regional arms restraint agreements, such as that in 1974 at Ayacucho in Latin America (which despite reaffirmation has hardly been implemented). France would be most affected by any such agreement in the Middle East, but all three suppliers would be seriously concerned. If the CAT Talks were any indication, suppliers are least likely to be interested in restraining transfers to the regions in which they predominate over competitors. NATO procurement would have to increase immensely to divert significant British and West German exports from the Third World, as there remains significant excess production capacity in both states, particularly in the ship-building industry.

Generally, aggregate trends appear to reflect mainly commercial, arms procurement and market cycle effects in slowing agreements or deliveries. Occasionally a major revolution, such as that in Iran, will wipe out, or a major war, such as in the South Atlantic, open up new export possibilities. Slowly mounting international and domestic political pressures, such as those applied in connection with South Africa and Chile, can have a moderating influence on arms transfers as well.

III.   Unilateral limitations

As major powers with extensive international interests, the second-tier suppliers long ago established government management of arms exports through licensing and have restricted or prevented certain exports in certain circumstances. Nevertheless, while export licence rules may discourage or disqualify specific deals, the vast majority of licence requests in each state are granted.

While all three states have asserted in principle that arms should not be dispatched to combatants in warfare or for internal repression, and have at times refused sales for such reasons, FR Germany and Britain appear to implement restrictions more stringently than France. In its quest for regional influence and trade as an alternative to the two superpowers, France has reportedly promised in specific sales agreements not to interrupt arms or spare parts supplies even in crises or war. The relative concentration of French exports to the Middle East as compared to the UK and FR Germany may in part reflect British and West German tendencies to look for export markets in regions suffering somewhat less upheaval, for example, Latin America and Asia.[16] However, these distinctions should not be carried too far, especially in light of Britain's major Saudi agreements of the 1980s, which carried no restrictions on the use or basing mode of Tornado fighters *vis-à-vis* Israel and Iran.

Second-tier suppliers are also concerned about the indiscriminate release of sophisticated technologies in weapon sales. For example, since 1978 the West German Government has required notification and approval of weapon design and blueprint exports, and since 1982 of *privately* negotiated as well as government-sponsored multinational co-production. France, which purports to scrutinize carefully prospective recipients of advanced systems,[17] also has led the way in the design of export-oriented ships, armour and aircraft in which the level of technology can vary or be modified.[18]

The government's role in arranging credit for Third World arms customers also is greater in Paris and London than in Bonn. Private or state banks carry the brunt of defence financing in the FRG, although the Federal Hermes trade credit guarantee agency has quietly underwritten more arms exports, especially of ships, than its formal role would indicate.[19] While there is no corresponding stigma attached to government financing of weapon sales in France, in 1968–73 Paris tended to discourage Third World credit purchases in the name of economic development and debt limitation, especially in former French colonies. Yet more recently, in heated competition with the USSR, the USA and Britain for sales to relatively large consumers, such as India and Saudi Arabia, the French Government has reportedly offered financing considerably below the interest levels agreed by the Organization for Economic Co-operation and Development (OECD) states. Paris has also sought to market the Mirage 2000 as a 'loss leader' with generous credit and repayment terms to debt-written states such as Peru.[20]

Finally, end-use or re-export restrictions are enunciated and applied by all three states, but enforcement of the provisions is rare. Indeed, concerted enforcement is thought to endanger the market position of second-tier suppliers by identifying them as 'unreliable'. Britain, for example, imposes end-use certification only in certain sales contracts where danger of re-export is considered great. It professes to rely on intelligence information to track down harmful re-exports and the threat of future sales bans to discourage them.[21] Generally, although France imposes re-export restrictions in most sales contracts, it poses few obstacles to purchasers' *use* of weapons. An exception was a ban on Israeli 'offensive' operations following the 1967 War, which was breached in attacks on Lebanon in 1968. President de Gaulle, responding to growing political pressure, then imposed an embargo on Israel and, for appearances sake, on Arab front-line states in 1969. These had extremely limited effects, as Israel essentially shouldered France aside and became a prime US arms client, thus showing the limits of second-tier supplier influence. While the French Government laboured during 1967–74 to justify continued arms sales to Arab states which were not 'battlefield' contestants, the embarrassing disclosure of Libyan re-exports of Mirages to Egypt in 1973 ended all pretence of an effective embargo, and it was lifted. Paris subsequently restricted arms sales to Libya itself, but more as a reaction to the latter's African adventures than to Middle Eastern warfare or unauthorized weapon re-transfers.

French restraints

France's unilateral arms transfer restrictions, like those of other second-tier suppliers, have been characterized as half-measures, often compromises for domestic or foreign political effect. In addition to the contorted logic of various Middle Eastern embargoes, France has imposed arms transfer restraints on Indochinese battlefield contestants in the late 1960s and at various times on Pakistan, South Africa, Libya, revolutionary Iran, Nigeria and Angola (the latter two during civil wars). However, at times France has also been willing to sell weapons to many of these same states and regimes directly or through third parties. Even when employed, restrictions have been leaky, as evidenced in Israel's famous seizure of fast patrol boats from Cherbourg in 1969, with the tacit co-operation of French officials. French spare parts continued to flow to Israel as well, during much of its embargo. French restrictions on Libyan sales have alternated with sales offensives, and restrictions have at different moments included controls on the types of weapon delivered, as well as 'temporary and selective embargoes on arms deliveries or on new contracts', all to little effect in disciplining the Libyan leadership.[22] In the Nigerian Civil War, France continued selling arms for a time to the FRG, but then switched to allow sales of French equipment to the Biafran rebels evidently to weaken Nigeria *vis-à-vis* Francophone Africa.[23]

Oddly enough, it was partly in the name of better Third World relations that François Mitterrand's Government de-emphasized prior Socialist Party critiques of the arms trade and lifted the restrictions of Giscard d'Estaing's Government on Libyan sales in 1981.[24] While Giscard d'Estaing had attempted to safeguard French North African interests through such sanctions, Mitterrand reasoned that Franco–Libyan relations could be improved through freer arms sales, a rationale that was to ring rather hollow during subsequent French military campaigns against Libya in Chad, a country in which Mitterrand had also attempted to use selective arms supplies and restrictions to various factions to wean them away from Libyan connections. Similarly, three gunboats, paid for by Iran but withheld by Giscard d'Estaing after the Iranian revolution, were released to Tehran by President Mitterrand.[25]

Basically, France continues a unilateral managerial approach to limiting arms transfers, vetting individual prospective recipients and deciding when to withhold certain weapons in certain situations to enhance French interests.

Looking beyond France's borders, there is no bureaucratic concern for the impact of French and rival arms suppliers' behaviour on regional and global security or on economic development in the Third World. The French military industrial complex can hardly look with equanimity on the prospect of decreased spending on arms by developing countries. Little or no attention is given to the impact on local stability of advanced weapon systems introduced into a region, such as supersonic aircraft in Latin America. Nor is much concern expressed for the arms races that might be provoked by the unregulated transfer of arms to a region such as South Asia or the Middle East where France has furnished arms to most of the principal rivals in the region at one time or another.[26]

France generally shuns broad doctrines or policy rules on restricting the arms trade and seems to have enunciated relatively few concrete decision criteria.

The largely nationalized French military–industrial sector basically draws government into the process of promoting and legitimizing arms sales. While French trade unions tentatively oppose increased arms sales,[27] in the midst of pressure for employment there has been no basic attack on the forces support- ing the arms trade, that is, the complex of military–industrial interests and state-supported weapon research teams. Unlike Britain and FR Germany, the issue of diversification or conversion from military to civil production has not been broached often by the government, labour or management. In the early 1980s the Socialists flirted with a reorientation away from Third World to European and North American markets, but failed to make the foreign policy changes, especially regarding NATO, which might facilitate such a shift.

British restraints

In a decidedly case-by-case orientation to the arms trade, the British Govern- ment maintains the watchword of 'flexibility' in rule application. The Defence and Foreign Ministries have generated tables which rank weapon systems as to technological sensitivity and rank prospective customers as to security risk or political acceptability. These lists are then compared in a rough calculus, especially in the early stages of controversial cases to determine appropriate release of technological information. The Treasury's ratings of credit-worthi- ness enter as secondary considerations as well. Recently, for example, credits were denied to its NATO ally Turkey, thereby aborting arms sales negotiations.[28]

Despite these seemingly objective criteria, the rankings can be rapidly changed depending upon political or economic circumstances. Export press- ures have resulted in calls for speedier downgrading of weapon security restrictions in the biannual review process. Despite political protest, Chile was quickly promoted from unacceptable status for arms shipments as an offset to Argentina during and since the Falklands/Malvinas War. India has presented problems because of security ties to the USSR, but Britain has nevertheless campaigned for and concluded major arms sales to India. The inadequacy of these evaluative ratings in predicting consequences harmful to British interests was demonstrated during the Falklands/Malvinas fighting, as the UK had largely trained and equipped the Argentine Navy.

In addition to effects on British security (including possible arms shipments to terrorists) and technology, other criteria and factors considered by the British Government in deciding on Third World arms export applications include questions of regional stability (an ill-defined concept), alliance interests and complications (e.g., potential conflicts with the USA in areas such as Latin America or the Middle East), delicate negotiations (such as those for the independence of Belize in Central America), Commonwealth ties (heavy pressure was applied to Britain about South African exports), nuclear non-proliferation, internal political repression abroad and economic interests. The latter two were especially important in the unpopular decision to continue supplying arms to the oil-producing Nigerian Government during the Biafran War.[29] Equipment judged useful in domestic repression was denied, for example, to Argentina, Uganda and Chile in the 1970s, and to Indonesia, Chile and Sri Lanka in the mid-1980s. However, equipment capable of use against domestic populations, such as helicopters and strike aircraft, has at times gone to both Chile and Indonesia since 1978, and no similar restrictions have been evident on shipments to India, Malaysia or the Sudan despite domestic unrest in those countries.[30]

British regional political interests have led since 1970 to selective embargoes against Honduras and Guatemala, regarding Belize (1970s); Taiwan, since the diplomatic opening to China; and Argentina and Israel, since the South Atlantic and Lebanese fighting of the early 1980s. In Israel's case, Britain's participation in the joint European Community embargo has continued partly because of a limited Israeli demand for British arms and because of interests in the Arab market. The UK has indicated that the ban will be lifted when Israel completes its withdrawal from Lebanon.[31] Spare parts shipments for Iran were held up temporarily during the US hostage dispute, and weapons have been denied to the PLO. The UN embargo on South Africa has largely been observed, although certain dual-purpose equipment, such as transport aircraft, have gone through under special provisions.

The Gulf War has been the occasion for rethinking British guidelines about the release of weapons to Third World states at war. The British approach has contrasted sharply with the joint British–US embargo against India and Pakistan during their 1965 fighting, and may reflect the growing ambivalence of Western arms suppliers about ending the Gulf War—that is, which side would be the preferred victor. Early in the conflict, the UK adopted a rule that exports of 'lethal' arms should be banned to both sides. Yet the ambiguity of this categorical definition, together with tempting commercial interests, strategic concerns, Iraqi battlefield reverses and the question of existing paid contracts with Iran, brought a reformulation in 1985:

(1) We should maintain our consistent refusal to supply any lethal equipment to either side;

(2) Subject to that overriding consideration, we should attempt to fulfil existing contracts and obligations;

(3) We should not, in future, approve orders for any defence equipment which, in our view, would significantly enhance the capability of either side to prolong or exacerbate the conflict;

(4) In line with this policy, we should continue to scrutinise rigorously all applications for export licences for the supply of defence equipment to Iran and Iraq.[32]

Obviously the criteria of conflict exacerbation and prolongation can be even more subjective than weapon lethality. The British Government has afforded itself more room to manoeuvre either to allow or disallow specific export licences, especially as the combatants have highly contrasting force configurations.[33]

The British Labour Party has been more responsive than the ruling Conservatives to interests critical of the arms trade, and Labour's record both in and out of office has been somewhat more restrictive about the arms trade to the Third World, especially on questions of human rights and domestic repression.[34] Nevertheless, it was a Labour Government which introduced the Defence Sales Organisation to rationalize and promote British arms exports in 1966, following similar developments in the USA. If Labour or the SDP–Liberal Alliance came to power, it is not entirely clear that the British arms trade would be curtailed.

Shadow defence spokesman Denzil Davies elaborated in 1985 upon what he termed a 'very difficult subject' for Labour:

My own view is that the Defence Sales Organisation [since renamed Defence Export Services Organisation] should be abolished but I recognize that there are many countries, especially Commonwealth countries, that still look to Britain for the purchase of arms for their defence. Therefore I cannot see the Organisation being immediately abolished, but I would certainly work towards getting rid of it. I would also be very concerned to change the rules to make it much more difficult for us to sell weapons of destruction abroad . . . I would change . . . to prohibit all sales unless there is a very good political reason for selling those arms. . . .[35]

Mr Davies also promised protests against military equipment exhibitions, joint efforts with trade unions to promote conversion, more public notice of arms transfers and destinations, and strict specific criteria about the supply of arms to states abusing human rights.

This would constitute a tightening of British procedures and standards, particularly in reporting sales and on questions of human rights. However, the Labour pronouncements also resemble the Thatcher Government formulations on issues such as exacerbation of international aggression or domestic repression. A great deal of definitional flexibility would remain about what constitutes such abuses, and about 'good political reasons' for selling 'weapons of destruction'. Labour's anguish about prospective job losses in the military sector is implied as well; during the 1986 parliamentary debates on the sale of Westland helicopter shares, much more was made, on both sides of the House, of US versus European ownership, and of the welfare and preferences of the workforce, than of the wisdom or viability of continued military helicopter sales abroad.[36]

West German restraints

The Federal Republic of Germany is unique among the three suppliers, with a legacy of legal and constitutional prohibitions against actions threatening international peace or promoting offensive war. While these legal structures have seldom been tested judicially, they make the sale of weapons abroad more controversial among the attentive general public than in France or Britain. Furthermore, despite the unrestrained growth of West German arms industries and exports since the 1950s, there is as yet no formal sales promotion agency in Bonn corresponding to the British Defence Export Services Organisation or the Directorate for International Affairs in the French Defence Ministry.

Only FR Germany among the three main European arms producers has indulged in blanket restrictions of arms transfers to states outside the circle of NATO and associated states, and particularly where war might threaten. However, the famous 'areas of tension' restrictions of the late 1960s and 1970s have been somewhat modified under the Schmidt and Kohl Governments to allow Third World sales where they can be shown to enhance 'vital' West German foreign policy and security interests, among states unlikely to use the arms in domestic repression, where regional tensions are unlikely to be increased or Western Alliance interests unduly harmed, and with at least the advice of parliamentary parties. This modification, a result of considerable inter- and intra-party debate, and clearly a move to facilitate lucrative sales to economically and strategically important states such as Saudi Arabia, has positioned the FRG much closer to Britain and France in judging arms transfer requests on a case-by-case basis. While Bonn has adopted a legalistic approach to arms transfers, the government has in the past failed to link its formal doctrines to well-defined foreign political as opposed to defence and economic priorities. Therefore, it has been argued that, with relaxed restrictions, arms exports to the Third World could come to substitute for a West German foreign policy regarding the Third World.[37]

Beginning under Chancellor Schmidt and continuing under Kohl, Bonn has shown greater interest in using arms for influence and improved relations. Chancellor Kohl has argued that a new generation of leadership means that the FRG is entitled to the full range of policy options available to major powers; a 'security partnership' with Saudi Arabia was subsequently announced. Whether for purely commercial or partly political interests, prior export licence denials for Egypt and Malaysia were lifted as well.[38]

Before its commercial sales push of the 1970s, FR Germany briefly experimented with arms transfers for political influence against the German Democratic Republic, especially in Africa. The failure and embarrassing consequences of these efforts, along with the still small volume of West

German arms production, made the enunciation of strong restrictions politically easy in 1968–71. Arms exports outside NATO were to be discouraged, with the sale of 'war weapons' prohibited in principle, although only for items mentioned in the War Weapons Control Act of 1961. 'Defence-related material', a separate category under West German law, was allowed to flow to the Third World, but not to 'areas of tension' such as the Middle East. The Foreign Ministry decided which were areas of tension, although no overall criteria were established. For instance, Libya was not allowed to import West German U-boats, although Chile was allowed to do so in the 1970s despite domestic repression and international disputes. A secret arrangement with France, since codified in the revised export regulations of 1982, allowed co-produced weapons to flow even to strife-torn areas and French clients such as Libya.

Under the 'areas of tension' guidelines, Bonn was selective and strict about where it would ship arms in the Third World. Most authorized direct exports were ships and submarines, for the benefit of the depressed West German shipyards. Finally, in the late 1970s, sensitivity about terrorism led Bonn to step up 'end-use' documentation requirements, although overseas licensed production still allowed for much evasion. Indeed, at one point in the 1960s Bonn attempted to require deposits to ensure compliance with end-use stipulations.[39]

West German debates about the wisdom of proposed exports to Saudi Arabia and Chile led to the redefinition and loosening of the export regulations by the Schmidt Government in 1982.[40] The three conventional political parties each developed proposals regarding the new doctrine, and the Green Party critically appraised the arms export business. Because the FRG has for so long been sensitive to its weapons being used in warfare among less developed states, and because, unlike France, the FRG still does not manufacture many more arms than needed for its own armed forces (as indicated in column 2 of table 8.3),[41] West German export restrictions continue and could be increased if political embarrassments occur. The ruling coalition government appears split on the appropriate loosening of export restraints, with CDU-FDP factions favouring some continued restraint and still prevailing over CDU-CSU groups desiring liberalized arms transfers. Of course, to be meaningful in limiting Third World access to West German weapons, restrictions would have to extend to the complex international channels for West German arms exports, so far an unprecedented occurrence. The closer the FRG comes to overt government-promoted arms sales and to arms 'overproduction', the less chance for unilateral renewal of tight restrictions.

With the decline in OPEC's importance to the West German economy, at least in the short term, together with persistent protest by peace and church groups and by elements of the military who are worried about the release of sensitive technology and the requirement for West German military instructors to be stationed abroad, there remains some prospect for a de-emphasis of Third World military markets. The FRG has long preferred multilateral diplomacy in

Table 8.3. Second-tier suppliers' economic dependence on arms exports

	Total arms exports, 1984 (national sources, $ b)	1984 arms exports as % of conventional arms production	Arms exports as percentge of total exports	Share of world exports of major weapons, 1981–85
France	3.8	50	3.9	10.6
UK	2.6	42	2.8	4.7
FR Germany	1.7	20	1.0	4.0
Italy	2.5	70	3.4	3.8
Spain	0.6	45	2.5	1.2
Sweden	0.3	25	1.0	0.2

Source: Brzoska, M. and Ohlson, T., 'The trade in major conventional arms,' SIPRI, *World Armaments and Disarmament: SIPRI Yearbook 1986* (Oxford University Press: Oxford, 1986), p. 336.

NATO and the EC, and would respond to expanded NATO conventional arms markets. West German trade unions, through a disciplined campaign by their leadership, have accepted the principle of reconversion far more widely than their French or British counterparts (jobs dependent on arms exports are not officially a valid criterion for 'vital' interests in the 1982 export guidelines), although their participation on company boards in 'co-determination' schemes tempers their opposition somewhat. Alarmed at government authorizations of easier defence exports to ASEAN (Association of Southeast Asian) states, at the preliminary authorization of export negotiations with Saudi Arabia, and at helicopter sales to South Africa, Chile and Iraq, the Social Democrats introduced a parliamentary bill, which was defeated in 1985—once again to ban war weapon exports to the Third World and to strengthen the Bundestag's role in controlling such exports.[42]

Arrayed against such interests in cutting Third World arms trade, however, are a complex of firms, including most of the major West German conglomerates, which rely on military business for at least a part of their turnover, as well as regional interest groups, as in Bavaria or the north, which are influential in the older political parties. Connections exist between the military, Defence Ministry and manufacturers to promote if not West German arms self-sufficiency, then a significant continuing production capacity. However, West German arms industries tend to depend less on arms production as a percentage of their total business than do the major British and French manufacturers. They could contemplate more easily a de-emphasis on or reorientation of arms exports; although they also strive to maintain weapon production capacities—some would say excess capacities. It is estimated that only 10 000 out of 240 000 jobs in the military–industrial sector depend directly on the Third World market,[43] and while West German trade balances have lately remained comfortably in surplus, the FRG's unprecedented post-war unemployment levels would have to drop considerably before serious tinkering with the arms export business would be expected, even from an SPD-led government.

In 1984, Foreign Affairs Minister of State Alois Mertes proposed (to little effect) a co-ordinated Western arms transfer policy in part to relieve the stigma and pressures on FR Germany for trying to sell arms to Saudi Arabia and the Middle East. Thus, the embarrassments long associated with FR Germany's arms trade could eventually lead to serious attempts at multilateral export guidelines (discussed below). Currently, however, the FRG can at least partially duck responsibility for sales through its low international profile and multifaceted supply arrangements.

All three second-tier suppliers have entered the military high-technology race, sometimes against and sometimes alongside the USA and Japan. However, profit margins and endangered production lines could also cause a renewed or at least sustained British, French and West German emphasis on marketing simple and lower-cost weapons. For example, expectations are that the new lightweight German Puma tank will be aimed both for the Bundeswehr and the Third World to compensate for the slow market in main battle tanks.[44] As the three suppliers move towards higher weapon technology, limits or restrictions on arms trade will move in that direction as well, and less sophisticated designs will be marketed more freely.

IV.   Multilateral approaches

Of the second-tier suppliers, the Federal Republic of Germany has the greatest potential interest in co-ordinated or multilateral limits on the arms trade. Traditionally, Bonn has tried to submerge its diplomacy innocuously in multilateral associations, and its arms trade involvements show this preference as well. With a late start in re-establishing production capabilities, especially in aerospace, and in view of possible surplus production capacity and faltering world demand for products such as surface ships, the FRG, and for similar reasons the UK, could come to favour international agreements to 'rationalize' the sale of arms and possibly apportion market shares.[45]

Among the current or historically enacted multilateral restraints on Third World arms trade have been: the Tripartite Declaration of 1950 regarding the Middle East; UN sanctions, embargoes and studies; and regional understandings such as that of Ayacucho. In addition, proposed or hypothetical approaches have included: the superpower CAT Talks; supplier co-ordination through the EC, NATO or the Western European Union (WEU); international arms trade and procurement registries; and a global consultative arms transfer committee. None of those enacted has made much of a dent in the international arms traffic, but they represent a class of restraints which could gain favour in future. In particular, multilateral approaches avoid some of the problems that unilateral restraints and embargoes historically seem to have stimulated—greater arms traffic from competitive suppliers.

Perhaps the most effective of supplier agreements was the Tripartite Declaration among the USA, the UK and France to regulate or balance arms shipments to the contestants in the Arab-Israeli conflict, in order to prevent a recurrence of the 1948–49 fighting. The agreement, which lasted until Egypt broke the Western arms supply monopoly to the region with the

Czechoslovakian–Soviet arms deal in 1955, also included British, French and US guarantees of Middle Eastern states' territorial integrity. A Near East Arms Co-ordinating Committee was formed to keep track of and balance the arms traffic, with a view to the security needs of states in the region. This mechanism proved generally inconvenient for the regional adversaries, and for the suppliers as well, since the USA and the UK had by 1953 developed interests in an anti-communist Middle Eastern alliance structure, including most Arab states. France also encountered the first Algerian anti-colonial struggles—thus developing common interests with Israel.[46] While the USA was particularly inclined to deny large-scale arms shipments to Egypt and Israel, and while Britain denied Egypt supplies during the Suez base dispute of 1953–54 and had little interest in supplying Israel, France—with a recovering arms industry and with the blessing of the USA—gradually became Israel's largest supplier. Britain and the USA tried to win other Arab states such as Jordan and Iraq through arms supplies.

The Declaration thus came to constitute 'more of a division of the market than a limitation on the sale of arms to countries of the region'.[47] It also has been criticized for failing to meet three basic criteria of successful supplier agreements: (a) that they be of limited duration and backed by intensive efforts to settle political disputes driving regional arms races; (b) that all relevant potential arms suppliers be included; and (c) that suppliers' regional political objectives not impede the arms supply necessary for a military balance acceptable to the conflicting parties.[48]

However, the agreement also illustrated the major arms suppliers' joint capability to prevent a regional arms race. Similarly the 1965 US–British embargo on India and Pakistan limited regional warfare, although opening the region to competitive Soviet and Chinese influence. Such capabilities were later somewhat eroded by indigenous arms production, the proliferation of major and minor arms suppliers, the anti-colonial ethic and worries about direct major power confrontation in the Third World (as in upholding security guarantees). However, the principle of supplier co-ordination, market sharing and recognition of recipient security needs stands as a precedent for future control efforts.

Although the United Nations Charter says little about arms transfers, the Organization has indulged in calls both for co-ordinated approaches to the arms trade and for specific embargoes. Of the former, perhaps the best known are a series of proposed resolutions advocating an arms trade register and a study of conventional disarmament and the arms trade in 1981. From the first UN registry proposals in 1965, Britain has been among the few major powers to lend support. Subsequently the FRG has come to favour such measures as well, calling for greater restraint by all arms suppliers and recipients, but premising agreement on prior arrangements to prevent the use of force in international disputes.[49]

In 1970, the UK made clear its willingness to promote control of the arms trade especially through regional agreements in co-operation with other suppliers and recipients.[50] At the UN Special Session on Disarmament in 1978, the UK included proposals for conventional arms control in the draft programme submitted with nine other Western states, and its proposal for consultations among major arms suppliers and recipients on the limitation of all types of international conventional arms transfers was adopted in the Final Document. Britain stressed the regional approach throughout the 1970s and into the 1980s, and in 1979 offered to participate in supplier-recipient talks once the Latin American/Caribbean states had agreed on possible measures of restraint. In relation to anti-terrorist concerns, the UK has also promoted a draft UN convention to ban the transfer of 'inhumane' weapons, such as mines, booby-traps, and incendiary and plastic fragmentation devices.[51]

In rationalizing its own continued arms sales promotions, the UK has consistently fallen back on the theme that cutting its 5 per cent share of global arms exports without multilateral restraints would have no significant beneficial effects. The Thatcher Government has also come to stress the right of self-defence in UN Charter Article 51 as a justification for sales to 'friends and allies', blaming the USSR and certain developing states for opposition to multilateral discussion of the arms trade.[52] In its own arms transfer reports, however, the UK remains unwilling to specify agreements and destinations except by region.[53]

At least in public pronouncements, the French Government has been much more sceptical than the UK and the FRG about the value of co-ordinated or multilateral measures. Linking arms exports to French autonomy and Third World influence, French leaders were extremely slow in responding to the UN Security Council's South African arms embargo of 1963; in 1970 France was still Pretoria's major supplier.[54] In 1968, however, during the height of his domestic difficulties with the left wing and while the bulk of French arms were still going to advanced industrialized states, President de Gaulle responded positively to Soviet and US calls for regional Third World arms limitations, particularly in the Middle East. France stated its willingness to examine the causes of arms trade if 'in particular cases, concerted measures could be decided upon and applied under a common accord'.[55] This approach eroded, however, both because the superpowers themselves were sidetracked by events such as Viet Nam and the Soviet–Czechoslovakian intervention, and because France was tempted to erode superpower arms hegemony in regions such as Latin America. France has come to view arms embargoes and joint supplier limitation as ineffective, merely spurring recipients' search for alternate suppliers or development of indigenous production.

Since de Gaulle's time, French leaders have manoeuvred to maintain freedom of action but have not entirely closed the door to multilateral restraints. At the 1978 UN Special Session on Disarmament, Giscard d'Estaing indicated a willingness to co-operate in regional arms limitations, provided that they were initiated by regional powers and included all the concerned parties. By implication, potential purchasers would have to define a satisfactory arms level. 'Real progress cannot be achieved from outside, through some form of cartel of producers or by unilateral action. It can be based only on the joint will of the countries concerned and their agreement on the aim and scope of a verifiable regional agreement'.[56]

Even before taking office, François Mitterrand confined his criticism of arms sales mainly to certain morally objectionable recipient states and did not advocate across-the-board reductions. Thus, multilateral restraint would appear to depend in part on major powers and consumer states mounting initiatives and forcing France's hand, plus diminished domestic economic, technical, political and bureaucratic pressure to produce and sell weapons—altogether unlikely short-term prospects.

Western approaches

Since the second-tier suppliers are NATO and EC members, one might expect common concern about the potentially destabilizing effects of arms transfers to important Third World regions, such as the Middle East or Africa. Yet on the whole, except for occasional consultations between the UK and the USA, and West German statements about arms exports and alliance interests, remarkably little co-ordination of NATO arms transfer policies is evident. NATO members continue carefully to limit 'out of area' concerns lest the Alliance's future be endangered by policy disagreements and competing priorities. Even when, for instance, the USA and France jointly intervened and co-ordinated policies in Lebanon, Chad and Zaire in the late 1970s and early 1980s, their approaches were decidedly unintegrated and did not extend to co-ordinated arms transfer limits.[57]

With a strong US initiative in the late 1970s, the prospect for a co-ordinated Western approach emerged on the eve of the CAT Talks. The Carter Administration intended to organize a conference of arms suppliers and consumers to extend arms control discussions to conventional weapons. Proceeding with unilaterally announced restraints, the USA applied 'moral suasion' to Western Europe. The Administration sought reduced sales promotions by all major suppliers and regional arms control agreements, and developed (unannounced) criteria to evaluate Western Europe's co-operation: (a) that other suppliers not fill the gaps left as the USA curtailed transfers, although they could maintain or even increase exports to their own traditional clients; (b) that other suppliers try to restrict the levels of sophisticated weapon technology released; and (c) that other suppliers consult with the USA before initiating new transfer agreements.[58] Naturally, such moral suasion did not sit well with the allies, for reasons of pride, politics and production.

Publicly, Britain, France and FR Germany indicated mild interest and tentative approval of the initial US proposals, but only if the USSR could be involved. Barring such involvement, and subsequently that of the recipient states, Britain and France particularly showed no interest in solely Western supplier restraint.[59] As a result, the CATT process thereafter focused exclusively on the ultimately fruitless USA–USSR talks.

Despite considerable doubt about such endeavours within the French bureaucracy, the French Government encouraged them, provided that a 'global framework' could be arranged. France's support of regional solutions to arms trade problems emerged soon after.[60] Similarly, Britain continued to stress its preference for regional approaches, and only as a seeming after-thought announced in 1979 that, 'we have also followed with interest the talks between the United States and the Soviet Union (which between them have over 70 per cent of the world's arms trade) on limiting the transfer of conventional weapons'.[61] The FRG had not yet changed their arms export guidelines and maintained the image of a relatively NATO-oriented arms marketeer, despite the reality of considerable and increasing Third World indirect sales.

Implied in the British statement is a hint of second-tier suppliers' basic objection to the CATT process at that time. They perceived themselves in a profoundly disadvantageous position in the international arms trade, and in relation to weapon technology and autonomy. In Europe, CATT restrictions appeared to imply a freeze on the status quo, which had the USA and the USSR dominant in the field of high-technology weaponry and its trade. West European defence budgets were tightly constrained, and the prospect of increased subsidization of arms production, increased domestic procurement or increased unit costs did not excite planners.[62]

If joint Western approaches are to be taken seriously and to work, they will require prior consultation and harmonization both of Western political and security policies regarding the Third World and of trade policy. Long deferred hard bargaining on the apportionment of Third World and NATO arms markets would be required.[63] This would probably entail a broader 'two-way street' in US weapon purchases and sales within the Alliance, and US willingness to restrict arms production capacity—perhaps on the model of farmland 'set asides'—or compensate smaller European suppliers in other ways, as in the purchase of civilian high-technology products.[64]

European approaches

On the European side, a nascent movement towards security policy co-ordination is detectable. In 1983, this came to include calls for common European Community arms procurement and transfer policies. Joint EC arms embargoes of Argentina and Israel during their 1982 war constituted a precedent for such co-ordination, although admittedly only on matters of primary concern to at least one key EC member.[65]

Stirrings of European interest in joint security policies and weapon procurement became evident in 1978, with a WEU (the organization with responsibility in defence matters) study claiming that the West European Alliance arms market could be economical even without Third World exports. Joint weapon procurement proved difficult, however, because only four states produced most of Europe's weapons and because national governments had varying force preferences. Article 23 of the Rome Treaty also allowed EC states to protect their security information and their domestic arms industries and trade. Further obstacles were encountered in co-production projects, over competition for project leadership and difficulty in translating experience in one type of arms production to another.[66]

A series of European Parliament resolutions followed during 1978–84, on co-ordinated security, conventional arms and industrial policies.[67] Yet while these were adopted at Strasbourg, the heated debate indicated a lack of consensus both within and among European countries, and there has been little subsequent implementation. Among the issues in contention were where any co-ordinated decision making should take place (WEU versus European Parliament versus NATO versus EC Council), and whether defence policy could be discussed in an EC context. Arguments in favour of greater co-ordination of arms exports, coming especially from certain British, West German and Danish conservatives, stressed the need to avoid Euro-arms trade fiascos such as the Falklands/Malvinas and Gulf Wars, and the untapped potential of the European as opposed to Third World arms market.

The Conservative majority could fall back on the EC Commission's strong support of cross-boundary arms industry co-ordination; by 1983 technocrats were citing the need for Europe to emerge as more competitive in high-technology fields to replace the dwindling coal and steel industries and to avoid over-dependence on the USA. An expanded and co-ordinated Euro-arms industry would fit the EC tradition of reduced protectionism, and could be conveniently labelled as 'industrial' or 'security' policy to avoid the defence issue. On the specific question of arms exports, the Commission tended to hold back, however, since it entailed the controversial 'sphere of political co-operation'.[68] The Conservatives thought it unrealistic to propose no EC arms sales to the Third World, and opted instead for guidelines to promote 'stability' and avoid harm to member states' political and economic interests. The EC could not presume to decide the security needs of the Third World, but certain types of equipment and technologies would be dangerous to export.[69]

Although they initially had opposed discussion of such issues in the EC, many Socialists eventually joined in proposing, if not ultimately voting for, the resolutions. Their concerns were somewhat similar to the Conservatives but went further, as they argued for specific export rules and bans. Socialists worried that a co-ordinated European arms industry would merely enlarge the Euro-military–industrial complex and result in an increased push for both NATO and Third World sales. They reasoned that restrictions on the West German model should be extended throughout Europe, perhaps in an arms export convention, to ban sales to the Third World, to confine exceptions to demonstrable common European foreign and security policy interests, with safeguards against arms delivery to governments violating human rights, and end-use clause enforcement and prohibitions of barter deals. Third World development issues would be addressed, and the USA and the USSR could be drawn into common arms export limits. Thus, the Socialist bloc hoped not simply to manage but to lower Europe's exports to the Third World. Most of their restrictive proposals and amendments were defeated, however, and most Socialists could not support the final resolutions.[70]

Euro-Communists and particular national political groupings from a variety of countries opposed the resolutions as well. While generally denouncing the arms trade, Communists did not want the EC dragged towards NATO-like defence debates and doctrines. There could be no joint approach to arms sales without agreement on a joint EC foreign policy, an unlikely prospect in the near term. Both leftist and rightist representatives of smaller countries, and particularly many from Denmark, opposed moves towards greater EC security co-ordination as risking British, French and West German domination. Denmark had opposed the Euro-arms embargo against Argentina as involving Denmark in the Falklands/Malvinas dispute, but by 1984 some Danish Socialists were willing to support establishment of a Euro-parliamentary committee on political aspects of security policy.[71] Dutch MEPs argued in 1983 that a joint arms export approach could link Europe to France in sales to the likes of Iraq. Greeks worried about a US 'trojan horse' in arms co-production with British, French or West German firms and objected to lack of requirements for arms transfer report to the Euro-Parliament.

Perhaps most tellingly, French Socialists opposed joint EC arms export restrictions as conflicting with French sovereignty. While favouring common industrial policies and joint projects to stimulate Europe's high-tech industries (presumably with French leadership), it was argued that the WEU was the only organ competent in defence matters: '. . . a common industrial policy in the arms field is diametrically opposed to the principle of French national independence. Arms strategy is central to the planning, organization, and deployment of France's entire military apparatus. This is not an industrial question, it is a question of defence'.

The Socialist government of France had supported the defence of Europe, but not necessarily a European defence, which could exist only with a single political authority. France viewed its European allies, with the exception of Britain, as sinking since World War II into 'military dependence, national egoism, debilitation, and even destabilization and neutralism'.[72] Thus the requisite common outlook for a Euro-defence policy was lacking.

The fractured nature of the defence debate has been evident *within* as well as among major EC countries and particularly within Britain and the FRG. Anti- and pro-NATO factions, anti- and pro-nuclear factions, anti- and pro-arms industry and sales factions vie for public support and votes. Even for those contemplating joint European approaches, larger and divisive EC projects come first, such as common agricultural, budgetary and monetary policies.

The question also remains as to what degree and at what point it is possible or desirable to merge European initiatives in controlling the arms trade with those of the superpowers and consumer states. Must interested parties wait until the international climate for renewing CATT processes is more auspicious, or can the processes be speeded with a greater sense of urgency as reflected in the

Palme Commission Report of 1982 and in calls for a NATO arms trade co-ordinating committee? The Palme Report urged arms suppliers to establish criteria for regulating arms transfers on an 'equitable' basis, with restraints defined in terms of 'quantities and qualities, geography and circumstances'. As seen, various interests would define 'equitable' differently, but the Report provides certain 'guiding principles' which might or might not clarify matters:

—No significant increase in the quantity of weapons which are transferred to a region.
—No first introduction of advanced weapon systems into a region which create new or significantly higher levels of combat capability.
—Special restrictions on the transfer of lethal weapons to warring parties, taking into account the inherent right of individual or collective self-defence.
—Adherence to the implementation of United Nations resolutions and sanctions.
—No transfer of particularly inhumane and indiscriminate weapons.
—Special precautions to be taken when transferring weapons, such as hand-held anti-aircraft weapons, which if they fall into the hands of individuals or sub-national groups, would be especially dangerous.

The Report went on to support resumption and expansion of the CAT Talks to include all major arms suppliers and to result in supplier–recipient talks in regions of tension. Regional security agreements and 'zones of peace' could be developed, with principles of restraint to be respected by supplying states.[73]

Apart from lingering ambiguities on such questions as 'legitimate right of self-defence', 'warring parties' and 'significant increases', there remains uncertainty about the advisability of European restraints in the absence of superpower agreement. Some would argue that European arms represent an important alternative to superpower arms exports and the resultant dependencies and temptations for superpower intervention in the Third World. Furthermore, a system parcelling out markets could work to the disadvantage of Third World arms purchasers by worsening the terms on offer in what has become a buyer's market. A tax on the arms trade, which has also been proposed in UN organs, might have similar effects but could also diminish the oversupply of weapons.

Is there likely, then, to be more multilateral arms export control in the EC or NATO? Incrementally, yes, but not in a Euro-arms export convention, at least in the short term. European parliamentarians, from where crises similar to the Falklands/Malvinas or Lebanon arise, as embarrassments such as those in the Gulf War and shipments to repressive regimes multiply, and as concerns about terrorism and inappropriate release of high-technology weapons mount, there will be increased pressure for joint supplier co-ordination and restraints. Indeed, there has been some informal convergence of separate British, West German and French principles governing the arms trade. However, common NATO rules are likely to develop only if accompanied by greater US willingness to purchase European arms or restrict the USA's own arms sales. And it is not clear to what extent France would participate in or attempt to impede either European or NATO co-ordination in this field.

V.   Conclusions

The leading second-tier arms suppliers limit their exports unilaterally to the extent of some concern about the release of sensitive technologies, and to a lesser degree about the reliability of recipients (for example, regarding support of terrorism) and the degree of domestic repression in the recipient state. While the British, French and West German Governments all mention a determination not to send arms to areas of ongoing warfare, the reality belies such restrictions, especially in the French and British cases and particularly in the Middle East. Regarding technology restrictions, the FRG appears particularly sensitive about armoured fighting vehicles, especially main battle tanks. The British watch carefully for equipment of use to the USSR or terrorists and pay some attention to domestic control potential. The French show concern about technology transfers but orient much of their weapon designs to export. For all three governments, technological restrictions appear particularly lax in the export of naval equipment. FR Germany and France are relatively free with licences to produce equipment abroad as well.

Prospects for increased restrictiveness in all such transfers depend upon several basic developments in the international arms markets and in international politics: (a) the resilience of Third World regional markets; (b) the political future of NATO and decisions about the Alliance's arms procurement; (c) superpower arms control initiatives and agreements; and (d) European security political debates about the benefits of military production.

Second-tier suppliers will increasingly be confronted by the choice of concentrating on sophisticated weapon systems primarily for the NATO market—with excess exports to wealthier or militarily ambitious Third World states—or moving towards the export of relatively simple designs, with few export restrictions, to a broad Third World market. In either case, Europe would contend with significant competition from other exporters. The choice will depend partly on the buoyancy of the Third World market. More fundamentally, it will depend on second-tier states' determination to stay in the weapon technology race. If the ability to produce aerospace systems, advanced naval systems, advanced electronic guidance and advanced fighting vehicles remains a high priority and a symbol of national sovereignty, then second-tier suppliers will have to come to terms with the US challenge and will look to market relatively higher-priced products.

Yet there are signs that Britain, France and the FRG cannot stay much longer in such a production league on the basis of mainly national efforts. Naval and helicopter production are kept alive only with intense government subsidy, with the most successful naval marketing in Third World-oriented designs (submarines and fast patrol boats). Mary Kaldor's contention that much of today's 'sophisticated' weaponry is a 'Baroque arsenal' could become an unavoidable European realization.[74] US and Japanese leadership in microchip and laser technology will complicate selection of a distinctively European defence product mix if traditional weapon systems are abandoned. Much will depend on the state of unemployment in Western Europe in the next decade, and available government defence budgets and R&D allocations in both defence and civilian sectors.

Government policy in this regard will also depend in turn on the future of NATO and Europe's security role. If the Alliance disintegrates, over such issues as nuclear policy or distrust of US leadership, European governments will be forced to spend more on conventional weaponry and will experience an expanded Euro-defence market. Temporarily, at least, they might turn away from Third World markets, although interest in longer production runs would eventually bring them back to such markets just as it did for the USA. If NATO is maintained, but with a decision to strengthen the 'European pillar', as appears increasingly to be the US preference, then many of the same tendencies would apply.

However, if the USA were to provide the inducement of a more open 'two-way street' in arms acquisition or to restrict its own arms marketing, and if France were drawn back into the NATO market, the need for Third World sales would shrink considerably. It is here that the best prospects for a Western arms transfer regime would emerge, with market sharing, mutual compensation and eventual consultation with the USSR and Third World customers.[75] If, on the other hand, NATO continues as is, with US domination of intra-Alliance arms trade and unresolved British, French and West German security and technology ambitions, then the Third World market will remain Europe's release valve.

Prospects for a greater European security role, of course, depend upon ironing out the differences apparent in the European Parliament, the EC and the WEU over foreign and defence policy. A consensus that arms sales need to be more carefully controlled is emerging, at least among British, West German and smaller state representatives. Conceivably, there could be an iron-clad rule against arms exports or resupply to states or factions engaged in military combat, unless compelling European security interests could be demonstrated to the Council of Ministers.[76] But French and Communist arguments that a co-ordinated European foreign policy is a prerequisite make considerable sense as well. Meanwhile, weapons of a particularly inhumane nature, or which would be especially useful to non-governmental groups, might be restricted from trade on the model of informal COCOM agreements on trade to the East bloc. Such rudimentary multilateral arms control steps could provide the precedent needed to encourage further development of an arms transfer regime.

Notes and references

[1] The author wishes to thank the US–UK Fulbright Commission for generously supporting this research, and the Centre for the Study of Arms Control and International Security at the University of Lancaster, UK, along with its Director, Ian Bellany, for playing host. The Centre for International Studies at the University of Missouri–St Louis, USA, provided additional support. Findings and conclusions remain, of course, the author's sole responsibility.

[2] Gordon, M. R., 'Western Europe leads in arms sales report says', *New York Times*, 14 May 1986, quoting the 1986 US Congressional Research Service Study by R. F. Grimmett, using 'classified US sources'.

[3] Brzoska, M. and Ohlson, T., 'The trade in major conventional weapons', in SIPRI, *World Armaments and Disarmament: SIPRI Yearbook 1986* (Oxford University Press: Oxford, 1986); 'The future of arms transfers: the changing patterns', *Bulletin of Peace Proposals*, no. 16 (1985), pp. 129–37; the *ADIU Report*, Arms and Disarmament Information Unit (Sussex University: Sussex, UK, 1985); US Arms Control and Disarmament Agency, *World Military Expenditures and Arms Transfers, 1985* (ACDA: Washington, DC, 1985); and Turner, J. and SIPRI, *Arms in the '80s: New Developments in the Global Arms Race* (Taylor & Francis: London, 1985).

[4] On various theoretical options, see Väyrynen, R., 'Curbing international transfers of arms and military technology', *Alternatives*, no. 4 (July 1978), pp. 87–113.

[5] Cannizzo, C. (ed.), *The Gun Merchants: Politics and Policies of the Major Arms Suppliers* (Pergamon: New York, 1980); Pierre, A., *The Global Politics of Arms Sales* (Princeton University Press: Princeton, 1982); and SIPRI, *The Arms Trade with the Third World* (Almqvist & Wiksell: Stockholm, 1971).

[6] Regarding Third World development opportunity costs in arms purchases it is worth noting that the three major second-tier suppliers are proportionally also among the largest development aid donors. The FRG gave 194 per cent more development assistance than it sold arms to the Third World in 1976–80; France gave 83 per cent more and Britain 54 per cent more. By comparison, the USA gave 14 per cent more assistance, Italy 35 per cent *less* assistance than arms, and the USSR 86 per cent less. In a sense, then, the second-tier suppliers have replaced part of the scarce Third World revenue they have obtained in the arms trade. See the report of the National Conference on the Church and Development, to the 'Ausschusses für wirtschaftliche Zusammenarbeit' (Bundestag: Bonn, 22 Feb. 1984), p. 150.

[7] Some have argued that it is misleading to equate Third World security needs with those of major powers. Warfare in the Third World involves many issues, some of which are no longer pressing in most of the industrialized world, such as border and ethnic disputes. Much of the military hardware exported to the Third World has been used for domestic control by entrenched elites. Most Third World conflicts have involved foreign intervention. Therefore, the 'appropriate' level of armament for Third World deterrence, regional balance or security could be far less, or different in configuration than that required elsewhere. See note 6, pp. 152–53.

[8] Taylor, T., 'The evaluation of arms transfer control proposals', in Cannizzo (note 5), pp. 167–85; and Betts, R. K., 'The tragicomedy of arms trade control', *International Security*, no. 5 (1980), pp. 80–110.

[9] On the welfare and security functions of states as related to the arms trade, see Kolodziej, E., 'National security and modernization: drive wheels of militarization', in *Third World Militarization: A Challenge to Third World Diplomacy*, ed. J. S. Mehta (L.B. Johnson School of Public Affairs: Austin, 1985), pp. 43–70.

[10] See Pfaltzgraff, R. L., Jr., 'Resource constraints and arms transfers: implications for NATO and European security', in *Arms Transfers to the Third World: The Military Buildup in Less Developed Countries*, ed. U. Ra'anen, R. L. Pfaltzgraff, Jr., and G. Kemp (Westview: Boulder, CO, 1978), pp. 159–75.

[11] Pearson, F. S., 'The question of control in British defence sales policy', *International Affairs* (London), no. 59 (Spring 1983), pp. 211–38; Pearson, F. S., '"Necessary evil": perspectives on West German arms transfer policies', *Armed Forces and Society*, no. 12 (Summer 1986), pp. 525–52; Pearson, F. S., 'Of Leopards and Cheetahs: West Germany's role as a mid-sized arms supplier', *Orbis*, no. 29 (Spring 1985), pp. 165–81; Kolodziej, E., *Making and Marketing of Arms: The French Experience and the International System* (Princeton University Press: Princeton, 1986), chapters 5 and 7; and Klein, J., 'France and the arms trade', in *Cannizzo* (note 5), pp. 127–66.

[12] Kolodziej, E. (note 11); 'French arms trade: the economic determinants', in SIPRI, *World Armaments and Disarmament: SIPRI Yearbook 1983* (Taylor & Francis: London, 1983);

Kolodziej, E., 'France and the arms trade', *International Affairs* (London), no. 56 (Jan. 1980), pp. 54–72.

[13] France joined the USSR as major Iraqi supplier, with British, West German and Italian equipment, co-produced systems and spares finding their way mainly to Iraq but in some cases to Iran as well, some as fulfilment of prior large-scale contracts. French sales to Iraq precluded a serious role for Paris as an Iranian or Syrian supplier, however. See SIPRI, *World Armaments and Disarmament: SIPRI Yearbook 1985* (Taylor & Francis: London, 1985); and Kolodziej (note 11), ch. 7.

[14] As of 1983, for example, more Third World weapon production was under way under German licences than under any other country's; the figures were: FRG, 44 licences; USA, 43; France, 26; UK, 22; Italy, 18; USSR, 13; Belgium, 7; Sweden, 5; and all others, 22. Thirty per cent of German licences were, however, for small arms and munitions. See the report by Herbert Wulf to the 'Ausschusses für wirtschaftliche Zusammenarbeit' (note 6), p. 217.

[15] See Kolodziej (note 10).

[16] Letter from John Simpson, University of Southampton (June 1986); letters from officials in the UK Ministries of Defence and Foreign and Commonwealth Affairs (May 1986); Edmonds, M., 'The British Government and arms sales', *ADIU Report*, no. 4 (Nov./Dec. 1982), pp. 10–13; Dillon, M., 'Arms transfers and the Federal Republic of Germany', in Cannizzo (note 5), pp. 104ff.

[17] See Chirouf, L., 'The French debate: arms sales', *ADIU Report* (July/Aug. 1981), pp. 15–17.

[18] The manufacture of export-oriented weapons can restrict as well as facilitate arms transfers to the Third World. When such systems are forced on reluctant military forces at home, as has sometimes been the case in France, military opposition to certain foreign sales can be generated. The French Dassault group reportedly had to seek Saudi funding for its Mirage-4000 twin-engine export fighter because of air force opposition to the venture. The military in any given arms-supplying state also tends to worry about being displaced in weapon acquisition by foreign sales. The UK Royal Air Force had to accept a later place on the Tornado production line in order to facilitate the Saudi sale. Armed forces have tended to lose such domestic procurement battles in recent years, contenting themselves with the secondary 'benefits' of longer production runs and foreign acceptance of their weapon systems. In the process, they have reportedly fostered greater awareness in government of their position on arms exports. See, for example, Kolodziej (note 11), chapter 5.

[19] See Pearson, 'Necessary evil' (note 11).

[20] The French Defence Ministry disposes of considerable funds in subsidizing and promoting arms exports and has a more elaborate apparatus of public and private banks, government credit and export agencies, and sales agents arranging Third World sales than either FR Germany or Britain. London has tried to keep pace, however, with the Export Credit Guarantee Department (ECGD) of the Treasury standing ready to protect against customer default and arrange and underwrite private (often non-European) bank loans to companies and customers. The British Defence Ministry is also committed to reimburse government-owned and semi-governmental arms exporters, such as International Military Services, in case of defaults. Third World customers are rated lower in credit-worthiness by ECGD than more developed states, especially for military sales, although oil-rich states and those with better repayment records are boosted in the ratings. See Kolodziej (note 11), chapter 6; Klein (note 11).

[21] Interview with UK Defence Ministry official, July 1986.

[22] Kolodziej (note 11), ch. 7.

[23] Stanley, J. and Pearton, M., *The International Trade in Arms* (Chatto and Windus: London, 1972), pp. 185–87.

[24] French Socialists had pledged to crack down especially on sales to colonialist, racist or fascist governments in the Third World, and to push for greater parliamentary control of transfers through a reporting system. However, once in office in partnership with the Communists, and later on their own, they were caught up in the momentum of arms sales.

[25] Chirouf (note 17).

[26] Kolodziej (note 11), ch. 5, p. 60 (manuscript).

[27] Unions specify that other states, and particularly the superpowers, must cut their arms exports first, that alternative production must be found for arms industries and that the government must pay for job losses. See Kolodziej, 'France and arms trade' (note 11), ch. 5, p. 68 (manuscript).

[28] Her Majesty's Government is responsible for making up shortfalls or facilitating interim financing in certain large arms deals, such as with Saudi Arabia, which involve barter rather than cash payment; varying markets for commodities make it difficult to predict the revenue of arms

barter agreements, and it has been argued that their terms violate EEC, OECD and GATT rules. See also Edmonds (note 16) and Pearson, 'The question of control' (note 11).

[29] See Edmonds (note 16) and Pearson (note 11); Stanley and Pearton (note 23), pp. 187–93; and interview with Defence Ministry official (July 1986).

[30] For indications that Britain sells arms to repressive regimes, see data compiled by the Campaign Against the Arms Trade, London.

[31] However, Israeli as well as Iraqi delegations were invited to the annual British Army Equipment Exhibition at Aldershot in 1986. See *The Guardian* (24 June 1986).

[32] Sir Geoffrey Howe, *House of Commons Official Report, Annex C*, Written Answers, *Hansard*, vol. 84, no. 172 (29 Oct. 1985), col. 454.

[33] Traditionally the British Government has tended to be less directly involved in the negotiations of arms exports than the more 'dirigist' French; most Third World customers would be expected to buy from British manufacturers rather than from government stocks. Increasingly, though, under the pressure of export interests, the highest government officials, including the Prime Minister, have promoted and campaigned for arms deals abroad, especially in the case of very large contracts. This has been seen most vividly in the successful competition against France for the Saudi aircraft sale, and in the unsuccessful attempt to edge out Paris in the sale of communications equipment to the US Army in 1986. (See, for example, Newhouse, J., 'Diplomatic round: politics and weapons sales', *New Yorker* (9 June 1986), pp. 46–69.) In the Tornado sale to Saudi Arabia, the British Government bought the aircraft from British Aerospace and dispatched them, along with spare parts, missiles and trainers, to Riyadh in return for oil shipments—oil to be disposed of through British commercial channels. Included as well were little publicized government agreements to buy older British aircraft from the Saudis and cover financial shortfalls; Saudi Arabia also insisted on 35 per cent offset arrangements (a difficult trick for British Aerospace to pump 35 per cent of £4 billion into the limited Saudi defence industry). Certain customers, like Saudi Arabia, remain bureaucratically conditioned to demand supplier-government backing and involvement in sales, despite the evidently growing trend among Third World customers, like Saudi Arabia, remain bureaucratically conditioned to demand supplier–government backing and involvement in sales, despite the evidently growing trend among Third World the more traditional 'arms length' governmental approach.

[34] Under a Labour Government in 1974, Lucas Aerospace was encouraged, especially by the Labour left, to undertake a major reconversion effort from military to socially relevant civil production projects and alternative technologies. Partly this was due to expected budgetary cutbacks and a possible recession affecting the defence sector. The enthusiasm and steam ran out of such joint government–labour management endeavours with the failure to agree on marketable products, worsening economic conditions and the Conservative victory in 1979. See the report of the Deutscher Gewekschaftbund to the 'Ausschusses für wirtschaftliche Zusammenarbeit' (note 6), pp. 190–91; and Vines, S., 'The Lucas Aerospace Corporate Plan', in *Democratic Socialism and the Cost of Defence*, eds M. Kaldor, D. Smith and S. Vines (Croom Helm: London, 1979).

[35] Campaign Against the Arms Trade, 'Iran and Iraq: arms sales and the Gulf War' (London: 1986), quoting statements of 29 Mar. and 17 Apr. 1985.

[36] The Conservative Government itself, or at least its main leaders, initially appeared most ready to allow Westland to sink if unable to find financing and foreign orders on its own. The constituency containing Westland was represented by a Liberal MP who strongly backed the employees in favouring the US funding bid. However, the Liberal Party itself has been committed to ending all arms sales, except in mutual defence treaties and launching massive job retraining schemes. In their 1979 manifesto the Liberals also called for a 'credible system of international controls of arms sales under the aegis of the United Nations'. In 1982 they called for the closure of the Defence Sales Organization, albeit with its functions to be assumed by another government agency. Reviewing the Falklands campaign, Liberal Leader David Steel advocated 'a European initiative to control and register the sale of arms to third countries'. The progressive restriction and reduction of arms sales under a Liberal government purportedly would begin with regimes which consistently and brutally violate human rights.

[37] Cowen, G., 'Arms exports and government policy: the West German experience', *ADIU Report*, no. 4 (July/Aug. 1982), pp. 5–9.

[38] Pearson, 'Necessary evil' (note 11).

[39] SIPRI (note 5).

[40] Cowen (note 37), p. 8; 'New arms export guidelines adopted'; *The Week in Germany*, no. 13 (German Information Center: New York, 7 May 1982), p. 2.

[41] See also Merryfinch, L., 'What They Say; What They Do: The British Government and

Military Exports', *Occasional Papers*, no. 3 (United World Education and Research Trust: London, 1985), p. 2; and Klein (note 11).

[42] As an indication of the stir caused in the FRG by the proposed Saudi sales agreements, see *German Tribune*, no. 1201 (Oct. 1985), p. 7.

[43] Pearson, 'Necessary evil' (note 11); and the report by the Deutscher Gewerkschaftbund to the 'Ausschusses für wirtschaftliche Zusammenarbeit' (note 6), pp. 180–84.

[44] *Financial Times*, 10 July 1986, p. 3.

[45] See, Lucas, M., 'West Germany: Can Arms Save the Export Giant?', *ADIU Report*, no. 7 (July/Aug. 1985), pp. 1–5.

[46] Evron, Y., 'The Role of Arms Control in the Middle East', *Adelphi Papers*, no. 138 (International Institute for Strategic Studies: London, 1977), p. 3.

[47] Klein (note 11), p. 158; see also Sampson, A., *The Arms Bazaar: The Companies, The Dealers, The Bribes: From Vickers to Lockheed* (Hodder and Stoughton: London, 1977), pp. 172–73.

[48] See Cahn, A. H., 'Arms transfer constraints', in *Arms Transfers to the Third World*, ed. Ra'anan *et al.* (note 10), p. 333, quoting Fuad Jabber (1972).

[49] Letter from a West German Minister of State (Bonn, July 1986).

[50] SIPRI (note 5), p. 300.

[51] *British Arms Control and Disarmament Policy: A Short Guide* (Foreign Office: London, Feb. 1979), pp. 11–12.

[52] When the UN study on conventional arms finally appeared in 1984, the Foreign Office mildly criticized the omission of British proposals for an arms trade, production and scrapping registry, mentioning that only Western governments appear willing to provide such information. The report's support for regional and supplier–recipient agreements and for reliable verification drew Whitehall's praise, however.

[53] See *Arms Control Disarmament Developments in the International Negotiations*, no. 12 (Foreign Office: London, May 1982), p. 18; *Arms Control and Disarmament Newsletter*, no. 24 (Foreign Office: London, Apr.–June 1985), pp. 44–47; and *Statement on the Defence Estimates 1986*, vol. 2 (Her Majesty's Stationery Office: London), p. 13. The British have argued that such non-disclosures are in deference to customer states' concerns about national security.

[54] The considerable amount of British and West German equipment which has got to Pretoria cannot be overlooked, in the German case largely through Paraguayan and other foreign connections or subsidiaries. Britain has dispatched more arms during periods of eased restrictions under Conservative governments, and both London and Bonn ship military equipment under 'dual use' civilian/military or 'non-lethal' categories. See, for example, testimony by Wolf Geisler to the 'Ausschusses für wirtschaftliche Zusammenarbeit' (note 6), pp. 223–33.

[55] Quoted by Klein (note 11), p. 159; see also Chirouf (note 17), p. 15.

[56] Speech of Louis de Guiringaud, Sep. 1978, quoted by Klein, J., 'Arms sales, development, disarmament', *Bulletin of Peace Proposals*, no. 14 (1983), p. 162.

[57] See also Blomley, P., *The Arms Trade and Arms Conversion*, discussion paper (Council for Arms Control: London, 1983).

[58] Franko, L. G., 'Restraining arms exports to the Third World: will Europe agree?', *Survival*, no. 21 (Jan.–Feb. 1979), pp. 14–15.

[59] See, for example, the 'ministerial reply' by John Gilbert, John Tomlinson and James Wellbeloved, 'Study into defence spending—summary of conclusions', in *Democratic Socialism*, ed. Kaldor *et al.* (note 34), pp. 545–47.

[60] See Pierre (note 5), p. 286; and Klein (note 11), pp. 160–61.

[61] Note 51.

[62] Sweden had deliberately restricted its Third World marketing and still maintained aircraft production, but only at considerably higher unit costs (offset by a high domestic arms procurement budget, the use of cheaper foreign component parts and a conscript army). See also Franko (note 58), pp. 16–22. In 1975, nearly 80 per cent of French arms exports consisted of aerospace and electronics, and French manufacturers of such products exported 50–60 per cent of their output.

[63] Prior to the CAT Talks analysts had proposed to the US Government and in technical journals a conventional arms transfer regime, or Conventional Arms Transfer Restraints (CATR), modelled after the London nuclear suppliers' 'Club', bringing the major arms suppliers into frequent consultation about guidelines. Regional market sharing arrangements or qualitative restrictions could be enunciated in a continuous forum, somewhat similar to that of the Tripartite Agreement. Arms balance and stability would be stressed, as distinct from disarmament *per se*. No requirement for recipient approval would necessarily be attached, at least initially. Perhaps for this

reason the plan evidently never reached the international discussion stage, but it represents an alternative approach if the major suppliers decide that Third World instability has become intolerable. Also countervening prevailing European preferences, it was proposed that multilateral regulation begin with joint US–West European initiatives, without necessarily waiting for the Soviet Union. Carter Administration failure to pursue such initiatives has been blamed on bureaucratic confusion and overload in Washington. See Pierre (note 5), pp. 292–301; and Haftendorn, H., 'Der International Rustungstransfer: Motive, Folgen, und Kontrollmöglich-keiten', *Europa-Archiv*, no. 33 (June 1978), pp. 331–40.

[64] Franko (note 58), p. 25.

[65] See Slaughter, R. L., 'The politics and nature of the conventional arms transfer process during a military engagement: the Falkland/Malvinas case', *Arms Control*, no. 4 (May 1983), pp. 16–30.

[66] Gregory, F., 'The Euro-Community and Defence', *ADIU Report*, no. 3 (Sep./Oct. 1981), pp. 5–9.

[67] These have been based on two 'Klepsch Reports', in 1978 and 1984; the Haagerup Report of 1982, the Fergusson Report of 1983, and a study by Defence experts, the Greenwood Report of 1981. The Klepsch Reports, by the Euro-Parliament's Political Affairs Committee, dealt with the question of joint European conventional armaments production and procurement under develop-ing common industrial and security policies. The Haagerup Report called for co-ordinated European approaches to the political aspects of security, and more effective consultation between the Community and NATO. The Fergusson Report focused on the supposed need for common defence industrial policies and common arms export guidelines. While somewhat pessimistic about establishing EC machinery for such co-ordination, the Greenwood Report advocated West European co-operation in military and civilian high-tech fields, through an intergovernmental Task Force for European Public Procurement and a European defence analysis bureau. The EC Commission subsequently softened this language, proposing a procurement 'forum' instead of task-force to exchange information on defence markets and policies. Both plans were considerably less than the European Arms Procurement Agency sometimes proposed by advocates of common Euro-security policies. See Gregory (note 66); and *Official Journal of the European Communities, Debates of the European Parliament*, 1982–83 Session, Annex 1–293 (13 Jan. 1983), pp. 221ff; 1983–84 Session, Annex 1–304 (11 Oct. 1983), pp. 53ff; 1983–84 Session, Annex 1–305 (26 Oct. 1983), pp. 155ff; 1984–85 Session, Annex 1–313 (11 Apr. 1984), pp. 108ff.

[68] See testimony by Commissioner Narjes, *Debates of the EP, Official Journal, 1983–84 Session*, 1–304 (11 Oct. 1983), pp. 74–75. The Commission has been only selectively involved in the arms export issue, admitting that arms 'counter trade' deals, e.g., UK–Saudi oil barter, probably violate EC rules, but proposing no action on the matter.

[69] Mr Haagerup, MEP, in note 68, p. 60.

[70] See the 'Debate on Arms Procurement', related to the Fergusson Report, *Official Journal* (note 67) (11 Oct. 1983), pp. 54–57.

[71] Debates on the second Klepsch Report, *Official Journal* (note 67) (11 Apr. 1984), pp. 108ff.

[72] Madame Charzat, MEP, in note 71, p. 72, and see pp. 61–62.

[73] *Common Security: A Programme for Disarmament*, Report of the Independent Commission on Disarmament and Security Issues, Olof Palme, Chair (Pan: London, 1982).

[74] Kaldor, M., *The Baroque Arsenal* (Hill and Wang: New York, 1981); on the dislocations and overcapacity in the German defence industry, see Wilke, P. and Wulf, H., 'Rüstungsproduktion in der Bundesrepublik: Industrielle Überkapazitäten und staatliche Finanzierungsengpässe', *Aus Politik und Zeitgeschichte*, 11 Jan. 1986, pp. 26–39.

[75] Renewed interest in Alliance and CATT arms export control surfaced in the US Congress in 1983 with a proposed resolution calling for a cartel-like arms supplier agreement. Sceptics still outnumbered proponents, however. See 'Would the French go along? International cartel to control conventional arms', *Defence Week* (28 Feb. 1983), p. 10. Third World arms importers would require compensation in the form of guaranteed supplies up to certain limits, and security guarantees, as well as compensatory technology transfers and investments in both civil and military production. The latter might complicate arms control prospects and anger Western arms manufacturers.

[76] Restrictions on second-tier arms supplies might not end regional wars where the combatants had large-scale superpower connections, but such restrictions could constitute heavy pressure to settle wars between states such as Iran and Iraq. Consultations with Third World arms suppliers such as China and Israel also would be required.

Paper 9. Arms transfer limitations: the case of Sweden

BJÖRN HAGELIN

I. Introduction

Official Swedish representatives often point out that Sweden is one of only a few non-aligned and neutral nations in Europe. This policy, coupled with a broad and advanced indigenous military industrial base, has led Sweden to play a not unimportant balancing and geo-strategic role in northern Europe.

There is, however, a tendency for all national leaders to magnify what is considered to be the positive images of national policy, such as the purported 'peace strengthening' effects of new military developments. Swedish officials are no exception. 'Sweden's conventional forces are purely for defensive purposes and pose no threat to anyone.' Sweden, moreover, has a very restrictive arms sales law and actively supports international arms control agreements.

The other side of the coin is that negative images are minimized or not even talked about. It is important to distinguish between declaratory policy and actual, manifest policy. It is also important to define what causes the manifest policy, especially if it contradicts stated policy. Swedish manifest arms export policy cannot be separated from general Swedish security policy. With this connection established, it is difficult to apply the arms export law as restrictively as the wording stipulates. In many respects, Sweden is representative of the 'third-tier' suppliers, and the pros and cons of arms transfer control in Sweden are thus also applicable in other countries. Moreover, the combination of a broadly based and advanced arms industry and a very restrictive declaratory arms export policy makes Sweden a pertinent example of the problematic issues treated in this book.

II. Background

The export of what in Sweden is called 'war matériel' has been controlled by the government since 1946. In 1934 a committee review, performed as a result of the attempt by the League of Nations to create national and uniform rules for foreign military sales, concluded that all production of war matériel—in Sweden mainly private—should be controlled by the government. The following year Parliament created such a law, and the War Matériel Inspectorate (known by its Swedish initials as KMI) was created for that purpose. The attempt by the League of Nations was unsuccessful, however, and in 1946 KMI was given the task of also controlling foreign military sales.

The then Swedish Prime Minister, Tage Erlander, on 25 April 1956 explained the government's position on arms exports. As his statement has been repeatedly referred to as the first major official presentation of the post-World War II rules—introduced in 1950—and since several aspects touched upon by Mr Erlander are still valid, it is worth quoting in some detail.[1] For example, he stated:

... that the Swedish manufacture of war materials is on the whole a political problem ... certain sections of this industry are highly developed. An essential condition for its high standard is unquestionably that a considerable part of its products are for export. If the production of ammunition was to be restricted to what is required to cover Swedish needs, it could not be kept anywhere near the technical level that is maintained at present. It is usually emphasized, especially in military circles, that a comprehensive domestic production of war materials is of great importance from the point of view of our state of preparedness.

This is still one of the major arguments for a Swedish overcapacity in the production of especially arms and ammunition by companies such as Bofors and FFV. The Prime Minister went on:

The export of war materials from Sweden nevertheless brings in its train various drawbacks of a political kind. The point can always be made that our exports 'disturb the balance of power' ... The Swedish authorities have not hitherto felt themselves obliged to avoid the political disadvantages of the export of war materials by taking the radical attitude that no exports should be permitted and that manufacture should be greatly restricted.

This is still the official view. Mr Erlander was then surprisingly outspoken:

Our licence policy has not been used in any attempt to avoid disturbing the balance in this area (the Middle East) between states that have been customers ... It is one thing to pursue a discriminatory export policy on the recommendation of the United Nations, but quite another to base export policy in critical times ... on the attitude taken to an existing conflict. Moreover, such a discriminatory export policy would not be very efficient in attaining a balance if it was not pursued jointly with other exporting nations.

In other words, it was not then, and is not today, contrary to Swedish policy to support opposing regional powers. It occurs today with regard to, for instance, India and Pakistan or to Argentina and Great Britain. However, later in his speech the Prime Minister declared: 'A new disturbing factor in the situation is the agreement on the export of war materials concluded last year between Egypt . . . and Czechoslovakia. This has completely thwarted the determination of the Western Powers to establish a certain balance in their exports.'

Thus, as long as the conflict was regional or non-hegemonical and not between East and West, there were no major policy questions involved for Sweden. It has been concluded by others that it was not restrictive Swedish rules but the Czechoslovakian agreement with Egypt in 1955, and with it the beginning of Soviet involvement in the Arab–Israeli conflict, that made Sweden embargo further military sales to Egypt.[2]

III.   The legislation

There are two sets of Swedish restrictions: unconditional and conditional. Unconditional restrictions result from international agreements or membership in international organizations such as the United Nations. For instance, Sweden embargoed war matériel sales to Portugal between 1963 and 1975, to Southern Rhodesia between 1965 and 1980, and to South Africa since 1963 as a response to United Nations Security Council recommendations and decisions.

The other set of restrictions are nationally imposed conditional restrictions. The basic rule is that the exportation of war matériel is prohibited. Exceptions are made on a case-by-case basis by either the government or the Minister for Foreign Affairs when there are no unconditional restrictions. Exceptions are accepted only when the foreign buyer is another government or its representative. No sales should, however, be permitted to: (a) a state engaged in armed conflict with another state, regardless of the existence or non-existence of a formal declaration of war; (b) a state implicated in an international conflict that could conceivably lead to armed conflict; (c) a state wherein internal armed disturbances are taking place; or (d) a state which, as a result of declared intentions or of current political conditions, can be expected to employ Swedish matériel to suppress human rights as specified in the United Nations Charter.

This means in reality all nations in so-called 'areas of conflict' such as the Middle East, where most nations can be expected to become involved in armed conflict. Since 1956 Israel and all Arab states with the exception of Tunisia are not allowed to receive war matériel from Sweden. Similarly, Iran and Iraq as well as other nations directly involved in armed conflict are on the prohibitive list. Earlier examples include the United States and other nations directly involved in the Viet Nam War, India and Pakistan during their wars in 1965 and 1971, and Argentina and Great Britain during the Falklands/Malvinas conflict. Examples of countries not already mentioned that have been or are excluded from receiving matériel from Sweden because of internal disturbances or political conditions are Chile, Thailand and Burma.

IV.   The neutrality factor

Sweden has one of the most restrictive arms export *regulations* in the world. But why are there export rules in the first place? One answer has already been given, namely, the international attempts by the League of Nations. Another is the national foreign or, more specifically, neutrality policy. Sweden is a relatively large producer of military equipment, and the producers are keen to sell to anyone who wishes to buy. For reasons of neutrality, however, 'free military trade' is not accepted by the Swedish Government. Regulations are thus necessary.

Another question of importance is why Sweden is a major producer of arms. The basic answer is twofold: first, Sweden has a long tradition of arms production—explaining its former role as a major European power—and a strong domestic industrial base. Second, the credibility of present Swedish security policy has been made dependent upon indigenous military production. The *implementation* of Swedish arms transfer limitations can therefore not be fully understood without some knowledge of Swedish security policy considerations.

Sweden's security policy is centred around neutrality. Neutrality in the strictest sense is relevant only for a situation in which there is, first, a war and second, one that does or might threaten Sweden's security. This wartime policy has important consequences for Swedish peacetime policies. It is by peacetime action or non-action that Sweden can show its determination and will to stay neutral in a war, thereby making its policy of neutrality credible. No commitment may be made in peacetime that prevents Sweden from fulfilling the wartime obligations of a neutral state under international law.[3]

The most fundamental condition for avoiding being drawn into war is to stay out of military alliances. The core of Sweden's security policy is sometimes phrased 'non-alignment in peacetime aiming at neutrality in wartime'. Closely related to this condition is not to become involved in any foreign economic, political or military relation that could seriously reduce Sweden's ability to decide over and implement national policies in a crisis or war. This policy of independence explains why Sweden has not, contrary to Austria and Switzerland, accepted any international neutrality guarantees. The conditions for Swedish neutrality are to be defined by Sweden alone.

Another basic condition is to be able to deter other states from attacking or using Sweden and the surrounding air and sea space for military purposes. The main 'war scenario' is an invasion which will be met before the attacker reaches the Swedish border. This demands a military force including an Air Force and Navy for 'forward defence'. It is moreover argued that a strong (in technological terms) and largely Swedish-built and nationally maintained defence force strengthens Swedish independence. This demands advanced indigenous military research, development and production. The Swedish security policy is therefore sometimes called 'armed neutrality'.

On the one hand, then, Sweden has a law prohibiting war matériel exports. On the other hand, arms transfers are officially viewed as increasingly important in order to sustain advanced indigenous military production. When the Swedish Government cannot secure that production by national military orders, arms exports must be permitted.

There are thus important push factors supporting Swedish arms sales, such as the security policy with its demand for advanced and permanent military production, the producers themselves, the War Matériel Administration (FMV, the government purchasing organization),[4] and to a certain extent the military leadership. But there are also important domestic pull factors limiting Swedish arms transfers. The law is one such factor, public opinion another, and the mass media is a third.

V.   Political push and pull

Since the 1950s, especially since the early 1970s, it has been officially recognized that Swedish arms sales must be permitted for economic reasons. During the 1960s the military personnel costs in particular began to increase. Together with inflation, more or less stable defence budgets in constant prices, and the development of new and expensive technologies, domestic arms acquisition rates have decreased. Foreign sales and international military industrial co-operation have, together with national rationalization and specialization, compensated for a reduced domestic military market in order to support advanced Swedish military production.

As in most countries with a relatively large military industrial base, there are several arguments for arms sales:

1. *The business economic argument:* Exportation results in longer production runs, which reduce the price of the final product and increase markets further. Military production thus becomes more profitable for the producer.

2. *The defence economic argument:* Reduced prices for military matériel means either that national military acquisition becomes cheaper for a given amount of goods, or that more matériel can be bought for a fixed sum of money.

3. *The employment argument:* Longer production runs lead to more secure employment.

4. *The first defence political argument:* Longer production runs permit prolonged preparedness for a sudden need to increase the production of that particular matériel (a 'crash' programme).

5. *The political economic argument:* Exportation results in increased total national exports, which lead to an inflow of foreign currencies and a better balance of trade.

To these five can be added two arguments that might be somewhat particular for Sweden, or at least for smaller industrialized countries:

6. *The second defence political argument:* The foreign sale of Swedish war matériel permits Sweden to obtain foreign military matériel and know-how that otherwise would be difficult or impossible to receive for a non-aligned nation.

7. *The international solidarity argument:* The buyer of Swedish war matériel avoids the negative political and/or military strings attached to sales from major military suppliers.

Export guidelines since 1966 have been partly formulated with the aim of permitting and increasing war matériel sales, although they have been officially presented as more and more restrictive.[5] Since most industrial countries protect their indigenous military markets, and since Sweden is not a member of NATO, the most promising markets during the 1970s were in the Third World and in particular Asia.

In parallel, public and parliamentary awareness of arms transfer problems increased. By the early 1980s an increasing portion of Swedish public opinion was explicitly critical of the political implications of Swedish war matériel transfers. Regardless of whether the value is high or low, arms sales always imply a political standpoint. An accepted delivery is a direct support to the recipient government and to international rearmament. A decision to refuse sales is an expression of official distrust or rejection of the policies of that foreign government. The sensitivity is evident from the praxis never to make public an individual military export decision.

The oldest and largest Swedish peace organization, the Peace and Arbitration Society, was founded in 1883. It argues, with support from other Swedish peace groups, that Swedish arms exports should be successively reduced and eventually stopped. Important political support comes from youth organizations of churches, from the Centre People's and Social Democratic parties as well as from the Women's Union of the Social Democratic Party. Certain sections of the trade unions have been indirectly engaged through discussions concerning conversion from military to civilian production.

The reasons for opposing Swedish arms transfers are several. The main focus of criticism is, however, on the inconsistency between Swedish regulations and disarmament policy on the one hand, and actual Swedish war matériel transfers on the other. The peace groups question the arguments listed above and the conclusions that large unemployment would necessarily follow from reduced sales or that it would result in a crisis for Swedish military production. They have found support in an official Swedish study of military production and possibilities for conversion in Sweden.[6] Other opponents, such as the Swedish Federation of Churches, which in 1984 issued a statement opposing Swedish war matériel sales, focus more on the normative issues and the 'merchant of death' effect from arms transfers. Sections of the churches holding shares in military firms have sold their shares in protest.

This debate, which started around 1979, led to a change in the Swedish restrictions: in 1981 the government proposed a new law against war matériel exports. It was based on guidelines from 1972, but with additions taking into account most of the public criticism. The government agreed to increase parliamentary advisory power with regard to recipient countries, international programmes and other issues of general importance; standard use of end-use certificates without defined time limits; governmental control of the sale of manufacturing licences; restrictions in military education and training of foreigners in Sweden; and regular and more easily available public information about Swedish war matériel sales. Each year since 1984 the government has presented a report to parliament on the war matériel sales of the preceding year.

It was also concluded that the 1972 guidelines saying that defensive, as opposed to offensive, matériel could be treated less restrictively should be interpreted with care since the meaning of defensive matériel is unclear. It is still possible, however, for a Swedish producer to supply contracted spare parts and ammunition regardless of conditional restrictions otherwise preventing exports, and thus even war. Contracted deliveries of spare parts for the Swedish Carl Gustaf anti-tank weapon to the Australian Army were stopped during its involvement in the Viet Nam War prior to 1972. After that incident few potential customers exposed to a threat of war wanted to buy Swedish weapons, which created severe problems for Swedish producers. The 1972 guidelines were aimed at overcoming this difficulty. Partly in order to retain foreign confidence in Swedish military assistance, the government accepted new sales of Bofors anti-aircraft guns to Indonesia in 1983 and 1984 despite public and parliamentary opposition.

Another difficult issue has been the sale of civilian technology and products that could be used for military purposes, that is, dual-use technology and equipment. This issue was raised in 1969, when the Swedish-produced MFI-9B light attack aircraft appeared in Biafra. It was sold as an unarmed civilian trainer equipped for dropping food supplies to the starving population. These aircraft were, after leaving Sweden, converted to attack duties and fitted with foreign rockets. After a public uproar the regulations were changed so that the MFI-9 trainer was then considered a military aircraft. The government concluded in 1981 that general guidelines are impossible to formulate. The government should instead make more case-by-case use of technical expertise,[7] but technical evaluations cannot solve political problems. During 1987, civilian, lightly armed Swedish boats sold to Iran quickly became a case in point and had important foreign policy implications owing to the US involvement in the Persian Gulf. The difficulties are even more apparent when dealing with activities other than the sale of equipment, for instance, education and training, consultative services and technical assistance.

VI. Policy application: the basic dilemma

The fact that the value of Swedish war matériel sales is low (in relative terms) is not because of lack of efforts on the part of industry. Swedish producers arrange special matériel demonstrations and participate in international military exhibitions in most corners of the world. Neither is the restrictive law the only explanation. A variety of factors, apart from domestic conditional and international unconditional restrictions, influence Swedish war matériel sales.

Successive governments have not appeared to want to unconditionally forbid Swedish war matériel sales. Instead, the most important restrictions, in rank order, seem to be international competition and critical public opinion. If Swedish producers did not have to face international competition, the figures for Swedish war matériel sales would be much higher. Sweden nevertheless is among the 15 largest exporters of major arms in the world. Since information about lost deals is not generally good news for public-relations-minded industries or the media, it is easy to assume from lack of information that political controls are effective.

The governmental controls are not unimportant but are here given third place. In fact, domestic public and parliamentary push for increasing restrictions explains why the list of war matériel has been extended and stricter political export regulations have been imposed—such changes have not emanated from the government, but have been the result of public criticism.

If the implementation of the guidelines were restrictive, Swedish sales would diminish, but the figures in constant prices show that there has been no decrease in the transfer of military matériel over time. War matériel sales are an effect of a worsening defence–economic situation. The relaxed export guidelines in 1966 and 1972 paralleled major reductions in the Swedish defence budget in 1968 and 1972. The present political dilemma in Swedish war matériel transfer policy is not how to reduce and stop Swedish war matériel sales. It is, rather, a conflict between a restrictive sales policy *and* foreign military sales in support of domestic military production. It seems economically impossible to give that support with a policy that unconditionally rejects military sales. On the other hand it is not politically possible to ease the export guidelines enough to solve the economic difficulties.

The Swedish Government has two main short-term alternatives: first, to let companies make more use of legal loopholes in present controls, that is, to sell dual-use equipment and technology (the category 'other' war matériel has in fact increased)—as defined by technical experts—as well as services, to participate in international military industrial co-operation and to sell military equipment via third parties. This alternative implies not accepting restrictions that close all loopholes and restrict industrial freedom of action. Second, although sales of war matériel and licences are controlled by the government, this does not mean that such sales are unacceptable. Domestic military production can be supported by not interpreting the guidelines unnecessarily restrictively. In fact, the increasingly competitive international market makes it necessary for the Swedish Government to support Swedish military sales, for instance, with export credits and financial guarantees. This was evident in the sale of Bofors artillery and other equipment to India during 1986, a case that caused turmoil in the Indian Parliament because of allegations of bribery.

Similarly, the government's explanations for continued sales to Indonesia and some other Third World countries show that internal armed conflict in the recipient country is no longer a prohibiting factor. Instead, it seems that the *intensity* of the conflict should be taken into account—that is, when the intensity has decreased or can be said to be 'low', sales can be permitted.

It was the view of the Swedish Government in 1956, as it is today, that a unilateral discriminatory export policy would not be efficient. 'If we don't sell, someone else will' is a common argument. But that argument could be inverted: 'we don't have to sell, since the customer can get what he wants from other suppliers'—unless, of course, the argument in reality has nothing to do with recipient needs, but is only in support of indigenous arms production and continued foreign sales. If that is the real goal, and if there is at the same time a restrictive export policy, 'war matériel' should not be too broadly defined and automatically applicable to all nations.

This is illustrated by Swedish export regulations regarding South Africa. The Swedish Government has not allowed war matériel sales to that country for 25 years. It has followed UN Security Council recommendations against sales to South Africa since 1963, thus long before the mandatory UN arms embargo of 1977. This, together with strong national and international opposition to the apartheid system, made it possible for the Swedish Government to strengthen its actions against the South African Government in opposition to Swedish commercial interests.

In 1977 the Swedish Parliament imposed a law prohibiting the sale to South Africa of war matériel as well as inventions of war matériel and similar know-how for both military and police use.[8] In 1985 the war matériel embargo was extended to include computers, computer programs, vehicles and gasoline. Even military imports from South Africa were prohibited. The general trade embargo has also been extended and, although there was not—by early 1987— a comprehensive Swedish trade boycott, all trade with South Africa has required a Swedish Government licence since July 1986.[9]

South Africa is clearly an extraordinary case. Special rules are applied to war matériel sales, and it is the only country with which all Swedish trade is restricted. Nevertheless, actions against South Africa show that the Swedish Government accepts that it is insufficient to prohibit only the sale of war matériel as defined by the export regulations if international armament controls are to be effective. Let us look at the arguments for extending the Swedish war matériel definitions in the case of sales to South Africa in order to define the margins for such unilateral Swedish restrictive actions.[10]

Three alternatives were considered in 1984: (a) to include all matériel 'of military importance'; (b) to include matériel bought by military or police agencies or for use by such agencies; and (c) to use unilateral definitions. The first alternative, although in line with the UN decision, was considered impractical and difficult to define and apply. Furthermore, such restrictive military trade regulations could hamper Sweden's trade with other countries.

The second alternative was found to be wider than what was suggested by the UN decision and was therefore not considered necessary. The third alternative, that is, to define other matériel than that mentioned in the Swedish list of war matériel, was therefore accepted. It was emphasized, however, that this was not a general extension of the Swedish war matériel list and would not, therefore, apply to other recipients. By defining the controls in this way, difficulties that would have resulted from the first alternative were avoided.

In summary, since the Swedish Government considers military sales a necessity, restrictions are only accepted within limits. The Swedish Government has not extended the regulations beyond the demands of public opinion or international organizations, and most restrictions are still conditional. Even though the case of South Africa shows that a broader view of regulations is necessary in order to effectively control legal international armaments, such regulations have not been accepted in principle. Actions taken against South Africa show, rather, a lack of will on the part of the Swedish Government to accept broad and unconditional prohibitions of military sales.

During the 1980s new issues related to military trade have also been raised, resulting in new demands for restrictive policies. It is no longer the legal sale of war matériel that is under fire, but illegal transfers of technology and matériel.

First, Sweden has been used by foreign suppliers as a 'port' for re-transfers of Western, mostly US, dual-use technology and goods to communist states. This was not illegal in Sweden before 1986 and is so only in a limited sense now. Good political relations with the United States are, however, necessary in order to receive the advanced goods, technology and services which are necessary for Sweden's military forces and arms industry. Since such re-transfers have for a long time been illegal according to US law, the Swedish Government and most other OECD governments accepted already during the 1940s informal solutions complying with US demands. The views of the US, French and British governments were taken into account when drawing up the Swedish export guidelines in 1950. It is noteworthy that the relaxed Swedish export guidelines of 1966 and 1972 paralleled not only Swedish defence economic reductions, but also a lessening of US embargo restrictions.[11] A law of June 1986 also formally prohibits the export from Sweden of imported high-technology end-items that are controlled in the country of origin, in reality the United States and West European countries.[12]

One Swedish dilemma is thus not only that exports have to be permitted in order to sustain advanced indigenous military production, but also that Sweden has to accept major-power politics in order for the production and the military force to be advanced. Sales to Ethiopia and to countries in South America during the 1950s and 1960s illustrate active co-operation between Sweden and the United States in the armament of foreign nations. Moreover, a comparison of Swedish Third World recipients between 1983 and 1986 with US security assistance recipients in the Third World for the same period shows that all recipients of Swedish war matériel also received US security assistance. One might therefore conclude that, although there are no explicit political or military strings attached, Sweden reinforces US–Western military values and policies in the recipient countries. This is supported by the fact that there are no major Swedish war matériel sales to communist states.

Second, the Bofors company has been accused of having deliberately violated Swedish military export regulations by either supplying military goods to countries that are not accepted recipients of Swedish war matériel, or supplying them to eligible recipients that have, with Bofors' consent, re-transferred them to unacceptable recipients. Such deliveries seem in several cases to have involved foreign companies and used the territories of other countries, both industrialized and others.

These two types of transfer show the need for stricter not only national but also international regulations. There is international co-operation between allies, between allies and non-aligned states, and between the non-aligned both in the production of military matériel and in the foreign sales of such goods. Swedish participation in international military industrial co-operation is not prohibited, and will most likely be eased for economic reasons, although it has been restricted for security policy reasons. Such increasing international co-operation will, most likely, be accompanied by reduced Swedish restrictions in the foreign sale of co-produced matériel.

The insufficiency of national controls is even more evident with regard to foreign licence manufacture. Some licence agreements, such as with Brazil for the manufacture of Bofors anti-aircraft guns, is reported to permit re-transfers and thereby side-step the control ambition.[13] However, even when such re-transfers are not permitted, controls are difficult to apply, especially when foreign sales are seen as necessary by the original supplier. Moreover, as time passes, design changes by foreign manufacturers will make end-use certificates impossible to apply. Despite the standard use in all Swedish war matériel sales since 1983 of end-use certificates without any specified time limit, the re-transfer of Swedish war matériel cannot be prevented by the Swedish Government.

It should be obvious from the above analysis that when arms sales are motivated by economic factors, or rather a lack of economic means for government purchases of indigenously produced matériel, this puts into question the government's will, first, to create unconditional and unambiguous regulations, and, second, to punish either a domestic supplier or a foreign recipient for violating re-transfer or other regulations. Rather, it is important to retain Sweden's international reputation as a reliable supplier. The regulations of 1972 were a step in that direction. The temporary Swedish embargo against war matériel sales to Singapore after its re-transfer of Bofors anti-aircraft missiles to the Middle East illustrates this point. The more mutual economic and industrial interests—between government and industry on the one hand, and between domestic and foreign industries on the other—that are created by military co-operation in production and sales, the more difficult it will be to control and limit military sales.

VII. Different approaches

Two of the most important and difficult problems for the control of conventional war matériel sales are, first, the economic and commercial relationships between production and sales, and, second, the political relationship between production and foreign and security policy.

It is necessary, therefore, to find solutions that do not imply that national security is defined in terms of sustained or increased arms sales. In discussing any approach to international military trade control arrangements, four themes are central: focus, scope, purpose and targets. The *focus* of controls means the definition of what is to be controlled. The focus depends on (a) the *purpose* of the controls, (b) the *scope* (the number of suppliers involved in the control measures) and (c) the *target(s)* (the nation(s) towards which the controls are aimed).

The important conclusion with reference to the focus is that when a total approach is *avoided* it is done with the knowledge of the decision makers. It should then come as no surprise if anticipated constraining effects in the target country are not achieved. If the purpose of the controls is disarmament rather than just arms control in the target nation, it is more important to take a total focus approach to military trade. Similarly, when the scope is narrow, the chances for success are reduced. This means that unilateral control measures are of limited value unless directed towards a target which is totally dependent upon this particular supplier. This is very rarely the case. Moreover, the effects can be overcome over time. The official Swedish approach—rejection of unilateral measures—is thus probably correct with regard to possible effects on the target nation.

There is thus a clear correlation between focus, scope and success. For control arrangements to be successful, both focus and scope need to be wide. It seems particularly important to include licences and services. Without such assistance it is difficult to maintain and use modern arms, as currently illustrated by the case of Iran. When the know-how to manufacture and support military matériel has been sold, on the other hand, it can never be retained. For future developments in global armaments and arms trade, therefore, the sale of manufacturing know-how and maintenance services might pose a greater threat than the sale of finished matériel.

Another conclusion from the analysis of military trade is that one can only in theory separate the Third World from other target nations. When SIPRI during the 1960s put the focus on the arms trade with the Third World, that perspective was important. Former colonies became independent, aspiring for recognition. The creation of a military force became important, and import of arms was the only possible way to do it. But modern armament relations are different. The armament process in many of these countries is currently a mixture of military imports, production under licence, some national military research and development as well as production of dual-use goods and technologies.

Today, there are crucial questions for discussion of trade control arrangements: Should the scope be limited only to the traditional producers, and the targets be only the developing nations? Should the latter be prohibited from arming themselves while the former continue with 'business as usual'? Or should military trade be considered a general problem, sustained by a global network of trade relations and as such only solvable if all nations are involved with equal responsibilities?

Supplier and recipient control arrangements cannot, in reality, be treated as two clearly different approaches if the purpose is general and effective control of international military trade. When they are, the effect will instead be a widening of the gap between those who have plenty of the most advanced weapons and those who have not.

Unfortunately, the political division in contesting power blocs, the mixed goals of military trade among military suppliers and the complex nature of military trade itself do not support the hope that military trade arrangements that are wide enough in focus and scope can be achieved. The United Nations is in no position to overcome these difficulties—it is a mirror of the world rather than a machinery to transform it. But it is not necessary to be trapped by the major-power perspective. Smaller states have less complicated purposes with their military trade. They ought therefore to be in a less complicated position to create a process towards restrictive military trade. Could Sweden be the initiator of such a process instead of passively waiting for others to agree?

In the Swedish debate an alternative has been suggested. The explicit aim is to avoid arming the Third World while continuing Swedish military production and trade. The proposal is based on military trade among the neutral countries in Europe. The most important partners for Sweden in such an arrangement would be Finland, Switzerland and Austria. This alternative is based upon the acceptance of certain common political and military criteria such as non-alignment, wartime neutrality as well as similar political outlooks and military demands. However, structural differences and asymmetries are among the main factors which complicate the realization of a fair and lasting neutral alternative based on continued armaments.

To solve the Swedish dilemma only by way of restricted international armament co-operation seems to be a difficult alternative. One cannot hope to reduce or stop Swedish military sales by creating a marriage with nations in a similar situation while permitting military production to continue more or less as before. Effective control arrangements must affect the circumstances for national military production. Swedish military sales are to a large extent the result of a military industrial base that can no longer be afforded. This, in turn, is caused by too ambitious a security policy. We are back to the neutrality factor introduced at the beginning. There is no bilateral arms race of which Sweden is a part. Rather, a general 'threat perception' forms the need for an advanced military defence. Sweden is involved in a race with technology itself. For a small country there is no hope of ever coming out on top of that race.

Even if an indefinite buildup of arms was possible, it is no guarantee of 'peace' or national security. J. David Singer, an internationally well-known peace researcher, has emphasized the insufficiency of armed security.[14] The point is that, should there be a major war in Europe involving the superpowers and should a party to the conflict deem an attack on Sweden as necessary, no realistic Swedish military defence could deter such an attack. This means that if there is no such necessity—defined by the military conflict rather than by the size and technology of the Swedish military defence—a different Swedish defence would be sufficient.

It seems that there is room for unilateral solutions in the case of Sweden. The military policy could be reformed to one that is more in harmony with the final security goal, that is, neutrality in wartime. The *minimum* condition would be a military defence that fulfils that demanded by a neutral state according to international law. It would be more 'defensive' than at present by a reduction of the forward defence. The goal to meet an invasion before reaching the Swedish border could be changed to one of strictly territorial defence. The army would then become more important than the air force. Indigenous military development and production should take advantage of Swedish skills rather than compete with international military technologies (the *maximum* condition). The producers would have to readjust to the domestic market. From these minimum conditions there could be many different possibilities for complements, but they would have to be agreed through the normal political decision-making process.

What is important is that there is an alternative that Sweden could realize unilaterally. After all, the conditions for Swedish neutrality are defined by Sweden alone. The structure of the domestic military industrial base can be changed in a direction that could reduce economic pressures and still fit the traditional Swedish security policy. If the above analysis is correct, there would also be less push for Swedish military sales.

Such a change demands strong political will and support. So far, the Swedish Government has shown no will to support a different military industrial structure. Even when industries themselves have been positive to conversion from military to civilian production, the government has refused to give political and, most important, financial support. The will to change could no doubt be supported by international actions. The 1986 Stockholm Conference Final Document was a small but still a step forward towards increasing military confidence building in Europe. If followed by concrete conventional arms reduction negotiations, Swedish disarmament steps could probably be accepted as part of a European disarmament process. For the Swedish political will, therefore, control arrangements in Europe are most important.

If a reduced Swedish defence posture could be accepted, the possibilities for a neutral military-security alternative might increase. The structural differences among the neutrals would be reduced, and the benefits from cooperation would increase. The still individual national defence forces could be created by emphasizing not indigenous production but neutral/military trade. The national forces would be created mainly from the common resources available in the neutral countries. Some 'core' indigenous production should be kept in each country, defined by the wartime demands of neutrality and the relative cost-benefits of certain production among the neutrals as a group. Non-neutral military trade would be reduced to a minimum.

With political courage and a long-term perspective, it might thus be possible for Sweden or the other neutral countries to find a role in arms control by creating a process aimed at reducing international military trade. Military trade control arrangements cannot, however, be looked at in a vacuum—they are influenced by domestic factors as well as by successes or failures of other arms control attempts. With the support of others, such a neutral seed might be allowed to grow to be not only a plant in Europe but also several similar plants in other parts of the world. Military trade zones based on minimum military requirements could be established. This would loosen the global network of military trade relations, detach strands of the 'global web' from each other and help pave the way for alternative or revised security concepts.

Notes and references

[1] *Documents on Swedish Foreign Policy 1956* (Ministry for Foreign Affairs: Stockholm, 1957), pp. 27–32.

[2] Stanley, J. and Pearton, M., *The International Trade in Arms* (Praeger Publishers: New York and Washington, DC, 1972), p. 195.

[3] See Andrén, N., 'Sweden's security policy', *Cooperation and Conflict*, no. 3–4; (Oslo, 1972); Hagelin, B., 'The margins of security: politics and economics in Sweden', *Policy Science*, no. 2, 1978; Vetschera, H., 'Neutrality and defense: legal theory and military practice in the European neutrals' defense policies', *Defense Analysis*, no. 2 (1985); Åström, S., *Sweden's Policy of Neutrality* (The Swedish Institute: Stockholm, 1977).

[4] Successive heads of the War Matériel Administration have since 1968 presented the agency's role as one in support of independent Swedish military production.

[5] The guidelines from 1950 have been followed by new ones in 1967, 1972 and 1983; see *Med förslag till lag om förbud mot utförsel av krigsmateriel mm*, Government's proposition 1981/82, no. 196 (Stockholm, 1981); *Svensk krigsmaterielexport*, betänkande av 1979 års krigsmaterielexportkommitté (Ministry of Trade: Stockholm, 1981), SOU 1981, no. 39.

[6] *In Pursuit of Disarmament: Conversion from military to civil production in Sweden*, vol. 1A, *Background–Facts–Analyses* (Ministry for Foreign Affairs: Stockholm, 1984); *In Pursuit of Disarmament*, vol. 1B, *Summary–Appraisal–Recommendations* (Ministry for Foreign Affairs: Stockholm, 1984); *In Pursuit of Disarmament*, vol. 2, *Special Reports* (Ministry for Foreign Affairs: Stockholm, 1985).

[7] *Svensk krigsmaterielexport* (note 5).

[8] Law 1977 No. 1127.

[9] *Dagens Nyheter*, 4 June 1986.

[10] *Med förslag till lag om förbud mot investeringar i Sydafrika och Namibia*, Government's proposition 1984/85 no. 56 (Stockholm, 1984).

[11] Hagelin, B., *Kulorna rullar* (Ordfront förlag: Stockholm, 1985), ch. 1; Holmström, M. and Sievers, T. V., *USAs exportkontroll: Tekniken som vapen* (Ingenjörsförlaget AB: Stockholm, 1985).

[12] *Aktuellt i Handelspolitiken*, no. 1, 1986, pp. 30–32.

[13] *Svensk krigsmaterielexport* (note 5), p. 76.

[14] Singer, J. D., *Explaining War* (Sage: Beverly Hills, 1979), p. 79.

Part III. Recipient control

Paper 10. Regional arms control in the South American context

AUGUSTO VARAS

I. Introduction

Arms control initiatives in South America have been closely linked to a set of factors related to domestic social, economic and political constraints, as well as to each country's power projection in the region. Sometimes they have also been used as individual strategems to legitimize each country's previous weapon purchases and maintain a relative superiority over its neighbours.

Against this background it is understandable that almost all the major initiatives to limit arms purchases and to control local weapon production have failed. The instrumental rationales for these initiatives vary according to changes inside each governmental coalition. In a given moment they are perceived as performing a positive internal function responding to a given local, social, economic or political conflict. But after the constraints presented by these local realities are over, the necessity for arms limitations tends to disappear. This autistic approach to the problem explains the recurring failures as well as the cyclical reappearance of such initiatives.

Up to the early 1970s Chile and Peru were the most active parties in this kind of initiative. The main reason for this was the high proportion of military expenditures in GNP of these countries. If compared to Argentina, Brazil and to other countries such as Colombia or Venezuela, it emerges that these countries spend less on military institutions and weapon imports and that they, on the other hand, have stronger economies than Peru or Chile. Accordingly, local economic factors have been a crucial aspect in motivating these initiatives.

This structural rationale for arms limitation initiatives in the region makes no distinction between military or civilian governments. Both military and civilian governments have used arms limitation talks as tranquillizers for local constituencies that are eager to cut down military expenditures. They have not primarily been the result of a political commitment to peace in the region.

There is also some linkage between, on the one hand, governmental policies aimed at the expansion of the domestic market and industrialization and, on the other hand, the initiation of arms limitation talks, but these efforts have not been sustained over time and through different administrations.

Other factors have exerted various influences on the willingness to initiate arms limitation efforts. Some international circumstances and conditions have, for example, favoured the initiation of arms limitation talks. A clear withdrawal of suppliers owing to considerations regarding local human rights conditions or ideological-political confrontations with regional governments has played an important role, but the international economic conditions that have limited the arms-importing capabilities of South American countries have been much more important.

Regional initiatives for limitation of inflows of weapons and the technology to produce them have also been related to South American relations with the USA and to the former's cyclical economic crisis. In effect, in the first period, immediately after World War II, arms limitations and intra-regional military balances were secured by the strengthening of the hemispheric military order lead of the USA. In the context of the Inter-American Reciprocal Assistance Treaty, signed in 1947, and through the Mutual Security Act of 1951 the USA transferred surplus military equipment and trained South American military personnel. These were the main instruments for the modernization and professionalization of South American military establishments. Bilateral military assistance pacts signed in the early 1950s between South American countries and the USA as well as the transfer of surplus military weaponry from the USA and the UK made possible such a policy. In 1963, funds for counterinsurgency training and equipment were provided to these countries to cope with guerrilla forces, while maintaining the intra-regional military balance.[1] Simultaneously with this type of military hemispheric relations, South American countries ventured from 1945 on a serious import-substitution industrialization process, allocating fiscal resources mainly to the civilian sector. In sum, industrialization processes, military balance considerations and the US containment of a regional arms race were the main factors explaining the ups and downs of initiatives to limit arms inflows into the South American area in the 1950s and 1960s.

This peculiar situation of the South American countries was reflected in the kind of conventional arms limitation initiatives that the region supported. Since in the 1950s and the 1960s military industries in the region did not produce the weapons the armed forces requested, these weapons had to be imported from the USA and the UK. These inflows were not directly linked to the availability of fiscal resources in the hands of the military. Accordingly, the rationale for almost all regional proposals for restricting these inflows in this first period was based on the need to develop confidence-building measures, decrease border tensions and allocate resources for development, coming not from arms and military technology imports but from reductions of military personnel.

Accordingly, in this first period, attempts to limit arms imports were a small part of larger proposals which stressed the need to decrease military expenditures. During the fifth Organization of American States (OAS) consultative meeting of foreign ministers, in Santiago in 1959, a resolution stressed the close relationship between disarmament and development and requested Latin American governments to progressively decrease military expenditures. In the same year, in the context of serious blockages to the import-substitution industrialization processes, the late Chilean President Jorge Alessandri stressed the need to decrease bilateral military tensions in the border areas, calling for a balanced reduction of military forces in the region but taking into account the real needs of the armed forces of each country, the hemispheric defence commitments and internal security concerns. In response, Peru proposed a meeting to discuss the Chilean proposal, and several preparatory meetings took place during 1960. The initiative did not survive since Argentina, Brazil and Peru were not in favour of a balanced reduction, and the latter insisted on restricting the application of the agreement to the South American context, not to the whole of Latin America as Chile had suggested.[2]

The same idea was stressed by the seventh OAS consultative meeting of foreign ministers in Costa Rica in 1960, repeating the above-mentioned concern but calling for a specialized conference on these matters. Similarly, in Punta del Este, Uruguay, in 1967 the statement of the presidents of Latin America indicated their intention to control military expenditures. Later, in the 25th General Assembly of the OAS, in 1971, it was recommended to the OAS Permanent Council to study the meaning and scope of the former declaration on the restriction of military expenditures.[3]

The hemispheric military order, led by the USA and more concerned with US strategic interests than with collective hemispheric security, collapsed in the late 1960s. The policy of weapon transfers and training for counterinsurgency alienated the newly professionalized military from their activities. Coupled with progressive or centre–left oriented governments, the South American military looked to Europe for arms purchases, starting a new wave of the regional arms race. The US reaction to the process that the Peruvian military government initiated in 1969—ordering Mirage fighter-bombers—was oriented 'to recapture the market for high-tech weapons lost to Europe during the counter-insurgency era', and 'president Nixon promoted the sale of supersonic fighters and other modern arms to Latin America'.[4] This change in the US arms transfer policy to South America, together with the new political standing of the armed forces in South American politics—partly owing to their modernization and professionalization—could explain that between 1964 and 1975 arms imports increased by a yearly average of 22 per cent, a figure much higher than the GNP rate of increase (5.8 per cent) or the increases in military expenditures (6.7 per cent), and even compared to the climbing external debt (16 per cent).[5] Thus, in the late 1960s a new arms race started in the region. This is the main factor which explains the growing interest in arms import limitation proposals observed during the 1970s.

II.   A period of concerns: the Ayacucho proposal

The South American arms race in the late 1960s and early 1970s coincided with an economic crisis in 1973 and 1974. Arms imports fell sharply from 1973 to

1974.[6] In addition, local arms industries had been developed or strengthened in the early 1970s, particularly in Argentina and Brazil. Thus, the regional arms race observed in the previous years had produced military imbalances in the area, and almost all South American governments were now prone to support some form of arms import limitation initiative. Accordingly, the nature of these initiatives in this second post-World War II period is characterized by the attempt to stop the sustained inflow into the continent of weapons and of the technology to produce them. Similarly, the nature of the main propelling forces in this period is different from those of the previous one, being also linked to marketing strategies of northern producers (licences, sub-contracts and co-production) in addition to regional demand.

On 9 January 1974, in the midst of the oil crisis, the Peruvian President proposed several measures to reduce military expenditures in the region, and on 15 February the same year the Peruvian Foreign Ministry invited the Andean countries' governments to work in this direction. A joint regional commission was created, consisting of the Andean countries plus Argentina and Panama. As a result, on 9 December 1974, the Declaration of Ayacucho was signed by the presidents of Bolivia, Panama, Peru and Venezuela and the representatives of Argentina, Chile, Colombia and Ecuador. The initiative tried to promote the idea of limiting military expenditures and weapon purchases, thus transferring resources to development and decreasing tensions among countries. The idea was to hold technical meetings to propose a regional agreement, but after five meetings of a group of experts (two plenary meetings and three working groups) this initiative collapsed.

Nevertheless, some positive improvements were made. It was clarified that the main goal to be achieved was limitations in the acquisition of arms and the reduction of military expenditures. In the first meeting it was recommended to develop confidence-building measures through co-operation among regional armed forces and the development of 'tempering border zones', limiting military personnel and installing only light anti-tank and anti-air defence weapons. These zones were to be surveilled by third countries. In this context different governments proposed to diversify the topics to be analysed. The Chilean Government proposed the compensated reduction of regional military forces. The Ecuadorian Government emphasized the freedom to decide the kind of weapons to be purchased within the limits of a reduction in military expenditures. Peru proposed the differentiation between offensive and defensive arms, and a regional control and verification agency was proposed.

In the second expert meeting held in Santiago on 1–5 September 1975, co-operation among military establishments was developed. The main ideas were to strengthen the interchange of military personnel; co-ordinate military industries and joint military research and development; prohibit toxic, biological and chemical weapons; determine ceilings for some weapon acquisitions; and define macro-economic parameters to be considered for standardization of information on military budgets.

Later, three working groups elaborated those proposals. The first working group met in Santiago on 12–23 December 1975: it analysed the issue of military co-operation. Its main proposals were to include police institutions in the interchange system and the idea of a technical commission for the analysis of the co-ordination of military industries and joint research and development activities. The second working group defined the main parameters to be used as limits of reference. Five main parameters were selected, namely: the rate of increase of the GNP; national income; exports; the GNP itself; and the external debt. Similarly, it defined the main concepts of military expenditures and military budgets. The third working group met in Caracas on 6–27 February 1976, and its main achievements were the list of forbidden weapons and of weapons to be limited. The main technical problem these talks faced was to define the area to be considered in the limitation proposals, that is, the Andean countries, South America or Latin America as a whole. In addition, the initiative was an all-embracing one, including almost all main aspects involved in an arms race process, instead of reducing it to a single-issue proposal.[7] Differences also arose on the idea to limit the import of weapons or to reduce military expenditures. The Chilean proposal for a built-down regional military balance was rejected.

The political difficulties that Ayacucho faced were also the product of the Andean Group crisis. The Peruvian initiative was launched in the context of the Andean integration efforts, which was the regional institutional actor selected to host it, but during 1974 and 1975 the Andean Pact suffered the Chilean defection and the blocking of its most important integration proposals. Accordingly, the Andean Group was not the best forum for the arms limitation initiative at that moment.

Nevertheless, strategic elements were also involved. The Chilean emphasis on a regional military balance was the product of a deeply rooted idea that an arms import limitation agreement could cement a regional military imbalance. As a matter of fact, Chile was at the time purchasing significant amounts of weaponry after a decade of scarce resources allocated to the military. The Argentinian, Brazilian and Peruvian rejection of this proposal should be seen in the light of the latter's intention to keep the current military balance unchanged. More specifically, Argentina and Brazil felt that a balanced reduction could endanger their arms industry and Peru saw it necessary to maintain its current military capability owing to the possibility of confrontation at both its northern and southern borders.

The same could be said about the list of permitted and prohibited weapons. There was consensus on the prohibition of biological, toxic and nuclear weapons, ballistic missiles, carriers, cruisers and nuclear submarines. Differences arose between Colombia, Chile and Ecuador, on the one hand, and Bolivia, Peru and Venezuela, on the other, regarding the range of missiles. The former supported the prohibition of long-range missiles, and the latter wanted to keep this option free and prohibit short-range missiles. Peru was against prohibiting artillery above 105 mm, and Colombia and Chile supported the prohibition of all types of bombers.[8] Here again it is possible to find strategic commitments that in the last analysis blocked agreements and prevented flexibility in these negotiations.

The idea to protect and to keep intact South American countries' conventional military deterrent has been a permanent concern in all discussions on arms import limitations. Even though the Ayacucho initiative initially integrated civilian experts in its meetings, it finally ended by being controlled by military officers and technicians. Accordingly, military security interests prevented the emergence of a new peaceful regional security structure. In addition, the fact that two military governments of different ideological orientation were active parties in the initiative, that is, Chile and Peru, polarized the main discussion and blocked an agreement. Nevertheless, it was demonstrated that, when confronted with severe economic difficulties, South American governments are prone to initiate arms limitation talks.

After the termination of the Ayacucho process itself four main meetings were held by the military institutions of Bolivia, Chile and Peru, in Lima in 1975, in Santiago in 1976 and in Bolivia in 1977. An additional follow-up was made at the meeting of the members of the Ayacucho Declaration during the UN special session on disarmament in May–June 1978 and in Washington, DC in June of the same year. Similarly, in June 1979 Argentina and Peru signed a declaration supporting the idea of Ayacucho, but these follow-ups could be explained mainly by the tensions generated by the Bolivian–Chilean talks in 1975 and 1976, and by the Argentinian–Chilean conflict from 1978 to 1982.

Other talks were held in September 1980, in Rio Bamba, Ecuador, by Colombia, Costa Rica, Ecuador, Panama and Venezuela with the attendance of Spain. They agreed upon a charter of conduct which called for peaceful resolution of controversies and reiterated the principles of the Declaration of Ayacucho. Measures of mutual confidence derived from these talks, but no arms limitation agreement on imports and production were made.[9]

In this context it should also be noted that civilian-initiated attempts to control arms inflows through restrictions on military budgets or expenditures— such as the Ayacucho process—have never considered the supplier's side. Due to this lack of comprehensiveness of the proposals and due to the absence of civilian experts and diplomats, the problem of limitation of weapon and technology imports has been handled by the military and those civilian groups with deeply rooted geopolitical thinking. No reasonable proposal on conversion of the inflow of military technology and products into a civilian one has been made. No common interests among suppliers and purchasers have been developed. A more coherent approach is still lacking.

In sum, owing to the all-embracing purpose and multi-issue orientation of the Ayacucho proposal, the increasingly polarized ideological divergences between some of its parties, the ambiguity on the geographical area to be considered, the inadequate institutional setting (leaving Brazil out of the talks) and the buoyant financial momentum, this arms limitation initiative did not prosper. Nevertheless, it has been the inspiration for the current third period of arms limitation talks.

III.   Unilateral actions and President García's proposal

A new regional concern about the need to limit the acquisition of arms—either imported or locally produced—emerged due to the debt crisis and the democratization process occurring almost simultaneously.

The debt crisis exploded in 1981 and 1982 after several years of international financial bonanza. The lack of control of financial inflows to South America produced a tremendous debt in the region. It had a twofold character. First, it was the highest figure ever reached, representing at the beginning of 1986 US $368 billion for the whole continent, increasing between 1975 and 1982 by 317 per cent. Second, the debt service—interest and amortization on loans expressed as a share of export revenues—jumped from 7 per cent in 1970 to 50 per cent in 1982. The strategic, political, economic and social consequences of this situation have created a serious crisis in the region.[10]

Simultaneously with the bankruptcy of neo-conservative experiments in South American economics, a democratization process occurred. Peru (in 1979), Ecuador (in 1980), Argentina (in 1983), and Bolivia, Brazil and Uruguay (in 1985) were newly democratized countries with new income-distribution concerns and high military expenditures. In all of them the armed forces used huge volumes of fiscal resources and part of the debt to purchase arms and maintain large military establishments.[11]

The Argentinian democratic Government initiated between 1983 and 1984 a serious attempt to control armed forces and military expenditures. The policy was oriented towards a reduction of military personnel, reallocation of units to their proper potential areas of action, the reduction of military expenditure by 50 per cent, increased civilian control of the military through a new concentration of duties in the Ministry of Defence, and the abrogation of 'commanders in chief' and its replacement by a 'joint chiefs of staff'.

A new Argentinian position implied a new arms-acquisition policy and the reduction of the overstocked arsenal piled up by the defeated military in the South Atlantic through the sale of some weapon systems. Nevertheless, as part of the policy to control and reorient the military towards non-political issues, the Argentinian Government also promoted the rationalization of the domestic arms industry and an expansion of arms exports. This implies that, whereas arms purchases have decreased, the import of technology to produce arms domestically has increased.[12]

In Peru the crisis has been particularly acute owing to the emergence of the ultra-leftist 'Shining Path' and the deadlock political situation the newly democratic government is facing. In this context President García in his inauguration address on 18 July called for 'a regional agreement for the reduction of arms expenditures and the freezing of arms acquisitions, recovering in this way the inspiration of the Ayacucho Declaration'. The proposal indicated the need 'to substantially reduce weapons purchases starting (in the case of Peru) with a reduction of already ordered Mirages a purchase currently in process'. The next day the presidents of Argentina, Bolivia, Colombia,

Panama, the Dominican Republic and Uruguay and representatives of Brazil, Chile, Costa Rica, Cuba, Ecuador, El Salvador, Guatemala, Haiti, Honduras, Mexico, Nicaragua, Paraguay and Venezuela signed the Declaration of Lima which states that they 'consider positive and convenient a balanced reduction of military expenditures and the allocation of more financial resources for the socio-economic development in their countries and agree to promote the adoption of additional measures to increase confidence in the region and particularly among border countries'. Later President García indicated that 'we have terminated armed ships (a cruiser) and our armed forces in the context of a new world are oriented to development'.[13] He also indicated that military expenditure will fall by 10 per cent and that 12 Mirages will be purchased instead of 26.

The Peruvian proposal has been received positively in South America, but no meaningful follow-up has been made with the exception of the Chilean–Peruvian talks (see below). Considering that President García's proposal was oriented towards a freeze on acquisitions of arms, both imported and locally produced, the main arms producers in the region, Argentina and Brazil, have only rhetorically supported the initiative. Colombia reacted positively and proposed a similar course at the last OAS meeting in Cartagena de Indias. Ecuador was sceptical about the future of an agreement of this kind, largely owing to a lack of political confidence in the Peruvian willingness for a real arms freeze. Besides, in Ecuadorian eyes, such a freeze would imply a bilateral military imbalance. Finally, the Ecuadorian fear that the ultra-leftist groups in Peru and in Colombia could extend their operations into Ecuadorian territory is an additional argument to maintain its scepticism.

The most important follow-up to the initiative has been the Chilean–Peruvian talks. In May 1986 the Joint Chiefs of Staff of the three armed forces met in Lima to discuss the Peruvian proposal. Nevertheless, instead of agreeing on a limitation of arms acquisitions the meeting ended in an agreement to enforce a set of confidence-building measures. The reason for this outcome is the different nature of Chilean and Peruvian military spending. The former has based its military capability on personnel, purchasing mainly weapons useful for counterinsurgency[14] as a result of 13 years of military rule. Peru, on the other hand, has based its policy on substantial arms purchases but not on military personnel. Accordingly, a reduction of or a freeze on arms acquisitions at this time will benefit Peru as against the Chilean Navy and Air Force.

This is yet another example of how differences in defence policies block agreement on arms limitations. Argentina and Brazil, as main producers, emphasized a freeze on weapon imports, not on arms acquisition or inflow of military technology. Chile and Ecuador favoured reductions of military expenditures without specifications on items to be reduced. Chile promoted a regional military balance. Peru and Colombia supported a reduction of arms acquisitions, since they both face financial problems to finance their armed forces. Venezuela, owing to its different strategic role in the Caribbean and supported by the USA as in the case of the F-16 sale, has been a passive element in all these initiatives.

Trying to remove some of these obstacles to the Peruvian proposal, Mercado-Jarrin proposed a formula consisting of a balanced freezing of arms purchased but not yet delivered, including those produced domestically by its allies. He proposed to reduce, in the period 1986–90, 50 per cent of the funds allocated for arms purchases in the previous five-year term, simultaneously with a freeze on the transfer of weapons ordered but not received.[15] This formula could be an alternative option for this new, frustrated arms control agreement.

IV.   South America and multilateral arms control agreements

Similar factors were at play in the multilateral agreements that were concluded with the participation of South American countries. The most important such agreement was the 1967 Treaty of Tlatelolco. In the context of a potential nuclear danger, a number of Latin American countries agreed on the principles and procedures of the Treaty. However, in the case of the two main 'near-nuclear countries', for example, Argentina signed the Treaty but has not ratified it; and Brazil signed and ratified it, but it has not entered into force for Brazil.[16]

Brazil has recently proposed a Zone of Peace in the South Atlantic. This initiative must, however, be seen against the background of several factors. The first is the permanent Brazilian interest to neutralize US proposals on a South Atlantic Treaty Organization including South Africa. For Brazil, this option is impossible to support since it would imply a crisis with its African partners which represent an important part of its foreign markets, especially the Sub-Saharan ex-Portuguese colonies. The second factor is the Falklands/Malvinas conflict which opened discussion of the presence of nuclear weapons in this area of conflict. The third factor is the Brazilian fear of a military imbalance in the region due to the presence of European military powers with higher technological military capabilities than those of Brazil. One of the lessons Brazil drew from the South Atlantic conflict was the need to modernize its Navy: Brazil has launched a $10 billion programme for this purpose. The final factor is the new Argentinian–Brazilian rapprochement, which is a good framework for deactivating a potential nuclear race between both countries.

A proposal for a Latin American Zone of Peace was made in May 1983 by the Chilean Peace Research Association. The initiative was presented in Argentina in November 1984, stating 'the total support and enforcement of denuclearization of Latin America; the elimination of all military bases and extra-regional military presence in the zone; the limitation and reduction of weapons in the region; and the acceptance of this new regional statute by the super-powers'.[17]

Finally, it is interesting to notice that in the early 1980s Colombia proposed the development of a Latin American mechanism of inspection of weapons and military personnel.[18] And in 1983 the Chilean Government proposed a Latin American Space Agency as a regional organization to preserve and to develop technologies for development. This Agency would develop a satellite verification and control system in the framework of the Tlatelolco Treaty and other agreements. A verification system *in situ* was also proposed.[19] None of these proposals has led to any affirmative political action.

V.   Future prospects

Arms and military technology inflows have been difficult to control in South America through multilateral agreement. Indeed, restrictions on arms imports and military expenditures have been unilateral, particularly those made by individual countries facing economic troubles, as in the case of Argentina, Brazil, Chile and Peru.

Nevertheless, these restrictions did not include the inflow of military technology for the domestic production of weapons. In these four countries, the previous arms-importing process has been transformed into an important inflow of licences. In non-producer countries, an increase in their import of finished weapons has been observed, as in the case of Ecuador, Colombia and Venezuela.

Considering the scenarios of this arms acquisition process and the problems that limitation agreements are facing in this region, it is possible to suggest a number of alternative procedures to cope with the problem.

First, before there can be any arms acquisition limitation, a process of confidence-building measures should be developed. Considering the previous all-embracing bias of regional proposals, bilateral initiatives on a single-issue base should be developed. Talks like the Chilean and Peruvian ones should be supported in other border situations.

Second, owing to the change to a regional security system produced by the Argentinian–Brazilian accord on integration, it is possible to redefine the South American role in the international military structure, finding a peaceful role for the region in it.[20] The development of military technologies for control and verification are an important part of this redefinition. This could decrease regional tensions and pave the way for future agreements.

Third, conversion of military technological inflow into the region could be envisaged, although this would to a large extent depend on, for one thing, supplier collusion. In such a programme of conversion, suppliers' support and joint efforts are crucial. The possibility to have joint ventures in other regions with civilian commodities produced by these industries could be a positive process, both to achieve a demilitarization of the indigenous military–industrial complex and as a way to keep suppliers' interest in conversion alive.

Fourth, owing to the debt crisis it is possible to include in the negotiations with creditors some conditions on the arms acquisition process. Since almost all South American countries are dealing with conditioned credits to pay their debt, it is in the supplier countries' interest to be part of a process of arms limitation.

Fifth, it is also possible to support unilateral restrictions on arms acquisitions and the enforcement of regional and global multilateral agreements supporting non-governmental organizations' actions for peace and development.

Finally, since limitation of weapon inflows or technology is closely related to domestic political and economic issues, the prevention of a growth of arms acquisitions is also related to the degree of civilian control over the military and over military budgets and military industries. Even though these are domestic political issues, they are not less important. Democracy and demilitarization of political life should be mentioned as one of the main pre-conditions for disarmament in South America.

Notes and references

[1] Klare, M., *War Without End* (Vintage Books: New York, 1972), pp. 276–79.

[2] Castillo, M. E., 'Control de armamentos: el case de América Latina', *Contribuciones*, FLACSO (Santiago), 1985, p. 5.

[3] CIESUL, *Gastos Militares y Desarrollo en América del Sur* (Universidad de Lima: Lima, 1980), pp. 85–86.

[4] Klare, M., *American Arms Supermarket* (University of Texas Press: Austin, 1984), p. 78.

[5] Varas, A., 'State crisis, arms race and disarmament in Latin America', in IPRA, *Elements of World Instability* (Campus Verlag: Frankfurt, 1980).

[6] See Arms Control and Disarmament Agency, *World Military Expenditures and Arms Transfers, 1985* (US Government Printing Office: Washington, DC, 1985).

[7] The reasons for the need to focus on single-issue initiatives are found in Varas, A., 'El efecto de la cooperacion sobre la paz regional', *Documento de Trabajo*, FLACSO (Santiago), 1986. A critical analysis of the Ayacucho process is given in Mercado-Jarrin, E., 'Perspectivas de los acuerdos de limitacion y desarme en América Latina y el Caribe', in A. Varas (ed.), *Paz, Desarme y Desarrollo en América Latina* (RIAL-GEL: Buenos Aires, 1987).

[8] Cortes, G., 'Los tratados de armamento en América Latina', *Seguridad Nacional* (Santiago), Mar. 1978, quoted in Varas, A., 'Controlling conflict in South America: national approaches', in eds M. Morris and V. Millán, *Controlling Latin American Conflicts. Ten Approaches* (Westview Press: Boulder, 1983), pp. 73, 74.

[9] Castillo (note 2), p. 19.

[10] Varas, A., 'The Strategic Implications of the Latin American Debt', paper prepared for the 26th Annual Convention of the International Studies Association, Washington, DC, 5–9 Mar. 1985.

[11] See Tullberg, R., 'Deuda relacionada con lo militar en América Latina', *Paz, Desarme y Desarrollo* in Varas (note 7).

[12] Insulza, J. M. *et al.*, 'Temas estratégicos en las relaciones de Europa y América Latina', preliminary report, EURAL, Buenos Aires, July 1986.

[13] See Mercado-Jarrin (note 7).

[14] Gazmuri, C., 'Las armas chilenas, 1975–1982', *Defensa y Desarme, América Latina y el Caribe* (Centre for Defense and Disarmament: Santiago, 1985).

[15] Mercado-Jarrin (note 7).

[16] For the full record of the participation of South American countries in arms control agreements, see Goldblat, J. and Ferm, R., 'Major multilateral arms control agreements', in SIPRI, *SIPRI Yearbook 1987: World Armaments and Disarmament* (Oxford University Press: Oxford, 1987), Annexe B, pp. 457–86.

[17] Lagos, G., Munoz, H., Portales, C. and Varas, A., *Democracia y Politica Exterior* (Chilean Peace Research Association: Santiago, 1983), pp. 19, 20.

[18] Castillo (note 2), p. 26.

[19] Castillo (note 2), p. 27.

[20] Varas, A., 'De la competencia a la cooperacion militar en América Latina', in *Paz, Desarme y Desarrollo* (note 7).

Paper 11.   Problems and prospects for arms control in South-East Asia

MUTHIAH ALAGAPPA and NOORDIN SOPIEE

I.   Introduction

For purpose of analysis it is important to recognize that there is not one but three South-East Asias: the market-oriented non-communist states of the Association of South-East Asian Nations (ASEAN); the communist states of Indo-China; and socialist Burma. The ASEAN states, although they continue to experience internal security problems in varying degrees, have enjoyed relative peace over the past 20 years, during which their economies grew at an accelerated rate. Brunei has one of the highest gross national products (GNP) per capita income in the world; Singapore belongs to the group of newly industrializing countries (NICs); Malaysia and Thailand have the potential to become members of this group; and Indonesia and the Philippines have made relatively good progress in economic development compared to other less-developed countries (LDCs). Since 1983–84, however, nearly all the ASEAN economies (except Thailand) have been experiencing a severe economic recession. Economic recovery in these countries is expected to be gradual and unlikely to repeat the spectacular growth rates of the 1970s and early 1980s.

The communist states of Indo-China are now united in a *de facto* federation under the tutelage of Hanoi. Bilateral treaties of friendship and co-operation covering political, economic, military and technical fields bind Laos and Kampuchea to Viet Nam (Hanoi refers to this as 'special relationships'). The Indochinese countries have not experienced peace for the past 40 years, during which their economies have stagnated: the combined GDP of Viet Nam, Laos and Kampuchea in 1985 was less than 15 per cent of that of the combined GDP of the ASEAN countries. Burma has followed an isolationist and passive neutrality course for over 30 years. While it has not experienced any major international conflict during this period, it nevertheless continues to experience severe internal security problems, and its economy has grown at a very slow pace.

The Vietnamese occupation of Kampuchea and the attendant threats, especially to the national security of Thailand, are viewed by the ASEAN countries as the biggest obstacles to peace and security in the region and have had the effect of polarizing and dividing the region into two blocs—non-communist ASEAN and communist Indo-China. This intra-regional polarization is reinforced by the involvement and alignment patterns of the great powers in the Kampuchean conflict, the international security arrangements of the countries in the region, and the increasing military presence of the global powers in South-East Asia. The United States, China and Japan support the ASEAN position on Kampuchea whereas the Soviet Union supports the Vietnamese position. The Philippines and Thailand have security treaties with the United States; and Malaysia and Singapore have security arrangements with the United Kingdom, Australia and New Zealand. Viet Nam has a security treaty with the Soviet Union. The United States has a strong military presence in the Pacific Ocean including the South China Sea, and the Soviet Union has steadily built up its military capability in the region. The latter is now seeking to establish its legitimacy as an Asian power. Thus, there are essentially four groups of actors (the ASEAN countries, the Indochinese countries, Burma and the extra-regional powers) whose views, interests and demands must be taken into consideration in evaluating the problems and prospects for arms control in South-East Asia.

The number of actors and their different but overlapping planes of interaction suggest that arms control in South-East Asia should be examined at the following three levels: (*a*) at the sub-regional level (i.e., within ASEAN and among the Indochinese states); (*b*) at the regional level (encompassing all states in the region); and (*c*) at the international level (encompassing all states in the region and the relevant extra-regional powers).

Before discussing the problems and prospects of arms control in South-East Asia it will be useful quickly to survey the history of arms control in the region.

II.   History of arms control

Arms control has not been an important feature of international relations in South-East Asia. The Kuala Lumpur Declaration of 1971 proposed to 'secure the recognition of, and respect for, Southeast Asia as a Zone of Peace, Freedom and Neutrality (ZOPFAN), free from any form or manner of interference by outside powers'.[1] Although the concept of neutrality embodied in this proposal has not been defined by ASEAN, it is possible to infer two objectives from the Founding Declaration of ASEAN of 1967 and the Kuala Lumpur Declaration of 1971: first, to make the region 'free of any form or manner of interference by outside powers' and to this end affirm 'that all foreign bases in the region are temporary . . . and are not intended to be used directly or indirectly to subvert the national independence and freedom of the states in the area or prejudice the orderly processes of their national development';[2] and second, to guide the states of ASEAN in the conduct of their foreign and security policies *vis-à-vis* the great powers. It is the intention that, to the extent possible, the Association and its members should follow 'active and independent' and 'equi-distant' policies in their political and military relations with the USA, the USSR and China.

From the above it is evident that the concept of neutrality and indeed the whole idea of ZOPFAN is intended to provide a broad framework for the management of international relations in the region. It is not an arms control proposal. It has, however, the potential to spawn measures of arms control such as the proposal to declare South-East Asia a nuclear weapon-free zone.[3] The proposal to declare the region a nuclear weapon-free zone is in fact the first and only specific proposal for arms control in South-East Asia. Although the formal undertaking by ASEAN to draft a treaty on a South-East Asia Nuclear Weapon-Free Zone (SEANWFZ) is of recent origin, there was a recognition of the idea in the Kuala Lumpur Declaration which took note 'of the significant trend towards establishing nuclear-free zones as in the Treaty for the Prohibition of Nuclear Weapons in Latin America and the Lusaka Declaration proclaiming Africa a nuclear-free zone, for the purpose of promoting world peace and security by reducing the areas of international conflicts and tension'.[4] It should, however, be noted that, given that none of the states in the region is a potential nuclear power, the SEANWFZ proposal is aimed at limiting the nuclear presence of external powers in the region.

There has been no proposal to control conventional armaments in the region as a whole, either by the suppliers of arms or by the recipient countries. Limitations on the level, deployment and use of conventional armaments have, however, been important features of the peace agreements in the Indo-China region. The 1954 Geneva Agreement on the Cessation of Hostilities in Viet Nam provided for the establishment of a demilitarized zone not exceeding five kilometres in width on either side of the demarcation line, and for a ban on the introduction into the two Viet Nams of fresh troops, military personnel, arms and munitions, and military bases.[5] The 1962 Agreement on the Neutralization of Laos provided for the military neutralization of that country. Laos was not to 'allow the establishment of any foreign military base on Laotian territory for military purposes, nor recognize the protection of any alliance or military coalition, including SEATO'.[6] The 1973 Paris Peace Agreement stated the need to respect the demilitarized zone (DMZ) established in 1954 and reiterated the clause in the 1954 Geneva Agreement on Viet Nam which declared that 'North and South Vietnam shall not join any military alliance or military bloc and shall not allow foreign powers to maintain military bases, troops, military advisers and military personnel in their respective territories'.[7] The parties to the 1973 Agreement also agreed to 'withdraw from and refrain from reintroducing into (Laos and Kampuchea) troops, military advisers and military personnel, armaments, munitions and war material'.

It is uncertain whether limitations such as these, contained in peace agreements, can be viewed as arms control measures; but what is certain is that they were conflict-specific with no validity for the entire region or even a sub-region. They were all violated in quick succession, thus indicating that a measure of arms limitation is only possible at a certain level of tension which makes arms control necessary and desirable to all parties concerned.

Although there is no formal arms control agreement currently operative in the region, the countries of South-East Asia are signatories to several international measures of arms control. This positive approach towards global arms control agreements, however, does not appear to have generated any impetus for the control of armaments among the countries of the region. An examination of the reasons for this will be useful in evaluating the prospects for arms control in South-East Asia.

III.   Problems of arms control

Three major problems continue to inhibit a positive approach towards arms control in the region: first, the continued existence of violent domestic and international conflicts; second, given the legitimate security concerns, the defence spending by countries in the region, especially by the ASEAN countries, is not unduly excessive when compared to countries in the Middle East, South Asia or North-East Asia; and, third, the many intractable difficulties associated with the limitation of conventional armaments.

Taken collectively, the region has not been free of internal and international wars since World War II (table 11.1). Although the ASEAN countries have enjoyed relative peace during the past 20 years, the fact that at least three of them (Malaysia, Thailand and the Philippines) experienced prolonged and high-intensity internal conflicts should not be overlooked. Moreover, the transnational dimension of domestic conflicts, especially those of an inter-ethnic character, and the consequent tensions between the countries (Malaysia–Singapore, Malaysia–Thailand and Malaysia–Philippines) should also not elude consideration. Two ASEAN countries (Thailand and the

Table 11.1. Major internal and international wars in South-East Asia, post-World War II period

Past wars

1.   The First Indo-China War (1946–54)
2.   The Second Indo-China War (1959–73)
3.   Revolutionary War in Laos (1962–75)
4.   Revolutionary War in Kampuchea (1971–75)
5.   Khmer–Vietnamese border war (1976–78)
6.   Vietnamese invasion of Kampuchea (1978–79)
7.   Sino–Vietnamese War (1979)
8.   The Huk Insurgency in the Philippines (1948–54)
9.   The Malayan Emergency (1948–60)
10.   The regional revolts in Indonesia (1952–62)
11.   The Indonesian confrontation with Malaysia (1963–65)

Ongoing wars/conflicts

1.   Communist insurgency in Burma
2.   Communist insurgency in Malaysia
3.   Communist insurgency in the Philippines
4.   Communist insurgency in Thailand
5.   Armed ethnic separatism in Burma
6.   Armed ethnic separatism in Thailand
7.   Armed religious separatism in the Philippines
8.   The war in Kampuchea
9.   The Sino-Vietnamese conflict
10.   The Thai-Vietnamese conflict

Philippines), because of their security treaties with the United States, were also involved in the conflicts in Indo-China until 1975.

An important characteristic of nearly all the conflicts in post-World War II South-East Asia has been the direct or indirect involvement of extra-regional powers, especially the United States, the Soviet Union and China. Conditions of war are hardly conducive to the institution of arms control, and the fact that external powers played an important, if not dominant, role in many of the international conflicts in the region implied that countries in the region were substantially constrained in their conduct of intra-regional relations. They did not have a major impact on their own strategic environment, and the external powers which did have the influence were not interested in arms control arrangements in the region.

There was, however, a noticeable improvement in the situation with the formation of ASEAN in 1967 and an increase in cohesion and understanding within the Association, especially in the post-1975 period. The development of ASEAN not only reduced tension and conflict among its members (which in itself is a significant achievement considering the fear, distrust and conflict that previously characterized relations among these states), but it also allowed ASEAN to engage in collective diplomacy on many issues of peace and security, in and external to the region. Likewise, the conclusion of the Second Indo-China War and the emergence in the post-1975 period of an unified and independent Viet Nam, Laos and Kampuchea can also be perceived as facilitating greater control of the South-East Asian strategic environment by the countries of the region. Concurrently the United States withdrew militarily from mainland South-East Asia including Thailand; China moved to improve its relations with the non-communist countries of the region; and the Soviet Union did not as yet have a significant military presence in South-East Asia. This favourable trend, however, was reversed by the Vietnamese invasion and occupation of Kampuchea which have *de facto* divided the region into two ideological blocs and again brought about a much higher level of foreign power involvement in the region. Although such a situation need not inhibit arms control talks, the continuation of the war in Kampuchea and the related high intensity of the Sino–Vietnamese and Vietnamese–Thai conflicts have negative effects for arms control in South-East Asia.

Equally important is the belief in nearly all the ASEAN countries that their current level of defence spending is inadequate or just barely adequate to meet legitimate security concerns. The concepts of the archipelagic state and the Exclusive Economic Zone have further increased the defence responsibilities, especially in the maritime dimension, of many states in the region. These states became increasingly unable or disinclined to rely on external powers to guarantee their national security, and they therefore proceeded to develop their own defence postures.[8] Indonesia—because of its experience during the 1945–49 war of independence, the sense of vulnerability arising from the vastness of its physical base (territory and population), and its firm commitment to the principle of an 'independent and active' foreign policy—was opposed to military alliances from the very beginning and adopted the doctrine of National Resilience as the basis of its defence and security. Malaysia, following the termination of the Anglo-Malaysia Defence Agreement in 1971 and the re-orientation of its foreign policy towards non-alignment, adopted a policy of Self Reliance in matters of defence. The separation from Malaysia in 1965 and the termination of the Anglo-Malaysia Defence Agreement, which also covered Singapore, implied that Singapore had to provide for its own defence. The lack of territorial depth, its limited population, its geostrategic location and its sensitivity to the linkages between internal and external threats led Singapore to adopt the concept of Total Defence. Although Thailand and, to a lesser degree, the Philippines continued to maintain their security treaties with the United States, they recognized the unreliability of US support in the post-Viet Nam period and undertook to modernize and develop their defence capability. Nearly all the non-communist countries in the region faced, or continue to face, very serious communist insurgency problems with which they have to contend on their own. Thailand is also concerned with the Vietnamese threat, which it ranks as the foremost external threat to its national security.

Viet Nam, Kampuchea and, to a lesser degree, Laos have, except for very brief periods, been at war since 1945 and have had to mobilize a major part of their resources to support the war effort. Viet Nam not only has to expend resources to continue the subjugation of Kampuchea but also has to counter the threat from China. Ironically, Viet Nam, which did not enter into any military alliance in its war against the world's foremost military power—the United States—has now deemed it fit and necessary to enter into an alliance with the Soviet Union to counter the threat from China.

Development of the defence capabilities identified above necessitated a relatively rapid buildup of the respective armed forces which, in most cases, had a very rudimentary beginning, given the fact that all but one of the states (Thailand) in the region did not become independent until the post-World War II period. (Brunei became fully independent in 1984.) Thus, many countries in the region, especially those in ASEAN, had to make dramatic increases in their defence spending, particularly during the period 1965–75. The combined military spending of ASEAN countries increased more than threefold with the average annual rate of increase at 13.2 per cent, more than four times the average annual rate of growth in total world military expenditure over the same period. Ron Huisken, writing in 1977, argued that, given this rapid rate of increase in ASEAN's military spending, there was scope for reducing the cost of preparations for war.[9] He projected that limiting the annual growth rate in defence expenditure to 5 per cent (as opposed to a 10 per cent growth rate) would result in a saving of $1.6 billion; and limiting growth to 2 per cent would result in a saving of $2.4 billion, which he argued could be more gainfully used for socio-economic development, for which the developing countries have a disproportionately large responsibility. He also argued that defence consumes skilled manpower and foreign exchange, both of which are in very short supply in developing countries.

Although defence spending has continued to increase in all the countries in South-East Asia (table 11.2), the annual rate of increase during the period 1975–84 is just over 6 per cent and only two percentage points above the annual growth rate in world military expenditure over the same period. Comparison of growth rates during 1975–84 with those of the period 1965–75 may, however, be misleading. Given the large base figure as of 1975, it is only natural that subsequent growth rates must decline. Therefore, comparison of the actual quantum of defence expenditure, its expression in terms of GDP and national budgets may provide a more accurate picture of the state of defence spending in the region. In absolute terms defence spending in South-East Asia increased from $6.23 billion in 1975 to $10.4 billion in 1984; the increase was 67 per cent. For the ASEAN countries the increase was 65 per cent, but as a percentage of the GDP defence spending it varied between only 3 and 8 per cent and, as a percentage of national budgets, between 8 and 23 per cent. The increase in defence spending during this period was largely, although not entirely, a consequence of a deterioration in the strategic environment (brought about by the Vietnamese invasion of Kampuchea) and the favourable economic circumstance of the ASEAN countries, both of which provided added momentum to the realization of the defence concepts outlined above. The economic recession in the ASEAN countries, however, has resulted in a dramatic cutback in defence expenditure, especially in Malaysia and Indonesia, despite the fact that the strategic environment had not altered very much.

Is there now a case for cutting defence expenditure or limiting its rate of increase? 'How much is enough?' is a question that has plagued every country, large and small, developed and developing, and its examination is beyond the scope of this paper. However, two points need to be noted. First, there is no precedence where sovereign states have agreed multilaterally to control or limit defence expenditure to a fixed ceiling.[10] Limitations have been on levels of armaments and/or their deployment and use. Reductions in defence spending can occur as a consequence of controls over the level or deployment, but this is different from accepting a prescribed limit on defence spending. In any case, verification and enforcement of defence spending are an exceedingly difficult if not impossible task, given the differences in definition, accounting procedures, sourcing, aid, and so on. The second point is that, whatever reduction in spending or decline in the rate of increase has occurred in the region, it is a consequence of unilateral decision rather than multilateral agreement but with due regard to the strategic environment, economic circumstances and other related factors. Therefore, the lesson to be drawn here is that some saving in defence expenditure may be possible through the building of greater mutual trust and confidence in the strategic environment.

The third major problem of arms control in South-East Asia is the universal one of the great many intractable difficulties associated with control of conventional armaments. The record of conventional arms control in the post-World War II period is abysmal. Although there have been talks on the control of conventional armaments, they were basically in the context of proposals for

Table 11.2. Military expenditure of South-East Asian countries, 1975–84

Figures are in US $ m., at 1980 prices and exchange-rates.

Year	Brunei	Indonesia	Malaysia	Philippines	Singapore	Thailand	Total ASEAN	ASEAN annual rate of charge	Burma	Viet Nam, Laos, Kampuchea	Total	Annual rate of change (%)
1975	54.4	1 976	883	857	413	(741)	4 924.4	..	161	[1 171]	[6 257.4]	–
1976	95.2	1 977	923	978	500	(913)	5 386.2	9.4	156	[1 281]	[6 823.2]	9
1977	96.1	1 914	1 059	967	556	(1 101)	5 643.1	4.8	181	[1 376]	[7 250.1]	6.3
1978	106.0	2 065	1 108	888	520	(1 382)	6 069.0	7.5	213	[1 522]	[7 804.0]	7.6
1979	189.0	1 963	1 249	821	532	(1 557)	6 311.0	4.0	227	[1 578]	[8 116.0]	4
1980	[191.0]	2 174	1 557	776	605	(1 476)	6 779.0	7.4	(246)	[1 661]	[8 686.0]	7
1981	180	2 449	1 856	784	677	1 574	7 520.0	10.9	[257]	[1 752]	[9 529.0]	9.7
1982	[200]	[2 564]	1 970	877	748	1 699	8 058.0	7.2	(263)	[1 867]	[10 188.0]	6.9
1983	(217)	[2 461]	2 090	843	816	1 822	8 249.0	2.4	(261)	[1 924]	[10 434.0]	2.4
1984	(279)	[2 662]	(1 829)	524	900	1 951	8 145.0	–1.3	(259)	[1 950]	[10 354.0]	–0.71

Source: SIPRI, *World Armaments and Disarmament: SIPRI Yearbook 1985* (Taylor & Francis: London, 1985), p. 274.

Key ( ) Uncertain data
[ ] Estimates with a high degree of uncertainty

General and Complete Disarmament (GCD) or arrangements among supplier states. In terms of regional arrangements or arrangements among recipient states (the two dimensions that are relevant to the discussion on South-East Asia) there are only two known attempts: the Central European Mutual and Balanced Force Reduction (MBFR) talks, which started in 1973, and the negotiations among the Latin American countries. The MBFR talks have so far not resulted in any agreement on the limitation or reduction of NATO and Warsaw Pact conventional forces.[11] In Latin America, after nine years of consideration, the countries of the region expressed in 1967 in Punta del Este 'their intention to limit military expenditure', but this was violated almost immediately.[12] Eventually the application of the Punta del Este Declaration was held to be 'the exclusive responsibility of each government in its own territory', implying that there can be no multilateral agreement governing defence expenditure. The subsequent Declaration of Ayachucho in 1974 called for 'the creation of conditions which permit effective limitations of arms'. A working group was convened in 1975 to work towards arms limitations, but the on–off negotiations appear not to have made any significant progress. The lack of success in these attempts stems mainly from the difficulties in determining the legitimate security concerns of the countries and what is a fair and equitable balance given these concerns. There is a whole host of other issues, including symmetry, verification and enforcement, which pose innumerable problems for conventional arms control. There is no reason to believe that these and related problems will not also plague any conventional arms control effort in South-East Asia.

Before turning to an assessment of the prospects for arms control in South-East Asia, it is necessary to deal with the proposition of an arms race in the region.[13] An arms race by definition implies that 'there should be two or more parties perceiving themselves to be in an adversarial relationship, who are increasing or improving their armaments at a rapid rate and structuring their respective military postures with a general attention to the past, current and anticipated military and political behaviour of the other parties'.[14] In fact, in every arms race so far, instances can be found of very specific responses to equally specific identified actions or anticipated actions on the part of the arms race rival. These conditions clearly do not obtain in South-East Asia. Although Thailand and Viet Nam are in an adversarial situation, they are not arming at a rapid rate against each other, and there is no specific action–reaction process under way. The purchase of F-16 aircraft by Thailand has been posited as a reaction to the anticipated delivery of the MiG-23 by the Soviet Union to Viet Nam. This proposition, however, does not give sufficient weight to several important factors, including the modernization programme of the Royal Thai Air Force launched in 1976 and the prestige and bureaucratic factors which underlay the Thai decision to purchase the aircraft. In any case, one squadron of F-16s is unlikely to alter significantly the strategic imbalance between Thailand and Viet Nam. Thailand, although it has embarked on a long-term force modernization programme, has not responded in any substantial way to match the military capability (hardware, personnel and experience) of Viet Nam, let alone gain military superiority.[15] It has also been triggered by purchases by Thailand and Singapore. Here again, Indonesia and Thailand are not in an adversarial relationship, and Singapore clearly is not a threat to Indonesia. It is possible to argue that Malaysia may have an adversarial relationship with both Thailand and Singapore, but it has chosen not to respond in kind to the purchase of the F-16 by these two countries. Although the defence spending of the countries in the region takes due account of threat perceptions, it is difficult to analyse their arms procurement programmes using the model of an arms race.

IV. Prospects for arms control

Given the problems outlined above, it is difficult to be optimistic about the opportunities for arms control in South-East Asia, but on the other hand the field is not entirely barren. Efforts can be directed towards creating greater trust and confidence in the regional strategic environment through a variety of confidence-building measures (CBMs). This objective can be approached on two levels: within the ASEAN sub-region and among all the countries in the region. At the ASEAN sub-regional level, confidence building has been developing at a steady pace but only among selected countries and on a bilateral basis. Bilateral co-operation can by definition help resolve or ameliorate bilateral problems and issues, but their impact on the sub-region as a whole is not significant. In any case, there are significant gaps in the network of bilateral co-operation which can only be bridged by multilateral co-operation at the ASEAN level. The sensitivities of the ASEAN countries towards an ASEAN security pact are well known and acknowledged and are not the objective of the line of reasoning advanced above. The proposal is for a forum to facilitate communication and discussion on issues affecting the regional strategic environment by officials involved in the planning and conduct of defence. Such a forum (an ASEAN Confidence-Building Measures Forum) can help to reduce distrust and misunderstanding and facilitate a more constructive approach to defence issues in the member countries.

At the regional level, as of now, there is no forum that encompasses all the countries in South-East Asia. The ASEAN and the Indo-China bloc countries operate as two distinct groups. Although ASEAN is open for participation to all states in the South-East Asian region, it is unlikely that the communist countries of the region will apply for membership or be accepted into the Association in the foreseeable future. In fact, as ASEAN makes substantial progress in economic co-operation it will become even more difficult for the communist states to become full participants in ASEAN. As such, there is a need for a forum that will facilitate the interaction of all states in the region to discuss issues of regional peace and security. There are, however, a number of difficulties to be overcome before this idea can gain acceptance in ASEAN. The ASEAN countries will not agree to participate in such a forum until the

Kampuchean conflict is resolved. They view any such participation as acceptance of a *fait accompli* in Kampuchea, which would be tantamount to a victory for Viet Nam. The idea of a South-East Asia Forum suffers, at least for the moment, from a negative image in ASEAN because a similar idea (a regional conference) has been advanced by Viet Nam to address all issues of peace and security in the region, including the Kampuchea issue.[16] Although a South-East Asia Forum may be unacceptable now, it is an idea that should not be lost sight of, and it should be pursued at the opportune moment.

On the international level, which encompasses all the countries in the region and the extra-regional powers that have a military presence in South-East Asia, control of conventional forces and armaments does not appear to be a realistic option. ASEAN, however, is studying the possibility of arms control on the nuclear plane. The principal motive for the SEANWFZ Treaty under study is not the fear of nuclear testing or dumping of nuclear waste which precipitated the South Pacific Nuclear-Free Zone (SPNFZ) Treaty, or the danger of nuclear war which resulted in the Tlatelolco Treaty, but a recognition by ASEAN of the need to breathe new life into the 15-year-old concept of ZOPFAN. Although declaring South-East Asia a nuclear weapon-free zone may not have an immediate and tangible impact on regional security or the security of individual countries, it is believed that the process has the potential in the long term to influence the strategic environment in South-East Asia. Viewed in this context, even a weak NWFZ agreement may be of value and will provide a framework for the conduct of international relations affecting the region during conditions of relative peace. It provides ASEAN and the other states with a symbol to be used at the opportune moment. This could not only put the USA, the USSR, China and the other nuclear powers under legal and moral pressure to limit their nuclear activities in the region; it could also contribute to the above-mentioned regional process of confidence building, aimed at reducing military expenditures and restricting the acquisition of conventional weapons in the region.

V.   Conclusion

A certain measure of common need (such as the desire to avoid unacceptable destruction and suffering, to halt an arms race, or to prevent excessive spending on defence), a level of political communication and understanding, and the absence of war are important prerequisites for any measure of arms transfer control. These prerequisites clearly do not obtain in contemporary South-East Asia, and control of conventional armament is therefore not a realistic option for the foreseeable future. The immediate requirement is for the forging of forums at the sub-regional and regional levels to facilitate communications and discussion of critical issues with a view to reducing tension and conflict in the region. Measures of arms control to strengthen the fabric of a stable and peaceful strategic environment may eventually emerge from agreements or understandings reached at these forums.

Notes and references

[1] The ASEAN Declaration on the Neutralization of Southeast Asia, 1971. For the text of the Declaration see Chawla, S., Gurtov, M. and Marsot, A.-G., *Southeast Asia Under the New Balance of Power* (Praeger: New York, 1974), pp. 145–46.

[2] Founding Declaration of the Association of Southeast Asian Nations (ASEAN), Aug. 1967. For the text of the Declaration see note 1, pp. 119–21.

[3] Joint Communiqué of the Nineteenth ASEAN Ministerial Meeting Manila, 23–24 June 1986. For the text see *19th ASEAN Ministerial Meeting and Post Ministerial Conferences with the Dialogue Partners* (ASEAN Secretariat: Jakarta, 1986), pp. 46–47.

[4] Chawla *et al.* (note 1), p. 145.

[5] Geneva Conference, Agreement on the Cessation of Hostilities in Vietnam, 20 July 1954. For the text, see Kahin, M. G. and Lewis, J. W., *The United States in Vietnam* (Dial Press: New York, 1967), pp. 348–66.

[6] Declaration on the Neutrality of Laos, 23 July 1962. For the text see *United Nations Treaty Series*, vol. 456, pp. 302–05.

[7] The Paris Peace Agreement, Jan. 1973. For excerpts of the text, see Chawla *et al.* (note 1), pp. 169–75.

[8] For a good discussion of the defence postures of the countries in South-East Asia, see the collection of articles in Chin Kim Wah (ed.), *Defence Spending in Southeast Asia* (ISEAS: Singapore, 1987).

[9] Huisken, R., *Arms Limitation in Southeast Asia: A Proposal* (Strategic and Defence Studies Center, Research School of Pacific Studies, Australian National University: Canberra, 1977), pp. 2–5.

[10] The European countries of NATO agreed to achieve a 3 per cent growth in their defence spending at the urging of the United States. This, however, was with a view to increasing rather than limiting defence expenditure. The attempt in Latin America to set a ceiling on defence expenditure failed.

[11] For details on the MBFR talks see Blacker, C. D. and Duffy, G. (eds), *International Arms Control: Issues and Agreements* (Stanford University Press: Stanford, 1984), pp. 296–305.

[12] For details of the negotiations among Latin American countries, see Duffy (note 11), p. 333.

[13] This proposition has been advanced by some political leaders and observers in and from the region; for example, see Richardson, M., 'The F-16 for South-East Asia; arms race or strategic balance', *Pacific Defence Reporter*, May 1985, pp. 17–19.

[14] Gray, C. S., 'The arms race phenomenon', *World Politics*, vol. 24, no. 1 (Oct. 1971), p. 40. See also Bull, H., *The Control of the Arms Race* (Praeger: London, 1965), p. 5.

[15] For details on the Thai defence buildup, see Alagappa, M., *The National Security of Developing States: Lessons from Thailand* (Auburn House: Dover, MA, 1987), pp. 119–26.

[16] Pham Binh, 'Prospects for Solutions to Problems Related to Peace and Security in Southeast Asia', paper presented at the seminar organized by CSIS, Jakarta, and the Institute for International Relations, Hanoi, 25–26 Feb. 1984.

Paper 12.   Third World arms control: role of the non-aligned movement

S. D. MUNI

I.   Introduction

In 1985 the world spent about $2.4 billion per day on arms and related activities, according to SIPRI estimates.[1] This is indeed an astonishing figure. The Third World's share of armaments—about 18 per cent of world military expenditure and 64 per cent of transfers of major weapons in 1985—has recently shown some sign of decline and stagnation. But this may not be a comforting sign as these levels are still significant in view of the Third World's feeble economic capabilities and vulnerability to conflicts. The recent indications of decline and stagnation in the Third World's share may also be a reflection of the overall recession and uncertainty in the world economy. They may prove to be of short tenure rather than a sustaining trend. It is therefore necessary that no let-up is allowed in the continuing concern for limiting armaments in the Third World.

Any success in limiting and controlling armaments in the Third World depends on many factors. Of critical importance is the approach of the Third World itself and the extent to which it is prepared to accept restraints. In this respect the role of the Non-Aligned Movement (NAM) is significant: not only because the NAM is the most authentic means of articulating the Third World's collective aspirations for peace, independence and prosperity but also because, among the 20 largest importers of conventional weapons in the Third World, 18 belong to the NAM.[2]

II.   Non-alignment, peace and disarmament

The NAM has always had a deep and abiding commitment to world peace and security. The Movement described itself as 'history's biggest peace movement' at the 7th Summit held in New Delhi in March 1983.[3] The NAM's commitment to peace dates back much earlier than its formal institutionalization in 1961. The initial moorings and moves that eventually led to the establishment of the NAM, like the Afro-Asian Conference held in Bandung (1955) and the Brioni meeting of the Heads of Governments of India, Egypt and Yugoslavia (1956), recognized that there existed a vital link between the struggle for peace and the endeavour for disarmament.[4]

These initial moves accounted for the NAM's emphasis on 'general and complete disarmament' as a vital means to achieve world peace. At the first summit in Belgrade in 1961, the Movement adopted a broad-based and comprehensive definition of general and complete disarmament. This included:

the elimination of armed force, armaments, foreign bases, manufacture of arms as well as elimination of institutions and installations for military training except for purposes of internal security and the total prohibition of the production, possession and utilization of nuclear and thermonuclear arms, bacteriological and chemical weapons as well as the elimination of equipment and installations for the delivery and placement and operational use of weapons of mass destruction on national territories.[5]

The concept of disarmament, so defined, was indeed so radical that the goal appeared to be somewhat unrealistic in the context of the then emerging international security situation. This broad-based definition, however, echoed the concern of the UN General Assembly during the late 1940s and the 1950s, in particular UN General Assembly resolution 1378 (XIV) of 1959 on 'general and complete disarmament under effective international control'. Until then, it seemed, the wounds of World War II, fought mainly with conventional weapons, had not been fully healed.

The 1961 NAM definition of disarmament had two important aspects. First, it accorded no specific priority to nuclear weapons and other weapons of mass destruction over conventional weapons. Second, the goal was that of the 'elimination' of all types of arms and war-supporting institutions and *not* their regulation, limitation or control. Regarding both these aspects, the position of the NAM made a major shift at the second summit. The broad-based concept has not been repeated by the NAM since 1961. The only exception was in 1978, when in the Tenth Special Session of the UN General Assembly on disarmament the non-aligned countries endorsed an expression which was similar to the 1961 concept. The Final Document of the 1978 UN Special Session stated:

General and complete disarmament under strict and effective international control shall permit States to have at their disposal only those non-nuclear forces, armaments, facilities and establishments as are agreed to be necessary to maintain internal order and protect the personal security of citizens and in order that States shall support and provide agreed manpower for a United Nations peace force.[6]

However, the NAM has recently started using the expression 'strengthening peace and security at a lower level of forces through the limitation and reduction of armed forces and conventional weapons'.[7]

III.   Shift in approach

The NAM did not sustain its 1961 stance on disarmament at the second summit in Cairo in 1964. It did not even mention the 'elimination' of conventional weapons and armed forces, but instead laid emphasis on controlling nuclear weapons. Welcoming the 1963 Partial Test Ban Treaty, the Cairo Declaration also 'urged the speedy conclusion of agreements on various other partial and collateral measures of disarmament proposed by the members of 18-Nation Committee on Disarmament'.[8] From the Cairo meeting onwards, the NAM was concerned mainly with disarmament and arms control measures in the nuclear field. The stated commitment to general and complete disarmament was accordingly qualified by adding the phrase 'in particular, nuclear disarmament, under effective international control'.

Why this sudden decline of interest in conventional disarmament? The answer can be found in the changing parameters of the international security situation. There were two sets of important developments in this regard. First, the escalating nuclear arms race among the great powers had acquired menacing proportions by the early 1960s. In addition, the Cuban missile crisis of 1962 and the entry of China into the nuclear weapon powers' club in 1964 were important developments that awakened the NAM leaders, meeting in Cairo, to the immediate prospects and frightening consequences of nuclear conflicts. The nuclear arms race has since then shown no sign of decay. The threat posed by conventional weapons has paled into insignificance against the fear of a nuclear holocaust. A number of studies have been made on the possibilities of accidental nuclear war, actual incidents of the threat of use of nuclear forces and the extent of nuclear weapon deployment in non-nuclear weapon countries of the Third World. The NAM, aware of these developments and their implications for world security, could not but reflect its fears; hence the increasing emphasis on nuclear disarmament and control of weapons of mass destruction.

The second set of developments was related to security in the Third World. The NAM started with the rather naive assumption that, since its aim was to avoid military conflicts, its members would not have to face any such conflicts. This assumption soon proved to be untenable. Third World countries became involved in three types of conflict. One was bilateral wars, such as India's conflict with China in 1962 and with Pakistan in 1965 and 1971, Egypt's conflict with Israel in 1967 and 1973, and the war between Iran and Iraq. A second type was the conflicts arising out of struggles for national liberation, such as in Algeria in 1962 and in many other African countries. Third, there were the conflicts imposed on Third World countries by the great powers through unilateral intervention under one pretext or another. One estimate puts the number of regional, local and internal wars between 1945 and 1983 at nearly 200.[9] According to another assessment of the frequency of major armed conflicts: in the 1950s the average was 9 a year; in the 1960s, 11 a year; and in the 1970s and thus far in the 1980s, 14 a year.[10] All these conflicts, in addition to other factors, added to the level of armaments in the Third World. The flow of arms to Third World countries received a further impetus as a result of growing domestic turmoil and instability on the one hand and expanding weapon production in the developed countries on the other hand.[11]

These developments have had a significant impact on the NAM's approach towards the question of conventional disarmament. While lamenting the great powers' failure in disarmament efforts and extending détente to the Third

World, the NAM increasingly emphasized the need to ensure the security of its members. One way to do so was to ask the great powers to guarantee the security of the non-nuclear weapon states and keep the latter out of the nuclear arms race.[12] Also, NAM members were urged to display greater mutual co-operation and solidarity in helping each other meet the respective threats to their sovereignty, territorial integrity and independence.[13] Under the NAM rubric, however, such mutual co-operation and solidarity were aimed 'against all dangers from outside'.[14] This concern for security thus provided the justification for the acquisition of arms rather than prompting any self-restraint or control.

The NAM pleaded for restraint on the flow of arms but only with regard to its perceived common adversaries, namely Israel and South Africa. The meeting of the NAM's Co-ordinating Bureau in Havana, Cuba, in May 1978 'condemned the Israeli military escalation in conventional arms and denounced its intentions of possessing nuclear weapons as a serious threat to peace and security'. The Bureau further asked the UN Security Council to call upon all states, 'particularly the United States of America . . . under Chapter VII of the United Nations Charter and irrespective of any existing contracts, to refrain from any supply of arms, ammunition or any spare parts thereof, to Israel, to ensure that such supplies do not reach Israel through other parties and to end all transfer of nuclear equipment of fissionable material or technology to Israel'.[15] Regarding South Africa, the NAM had been pleading for a mandatory arms embargo by the UN Security Council.[16] This was achieved in 1977 under Security Council Resolution 418. The NAM has since then constantly pleaded for implementation of, and adherence to, this resolution by the Western powers.[17] In 1984, at the initiative of the non-aligned countries, the UN General Assembly carried a resolution with an overwhelming majority, imposing comprehensive sanctions against South Africa and asking the Security Council to take appropriate action under Chapter VII, so as to prohibit all co-operation in military and nuclear fields with that country. The resolution further called upon all governments to terminate all military and nuclear collaboration with South Africa.[18]

Following the NAM summit in Harare in September 1986, there have been suggestions from some of the non-aligned countries in the UN General Assembly that a mandatory embargo be placed on not only the arms imported *by* but also the arms imported *from* South Africa. For this, 'revocation of all agreements or licences' in the military-related fields with South Africa was urged upon the members of the United Nations.[19]

IV.   Specific arms control measures

The shift in the NAM's position was thus towards emphasizing nuclear rather than conventional disarmament. In this shift, the idea of control and limitation of arms substituted for the earlier call for their elimination. This was with a view to reaching immediate, realistic and practical solutions. Theoretically, however, the concept of arms control was seen as a necessary step towards general and complete disarmament and not as an end in itself. This was made clear in various documents of the NAM meetings. Arms control, detached from disarmament, was not compatible with the thrust of non-alignment. Arguing this, India said in the Preparatory Committee meeting of the Second Special Session on Disarmament in 1982:

the expression arms control . . . carried the unacceptable implication of control without disarmament and the concept of a given group of countries gaining the permanent capacity to control all other countries in the manner of possessing arms. One wonders then, whether the game of disarmament in the nuclear age was *inter alia*, an effort by the great powers to control smaller countries, something like a modern version of colonialism and imperialism.[20]

Nuclear, chemical, biological and other weapons of mass destruction

The immediate and greatest danger to human survival and international peace is posed by nuclear weapons and other weapons of mass destruction. The NAM has strongly and consistently pleaded for control and eventual elimination of such weapons. The great powers have a major responsibility for the development, production, stockpiling and possible use of such weapons. Therefore, the NAM has been directing its efforts towards these great powers in three different but interrelated ways. First, it issued special appeals and messages to the great powers to take effective steps for controlling nuclear weapons. Second, the NAM has tried to build strong public opinion and initiate moves in the United Nations to bring about restraint on the spread of nuclear weapons. Third, the NAM has lent its support to the important measures—unilateral, bilateral or multilateral—aimed at controlling and limiting nuclear and other more harmful weapons of chemical and biological types.

While it has been both realistic and convenient for the NAM to stress the role of the great powers in nuclear arms control and disarmament, it would be unfair to say that the non-aligned countries have been opposed to restraints on their own activities with regard to nuclear weapons. At the Cairo summit in 1964, in pleading for nuclear restraint on the great powers, the non-aligned leaders also asked them not to disseminate nuclear weapon technology. By implication, this was to affect all non-nuclear power states including the non-aligned countries. The non-aligned leaders further declared at Cairo 'their own readiness not to produce, acquire or test any nuclear weapons and call on all countries including those who have not subscribed to the Moscow Treaty to enter into a similar undertaking'.[21] The NAM members have persisted in their commitment 'not to produce, acquire or test' nuclear weapons. Notwithstanding this commitment, the 1968 Non-Proliferation Treaty (NPT) has not been formally endorsed by the NAM. The Lusaka summit, which took place soon after the NPT entered into force (September 1970), did not even refer to it.

However, this should not lead to the false conclusion that the non-aligned countries favoured nuclear proliferation. In fact, more than 75 per cent of the

NAM members had become signatories to the NPT by 31 December 1985. At the same time, more than two-thirds of those who have not signed the NPT are also non-aligned countries. The case of these countries for not signing the NPT rests on two arguments. First, it is claimed that the Treaty is 'paternalistic and discriminatory' against the non-nuclear weapon states. In particular, the NAM has from the beginning asked for unhindered transfer of nuclear technology for peaceful purposes from the developed to the developing countries. Second, some of the non-aligned countries did not sign the NPT because of their perceived regional security concerns and roles,[22] which made a regional approach to arms control in the nuclear field assume significance. The NAM has, from the beginning, endorsed this regional approach. In 1964, the second NAM summit welcomed the initiatives of African and Latin American countries in this regard. Similar proposals to denuclearize regions in Europe and Asia were also supported as 'steps in the right direction because they assist in consolidating international peace and security'. The nuclear powers were asked to respect the denuclearized zones.[23] This position has been consistently maintained.

Some of these lingering proposals in Africa, the Middle East, South Asia and the Indian Ocean have been bogged down in regional conflicts and rivalries. In Africa, the Middle East, South Africa and Israel, the suspected 'hidden' nuclear weapon states have refused to undertake any regional or other obligations to restrain their nuclear ambitions and capabilities. Israel, within a year of lending its token support to the Middle East nuclear weapon-free zone, carried out a massive attack with impunity upon Iraqi nuclear facilities in June 1981. In South Asia, both India and Pakistan have stated their commitment to non-proliferation and accepted the principle inherent in the regional denuclearization proposal, but the divergent security preoccupations of India (with Chinese, US and Soviet nuclear presence in the Indian Ocean) and Pakistan (with India) do not allow them to relinquish the nuclear option. The NAM has covered this dilemma of regional security preoccupations in the regional denuclearization proposals by saying that such arrangements should be based upon freely arrived-at regional consensus, keeping in view the special characteristics of the region concerned. This is evident in the NAM deliberations on the issue since the Havana summit, where Pakistan was admitted as a non-aligned member.[24] There is no hope that in the near future the prevailing stalemate on regional denuclearization in South Africa will be resolved.

Conventional weapons

The NAM declaration and communiqués since the 1964 Cairo summit have said little on the question of the conventional arms race that could be construed as having restraining implications for the Third World. The NAM's position on three specific and related issues may be an exception.

First, the NAM has frequently raised the question of the growing waste of economic resources on the arms race and has asked for such waste to be stopped and the resources thus saved to be utilized in the development of the developing countries. The NAM realizes the close nexus between disarmament and development and has found military spending 'inconsistent with efforts aimed at achieving the New International Economic Order'.[25] Specific proposals for the reduction of military budgets have, however, not found favour with many Third World and industrialized countries. The latter, being heavy spenders, have been asked to demonstrate political will and take the lead. No viable comparative criteria for an evaluation of military expenditures have been evolved, despite numerous studies and expert reports.

Second, the NAM has endorsed regional approaches to peace and demilitarization as a positive step towards achieving general and complete disarmament. Accordingly, proposals and initiatives for regional demilitarization or arms limitations such as in Africa (1964), ZOPFAN (Zone of Peace, Freedom and Neutrality) in South-East Asia (1970), the Indian Ocean as a Zone of Peace (1971), the Ayacucho Declaration in Latin America (1974), and zones in the Middle East, South Pacific, Europe, Mediterranean, and so on have been welcomed. The criteria on which the NAM has endorsed the regional approach to arms limitation is the same as in the case of nuclear weapon-free zones: namely, that such arrangements should be arrived at freely among the states of the region. Since the Ayacucho Declaration of the eight Andean countries in 1974 was considered to fall short of this criteria, it was initially ignored. Subsequently, the same declaration was welcomed when in 1978 its scope was broadened and countries such as Cuba were also included.[26] It may not be out of place to note here that the NAM summit in Harare did not take any notice of the Contadora Group's initiative in finalizing a treaty for regional arms limitation. Reiterating the basic criteria for regional arms limitation, the 1986 Harare summit said that, on the basis of 'undiminished security' and within the framework of 'general and complete disarmament':

. . . where the regional situation so permits at the initiative of any or all of the states so concerned and with their concurrence, states should consider and adopt measures at the regional level with a view to strengthening peace and security at a lower level of forces through the limitation and reduction of armed forces and conventional weapons.

For the success of such regional efforts, the leaders at Harare called upon the major arms suppliers to help and co-operate.[27]

As a third exception to its otherwise docile attitude towards the conventional arms race, the NAM has shown serious concern for new technological advancements in conventional weapons. It has called for the prohibition of such weapons, particularly those which are excessively injurious and of an 'indiscriminate and cruel nature'. It has welcomed the UN convention on the subject which came into force in December 1983. The NAM is worried that such weapons, because of their severe effects, tend to 'obscure the distinction between nuclear and conventional weapons and thus legitimize the possession of nuclear weapons and other weapons of mass destruction'.[28] It is important for the NAM that this distinction and the priority of nuclear over conventional disarmament and arms control are maintained. For the same reason, the NAM rejected the concept of winnable and limited nuclear war, because, among other things, it also aimed at blurring the distinction between nuclear and conventional warfare.[29]

The running thread in the NAM's position on all the three issues mentioned above was that the great powers were mainly responsible for quantitative and qualitative escalation in conventional armaments. As such, they were to take a lead in controlling or limiting these armaments.

The Third World had to confront the great powers on the question of conventional armaments outside the NAM forum, in the United Nations. Since 1965 (i.e., following the second NAM summit, where reference to conventional disarmament was avoided and when the flow of conventional arms to the Third World started to attract attention) the UN has witnessed an intensive debate on the ways and means to restrain conventional armaments. The lead in initiating this debate has mostly come from the Western great powers and their Third World allies and associates. These countries have put forth proposals for regulating arms transfers and limiting the arms buildup in the Third World. The important ones included: maintaining an arms transfer register, monitoring national and regional transactions in conventional arms, voluntary restraints, reduction of military budgets, restraints on production lines, regional arms limitation arrangements, a fee on arms sales to build funds for UN development assistance, and so on.[30] The UN debate on these issues in the General Assembly, the Disarmament Commission and the Committee on Disarmament has been lively and extensive, but nothing concrete has emerged from the debate, which continues to engage the interests of the great powers and the Third World.[31]

Most of the conventional arms control proposals made by the Western powers and their associates in the UN have not found favour with the majority of the Third World countries. Most important was the assertion that the great powers, by raising the issue of conventional arms control, were trying to divert attention from the vital question of nuclear disarmament. During the first UN Special Session on Disarmament in 1978, the non-aligned countries strongly resisted the Western attempt to link, for equal treatment, the two questions of nuclear and conventional disarmament, so that progress in the two areas could advance on a parallel basis. It was only to avoid such a link that the Third World even accepted the compromise of starting negotiations in the two areas at the same time.[32] The Third World countries held on to this position when the question again came up during the second UN Special Session on Disarmament in 1982.

The non-aligned countries brought up the question of the responsibility of the countries having the largest and most modern arsenals of conventional weapons. Thus the proposal for restraint on transfers was countered with restraint on production. It was also repeatedly asserted by a large number of non-aligned countries that access to conventional weapons was essential for the preservation of their sovereignty, independence and territorial integrity and in their struggle for liberation from colonial rule.[33] Supplier-initiated restraints on the transfer of weapons and technologies thus could possibly diminish security and cripple the liberation struggles of the Third World. Accordingly, the NAM did not show enthusiasm for the Conventional Arms Transfer Talks (CATT) between the superpowers in 1977–78. The NAM ministerial meeting in Luanda (September 1985) disapproved of superpower talks on disarmament issues, since that diminished the potential for what was regarded as necessary multilateral negotiations. If these talks had succeeded, yet another channel for the great powers to dominate the Third World would have come into existence. They did not want a London Club of suppliers in the conventional arms field as well. The Third World could only accept that the suppliers negotiated suitable measures under certain conditions with the recipients, in order to limit the buildup of conventional arms. Accordingly,

consultations should be carried out among major arms suppliers and recipients countries on the limitation of all types of international transfer of conventional weapons . . . on the basis of the undiminished security of the parties . . . taking into account the need of all States to protect their security as well as the inalienable rights to self determination and independence of peoples under colonial or foreign domination . . .[34]

The considered answer of the NAM to the question of the conventional arms buildup in the Third World was to root out the basic causes of conflicts and tensions that lay in colonial and racial domination, economic disparity, military alliances, bases, the presence of foreign troops and interventions.

The only proposal of the Western powers that found comparatively wider acceptance in the Third World was the regional approach to limitations of armaments. Here again, the Western position, which had been articulated by the USA since 1966 and elaborately defined in 1970, was not acceptable to the Third World. The USA—from the point of view of the Third World—had tried to twist and dilute the earlier position on this subject, adopted by the Eighteen-Nation Disarmament Committee (ENDC) in 1966, wherein two basic principles had been underlined, namely: (a) that arrangements for regional arms control should come from within the given region, including all important regional members, and (b) that such arrangements be respected by all the potential suppliers of weapons to that region. The USA wanted to change this and submitted a working paper to the Conference of the Committee on Disarmament on 12 August 1970. In this paper, the USA introduced the idea of 'unilateral action' by one or more regional countries. Such action could then become the basis for outside suppliers to refuse to supply certain types of sophisticated equipment to the countries of that region, including to those which had not endorsed the 'unilateral action'. This position could be used by the USA or any of the suppliers of major arms to influence the military balance and overall security situation in a given region. That is why it was not acceptable to many Third World states; they have therefore tried to introduce various qualifications to the idea of regional arms control arrangements.[35]

It should indeed be unrealistic to assume that there is complete unanimity among the Third World countries on all these issues related to conventional arms control. For that matter, such a vast and diverse grouping as the Third World cannot reach complete unanimity on any issue. Many of the non-aligned countries have tended to look at the question of conventional disarmament from a narrow perspective and in isolation from the objective of general and complete disarmament, particularly nuclear disarmament. This is contrary to the stated NAM position and in sympathy with the moves and initiatives advanced by the Western powers. Countries like Egypt, Ghana, Singapore, Zambia, Pakistan and Indonesia have consistently tried in the UN, as well as in the NAM meetings, to shift emphasis from nuclear to conventional disarmament. Even at the latest NAM summit in Harare, this was evident in the amendments moved by Pakistan, North Korea and Iran, on 28, 29 and 30 August, respectively, to the draft prepared by the working group on International Security and Disarmament.[36] The deviant behaviour of the minority of the NAM members in this respect may be understood either on the basis of the strategic proximity of some of these countries to the great powers (as in the case of Egypt, Pakistan, Singapore, Indonesia, etc.) or in the light of their regional and bilateral security pre-occupations with co-members of the Movement (as in the case of Iran, North Korea and Pakistan). The NAM has absorbed such diversionary pressures from within, partly by showing accommodation on less substantive aspects and partly by letting the weight of consensus decision making assert itself.

Prospects

The question of arms control in the Third World has been talked about extensively for the past two decades without yielding any significant results. The main reason is the almost complete lack of sincerity and necessary political will behind this talk.

The prospects of the NAM playing a meaningful role in advancing the cause of arms control in the Third World are not encouraging. To begin with, the NAM is more seriously concerned with arms control in the nuclear, chemical, biological and conventional arms fields, at the level of the great powers rather than in the Third World. The imperatives of the international security situation justify this one-sided concern. In addition, there are constraints inherent in the organizational composition of the NAM. It can do nothing about those Third World countries which are not members of the Movement. Even for its own members, there is no mechanism to ensure adherence and compliance, particularly since the major Third World arms importers, manufacturers and military spenders also happen to be the leaders and influential members of the Movement. Above all, the subject of arms control is so complex and sensitive that it can hardly be thrashed out in a grouping of such size and diversity. The interests of the states in this respect are not always mutually compatible.[37]

The blame for the failure of arms control in the Third World cannot be put on the Third World alone. This is a highly political issue caught in the quagmire of

East–West rivalry and North–South control.[38] Various dimensions of global security are so closely interwoven that it is unrealistic to segregate them to achieve viable solutions. This may explain why the regional arms control approach has made only limping progress. Many regional arms limitation proposals (like ZOPFAN in South-East Asia, zones of peace in the Indian Ocean, the Middle East and Africa, and the Declaration of Ayacucho in Latin America) have made little progress in concrete terms, although the NAM has endorsed them. The reservations of the great powers in offering binding commitments constitute one of the main hurdles.[39] In the absence of such commitments, the Third World would neither feel motivated nor be effective in the field of arms control. Reference is sometimes made to the arms control imperatives, both for the great powers and the Third World countries, inherent in the dynamics of an ever expanding 'arms bazaar'.[40] But such imperatives are more than matched by incentives to proliferate, inherent in the same dynamics.

Notwithstanding these factors, the NAM remains acutely aware on two counts. One is that it has high stakes in reducing and eliminating the dangers of nuclear war; and second, that the financial and political costs imposed by the buildup of conventional arms cannot be perpetually enhanced. As a result, the NAM should and would persist in arousing and articulating world public opinion against prospects of nuclear conflicts and root causes of conventional arms races.

There is one area beyond this general approach where the NAM can make a significant impact, namely in initiating and concreticizing confidence-building measures that can contribute to reducing regional and global tensions. The NAM had hailed moves in Europe such as the Helsinki Accord and the Conference on Security and Co-operation in Europe as well as the talks on Mutual (Balanced) Force Reductions. The Movement is also inclined to see whether similar moves could be initiated for Third World regions. There again, the co-operation of the great powers is crucial. At the same time, much can be done by the Third World itself to reduce its own inter-state tensions and conflicts that lead to external interventions and arms buildups. It is unfortunate in this respect that, even after more than a decade of efforts on the part of countries like Yugoslavia and Sri Lanka, the NAM has not succeeded in evolving a mechanism for settling disputes between its members. The NAM's pathetic failure to influence the course of the Iraq–Iran War so as to bring it to an end is ample testimony of its internal weaknesses. Such weaknesses need urgently to be removed; in order to get out of the situation of pathetic helplessness, the NAM must rise to the occasion and transform itself into the moral, effective force that it was in the early phase of its evolution, when it radiated moderation on the global security situation. Its internal organizational cohesion, ideological commitments and moral integrity were its principal assets. These assets have gradually been dissipated owing to the ever-increasing pressures of global as well as regional and national security imperatives for the non-aligned countries. There is considerable scope for the NAM to take firm steps to regain some of its lost moral *élan* and strength.

First, while rejecting such partial and narrowly oriented concepts as 'arms control', paraded by the great powers, the Movement should firmly assert the endorsement of broad-based, realistic concepts such as 'common security' (defined by the Palme Commission) and 'comprehensive disarmament' (previously stressed by the NAM). Anything short of these comprehensive approaches should not be lent credibility and legitimacy by the NAM, even in the name of step-by-step approaches, because the experience of past decades in the field of disarmament shows that small steps have often proved to be distractions from and counter-productive to the ultimate, cherished goals of peace and disarmament.

The NAM ought to realize that it has to bridge the gap between its precepts and principles, on the one hand, and the practices and behaviour of its own members, on the other. Accordingly, the NAM cannot expect any response, let alone compliance, from the great powers on the issues of nuclear disarmament unless the willingness of its members is demonstrated through meaningful action on the questions of nuclear non-proliferation and conventional disarmament. For instance, the NAM has been constantly pressing for a comprehensive test ban and nuclear freeze on the part of the great powers. Should the NAM not accept a voluntary freeze or moratorium on the purchases of major and sophisticated conventional weapons by its own members, at least for a few years, on an experimental basis? Such resolve, if sincerely adhered to by all the NAM members, would have two important implications. In general, it will not alter the existing regional military balances in the Third World; and at the same time, it will hurt the suppliers of major weapons by freezing their markets for the stipulated period. The bonus advantages would include a thaw in regional tensions and hostilities and more resources for internal development for the NAM countries. It is possible that such an idea might not be fully effective, but it could then be abandoned. Then the Third World could say with greater credibility that it is serious about reducing the flow of arms in the world.

The NAM would be failing in its moral duty if it did not address itself to these and related questions through some form of concerted action.

Notes and references

[1] SIPRI, *World Armaments and Disarmament: SIPRI Yearbook 1986* (Oxford University Press: Oxford, 1986), p. 211.

[2] SIPRI (note 1), table 7.7, p. 344.

[3] Keynote address of Mrs Indira Gandhi, Prime Minister of India, at the opening of the Seventh NAM Summit held in Delhi, in March 1983. Text of the Final Documents, Annexure II (mimeographed).

[4] For the texts of the Bandung Declaration of 1955 and the Brioni Joint Communiqué of 1956, see Mates, L., *Non-Alignment: Theory And Current Policy* (Oceana: New York, 1972), pp. 371–81.

[5] Belgrade Declaration of 1961, Section III, para 16. See the text in *Two Decades of Non-alignment: Documents of the Gatherings of the Non-aligned Countries, 1961–82* (Ministry of External Affairs: New Delhi, 1983), p. 8.

[6] 'Final Document of the Tenth Special Session of the U.N. General Assembly', para. III, *The United Nations Disarmament Year Book*, vol. 3 (United Nations: New York, 1978), appendix 1.

[7] See, for instance, paras 46 and 47 of the NAM Bureau meeting held in New Delhi, 14–20 April 1986, and para. 52 of the Declaration of the Harare NAM Summit, 1–7 Sep. 1986 (mimeographed).

[8] Cairo Declaration of 1964, Section VII in note 5, p. 23.

[9] Gasteyger, C., *Searching for World Security: Understanding Global Armament and Disarmament* (Frances Pinter: London, 1985), figure 7.1, pp. 91–92.

[10] Sivard, R. L., *World Military And Social Expenditure* (Washington, DC, 1983), p. 20. The literature on conflicts in the Third World is growing fast. See, for instance, Kende, I., 'Local war 1945–1976' in A. Eide and M. Thee (eds), *Problems of Contemporary Militarism* (Croom Helm: London, 1980); Small, M. and Singer, D., *Resort to Arms: International and Civil Wars 1816–1980* (Sage Publications: Beverly Hills, CA, 1982); Gaddis, J. L., 'The long peace', *International Security* (Spring 1986), vol. 10, no. 4, pp. 99–142; Soedjatmoko, 'Patterns of armed conflict in the Third World', *Alternatives* (1985), pp. 477–93.

[11] Causes of the arms buildup in the Third World have been discussed in Muni, S. D., *Arms Buildup and Development: Linkages in the Third World*, Canberra Papers on Strategy No. 22 (Australian National University: Canberra, 1980).

[12] See, for instance, the Colombo Declaration of 1976, 'Resolution on Disarmament', para. 1, in note 5, p. 232.

[13] Muni, S. D., 'Non-alignment and the Security Parameter', *International Studies*, vol. 20, no. 1–2 (Jan.–June 1981), pp. 159–72. Also Bebler, A., 'Security aspects of non-alignment', *International Studies*, vol. 14, no. 2 (Apr.–June 1975), pp. 289–302.

[14] Algiers Declaration of 1973, para. 67, in note 5, p. 97. Yugoslavia proposed at the Colombo Summit (1976) that the functions of the NAM Ministerial Consultative Committee be expanded to include consideration and finalization of urgent, collective action in the event of an aggression against a member country. *The Hindu*, 18 Aug. 1976; *The Times of India*, 3 Aug. 1976.

[15] Havana Communiqué, para. 36, in note 5, p. 276.

[16] Colombo Declaration, Section VI, para. 60, in note 5, p. 5196.

[17] Note 5, pp. 279, 280, 349, 366, 374, 597ff.

[18] Resolution 39/72 A was carried by 123 votes in favour, 15 against (Western states) and 15 abstentions.

[19] Statement by Indian delegation, *Indian Express*, 4 Oct. 1986.

[20] As summarized in *UN Disarmament Year Book*, vol. 7 (New York, 1982), p. 42.

[21] Cairo Declaration of 1964, Section VII, in note 5, p. 23.

[22] Thus Pakistan's approach to accepting nuclear restraints is guided by what India does. Pakistan has taken a position that it would sign the NPT if India did the same. India on the other hand underlines its pre-occupation with the Chinese nuclear weapon programme and the fact that China has not signed the NPT. Similarly, the competition between Brazil and Argentina in Latin America keeps both of them uncommitted to the NPT, notwithstanding the fact that they have signed the Treaty of Tlatelolco. Apprehensions about the nuclear capabilities of Israel and South Africa influence the decision of some of their neighbours on the NPT.

[23] Cairo Declaration of 1964, Section VII, in note 5, p. 23.

[24] Havana Declaration of 1979, para. 211; New Delhi Ministerial Meeting Communiqué, 1981 paras 35 and 38, in note 5, pp. 221 and 502 respectively. See also New Delhi summit, 1983, no. 3, para 31, p. 10 (mimeographed).

[25] Colombo Summit, Political Declaration, 1976, para. 136, in note 5, p. 202.

[26] Belgrade Ministerial Meeting, July 1978, para. 131, in note 5, p. 310. Under the broadened scope, the participating countries had 'agreed to exchange information and work towards a regime of restraints on arms transfers'. Pierre, A. J., *The Global Politics of Arms Sales* (Princeton University Press: Princeton, 1982), pp. 283–84.

[27] Harare Documents, no. 7, Section IV, paras 51 and 53.

[28] Harare Documents, no. 7, Section IV, para. 33.

[29] Ministerial meeting, New York, 25–28 Sep. 1981, Section II, para. 6, in note 5, p. 542.

[30] For a detailed background of these proposals, see, *UN Disarmament Year Book*, vol. 1 (New York, 1976). Pierre (note 26), Part IV; and *United Nations Study on Conventional Disarmament*, Sale No. E.85.IX.I (New York, 1985).

[31] Accounts of these debates are summarized in *UN Disarmament Yearbooks*, published annually since 1976. See also Pierre (note 26); *Study on Conventional Disarmament* (note 34); United Nations, *Study on All Aspects of Disarmament*, Sales No. E.81.IX.2 (New York, 1981); and US Department of State, *Conventional Arms Transfers in the Third World*, Special Report no. 102 (Washington, DC, Aug. 1982).

[32] Final Document, para. 22, no. 6, p. 476.

[33] *UN Disarmament Year Book*, no. 35, vol. 2 (New York, 1977), pp. 242, 267.

[34] Final Document, para. 85, no. 6, p. 483.

[35] For details of the US Working Paper, see *Official Records of Disarmament Commission*, Supplement for 1970, Annex C, Section 36 (CCD/307).

[36] Texts of the Amendments moved, PC/CRP. 6, 28 Aug. 1986; PC/CRP. 24, 29 Aug. 1986; PC/CRP. 31, 30 Aug. 1986 (mimeographed). Also see, *The Hindu*, 3 Sep. 1986.

[37] Hafterodorn, H., *The Proliferation of Conventional Arms*, Adelphi Papers No. 133 (IISS: London, 1977), pp. 33–41.

[38] Dubey, M., on 'Conventional disarmament', *Subregional Conference for the World Disarmament Campaign*, Sweden, Apr. 1985 (United Nations, Department of Disarmament Affairs: New York, 1985), pp. 73–79. In the same source John Simpson has argued for the urgency of conventional disarmament and the Third World's responsibility (pp. 97–104).

[39] *Common Security: A Programme for Disarmament*, The Report of the Independent Commission on Disarmament and Security Issues Under the Chairmanship of Olof Palme (Pan Books: London, 1982). See also Galtung, J., *There are Alternatives: Four Roads to Peace and Security* (Spokesman: Nottingham, 1984).

[40] Brzoska, M. and Ohlson, T. (eds), *Arms Production in the Third World*, SIPRI (Taylor & Francis: London, 1986), pp. 289–90. Landgren-Bäckström, S., 'The transfer of military technology to Third World countries', in H. Tumoi and R. Väyrynen (eds), *Militarization And Arms Production* (Croom Helm: London, 1983), pp. 193–204; Katz, J. E., *Arms Production in Developing Countries: An Analysis of Decision Making* (Lexington: Toronto, 1984).

Part IV.   Integrating approaches

Paper 13. Arms transfer control and proposals to link disarmament to development

JACQUES FONTANEL and JEAN-FRANÇOIS GUILHAUDIS

I. Introduction

The idea of there being a link between disarmament and development is a very old one. Economists believed two centuries ago that military expenditure was improductive and had a negative effect on the world economy, but proposals to establish an institutional link between disarmament and development are recent. They have mostly appeared in the 1970s and 1980s. The problem of underdevelopment is certainly one of the oldest, but its theory and economic policy are intimately related to the process of decolonization. The considerable inequality of development between states, the responsibility of colonial states for underdevelopment now admitted by most analysts, and the growing power of the Third World in the international community have aroused international concern for the developing countries. The need for disarmament has become greater because of increasing military expenditure, the arms race between East and West and even in the Third World, and the terrifying effects of modern weapons. Since it could be possible to have the same international security with fewer weapons, the arms race is scandalous when seen in the framework of underdevelopment problems.

A recent UN document for the International Conference on Disarmament for Development—initially to be held in Paris in 1986 but postponed until 1987 and held in New York—gives a list of no fewer than 19 state proposals, among which 11 were made after 1973 and 6 since 1984.[1] Until now, France and the Soviet Union have been the two leading states in the field of proposals concerning disarmament and development. As early as 1955, President Edgar Faure proposed the establishment of an international fund for development and mutual assistance. According to this plan, states would agree to reduce a growing percentage of their military expenditures annually and to transfer these resources to an international fund. This fund would decide on a uniform definition of military expenditure, and states would be obliged to communicate all documents pertaining to their defence budgets. A part of the resources assigned to the fund would be put at the disposal of the donor countries, and another part would be available for international aid transfers. Edgar Faure's plan did not receive any agreement from the international community.[2] Some of his ideas were again put forward in 1978 when France proposed, at the first UN special session on disarmament, to establish an international fund.[3] The project was institutionally ambitious but modest regarding the revenues which were to be transferred to developing countries. France once again improved its proposal in 1984 and asked for an international conference.[4]

Soviet proposals since 1956 have focused on military budget reductions. In 1973, the USSR asked for a reduction of 10 per cent of military budgets of the permanent members of the UN Security Council.[5] According to Soviet views, 10 per cent of these funds ought to be reallocated to the economic and social development of underdeveloped countries. In 1973, Mexico called for an expert study on technical problems linked to the definition and comparison of military expenditures. The UN General Assembly passed a resolution supporting both the Soviet and the Mexican proposals.[6] With the exception of Mexico, and previously of India (1950)[7] and Brazil (1964),[8] the developing states have not paid much attention to the idea of disarmament for development. It has mainly been an idea developed by the great powers. Nevertheless that situation was recently modified. Senegal (1978 and 1984),[9] Tunisia (1984),[10] Mexico (1984)[11] and Sri Lanka (1985)[12] have also submitted proposals.

Even if there exist important differences between these proposals, they all conceive of the idea of disarmament for development in the same way. Their purpose is to promote disarmament in states that are well developed and armed in favour of aid transfers to underdeveloped, poor and less armed states. For example, Soviet proposals identify as donor states the five permanent members of the Security Council and, further, other major states which are well developed and armed.[13] The French proposal of the international fund more or less agrees with this solution. In principle, the fund would be filled by resources coming from disarmament, but as long as there is no disarmament it will be firstly fed by contributions mainly from states possessing nuclear weapons.[14] Thus, both France and the USSR propose not to receive funds from the Third World. Furthermore, they do not propose to use the idea of disarmament for development for limiting arms transfers to developing countries. Other proposals which have been made on disarmament for development or on the reduction of military expenditures generally share that view. Disarmament for development has, until now, been required mainly from developed states, using funds from industrialized states.

It is easy to explain this prevailing concept. Any attempt to ask developing states to be among the donors in the disarmament for development process would confront the principle of the main responsibility of the great powers, especially the superpowers, in the arms race and disarmament, which is well established and has been ratified by the first UN special session in its Final Document.[15] It would also mean that the Third World would be seen as truly participating in the arms race. Such an idea is unacceptable for Third World states and furthermore is not sustained by all the great powers.[16] It seems to be extremely difficult to change the present approach. Third World countries are in the majority in the UN General Assembly. Any effort in this direction would undoubtedly be at a very high political cost. That is all the more true as military expenditure in the Third World is presently decreasing.

In such a context it is interesting to observe that some developing states are partly diverting from the common approach. Thus Senegal proposed a tax of 5 per cent on the military budgets of all states.[17] Tunisia is in favour of compulsory contributions to an international disarmament fund for development linked to arms transfers.[18] In the Tunisian view, these contributions would be paid by arms-exporting states. But since most arms transfers are intended for developing states, such a proposal entails arms transfer controls in the Third World, owing to the higher costs it would incur. With the previous remarks in mind and without forgetting that none among the proposals in favour of disarmament for development or reduction of military expenditures has succeeded, it may still be of interest to explore whether disarmament for development can help arms limitations in the Third World. One can especially examine: (*a*) whether and how the adoption of such proposals would affect the level of arms imports and arms production technology in the Third World, and (*b*) whether linking limitations of arms to the Third World with development aid makes such limitations more attractive for the states involved.

II.   Limitations on arms transfers and arms production

Every negotiation on arms transfer limitations confronts three main difficulties:

1. The definition of weapons is not universal: the notion of military products is ambiguous and depends on various circumstances. In wartime, for example, any product can be considered as a weapon for the defence of a country. In peacetime, it is often difficult to know the real nature of products which can be used in either civil or military fields.

2. Will the geographical coverage of the limitation concern the whole world, or only special zones? How can the list of the states which would have to participate be constructed? Is it conceivable to limit or even to forbid arms transfers to states which do not produce arms?

3. An international agreement must be verified. But, in the arms trade, secrecy is the usual practice.

Beyond these general problems, special difficulties appear in connection with each specific effort to promote arms transfer limitations.

Arms import limitations

The proposition that Third World states should decide to reduce or stop their arms imports from developed countries is usually based on the negative economic effects resulting from regional arms races. However, arms import reductions may have various effects on the national economy. If these reductions are not counterbalanced by national military purchases, the country will actually increase its total reserve of foreign currencies or reduce its debts. But if an import substitution policy is applied, then direct and indirect effects will be more complex.[19] They depend on the possibilities for the country to export its weapons, if it does not want to produce a very expensive product without economy-of-scale effects. Arms production is characterized by very high costs for research and development, steep learning curves and a need for long production. They produce tendencies towards monopoly in the market.[20] The theory of the industrialization of the Third World is not applicable to the arms industry, since increased competition pushes world market prices down towards short-run marginal costs. Large producers can produce more cheaply and undercut competition. Third World states are not—as a rule—able to produce very sophisticated weapons.[21] So, an arms import reduction in the developing countries without a reduction of military expenditure is a political decision which is certainly very expensive. If a government wishes to establish an indigenous arms industry in order to ensure national independence, it will need various informal and formal barriers to protect its arms industry, and this will involve buying its products far above world market prices. In purely commercial terms it is a risky and unattractive market, because of a long product-development cycle, international competition, and the large amount of research and development included in the production of weapons.

A reduction of the arms trade with the Third World makes no real sense in terms of disarmament and development without a reduction of military expenditure. The lack of such a reduction would favour the rise of new arms producers. One may doubt that such a result would in any way be a positive change. The main reasons for establishing arms industries are political in nature, based on security concerns and the will to be more independent by becoming self-sufficient. But some governments, following inward-looking import-substitution strategies for economic development, use arms production as a vehicle for the industrialization of their countries. They believe that there are technological spin-offs from military industrialization, that military industries have backward linkages and create effective demand for inputs produced by the civilian system, and that the costs of foreign arms are becoming prohibitive both for their balance of payments and for their foreign currency reserves.[22] However, military technology constraints on civilian and military products are very different. The spin-offs of the military sector are not so important, partly because of military secrecy. For instance, it has been demonstrated in the case of India that in none of the main industries has the industrial spin-off from military expenditure had any significant positive effects.[23] In general, the country must compete on external markets for the scale effects useful for military industries, increasing its dependence on international arms transfers. The general effects of arms industry for under-developed countries do not seem positive in the long run, given the relatively poor integration between military and civil industrial sectors, the weakness of the spin-off of military R&D on the civilian sector, the need for considerable imports of components or sub-systems in weapon production, the negative effects on the national debt[24] and the constant need to sell weapons on the international market.[25] If a reduction of the arms trade leads to the development of new arms industries in the Third World, then the remedy is worse than the disease. A reduction of military expenditure must be included in a negotiation on the reduction of the arms trade. But the main obstacle to arms import limitation, either quantitative or qualitative, lies in the right of developing states to acquire the means to preserve their security.

Arms export control

The idea of a limitation on arms transfers that is initiated by the great powers deserves some examination. For example, the informal London Suppliers Club for major nuclear technology has been trying to limit the proliferation of military nuclear technology.[26] It has been partly successful, but by the late 1980s several developing countries, with the help of industrialized countries, have obtained the technological potential to produce nuclear weapons. Export cartels are able to restrict the proliferation of certain weapon systems in the short run, but it is very difficult to retain the homogeneity and the solidarity of the Club in the long run. The efficiency of embargoes[27] is a matter of dispute for many economists and politicians. Usually, economic measures fail in the long run, either because various economic interests of the partners are conflicting or because opportunity costs for the opponents are very different. As argued in part III of this book, it seems unlikely that it would be possible to obtain a limitation of arms exports to the Third World: because the economic interests involved are far too important for many industries in developed countries, and because socialist and capitalist states compete in the world for ideological and strategical supremacy.

Even if an agreement on arms transfer control were accepted by the major powers, a lot of short-term problems would arise, such as pressures from military–industrial lobbies, the additional costs of some weapons for the exporting countries, the dependence of employment on arms exports, the temptation of developing countries to keep up with the technological developments of the developed countries, the strategic disequilibrium of some regions or the development of an international black market. In the long run, the discrimination between developed and developing countries created by such transfer control could become intolerable to the Third World.

Tax on international arms transfers

This proposal from the report of the Brandt Commission[28] was supported by former French Prime Minister Laurent Fabius[29] and, in a way, by Tunisia.[30] The main idea is to establish a tax on arms transfers for the benefit of development aid. In order to have a correct perspective on this tax, one needs to observe that: (a) arms transfers represent only about 3–5 per cent of military expenditures,[31] and (b) 65 per cent of the arms transfer transactions affect developing countries. Therefore, the productivity of the tax would be low and, even if it was paid only by developed states, it would especially affect developing states, with the exception of countries that produce their own weapons or buy only small quantities of foreign arms, because it is easy for arms producers to increase the prices of weapons in order to recover the amount of the tax. Arms transactions are very complex.[32] The transfer often takes place as part of a package involving equipment, spares, training, access to technology, and so on. With arms transfers, other arrangements are negotiated in the civil sector. The real transaction price is then seldom well defined. Furthermore, any attempt to ask developing states to pay a part of the tax would raise the question of their right to preserve their national security and incite them to create or to increase their military industry at a very high cost.

III.   Proposals on disarmament for development

Three main proposals on disarmament for development have been made: aid to developing and low-military-expenditure countries, the reduction of military expenditures and the creation of an international disarmament for development fund.

Aid to developing and low-military-expenditure countries

Several types of proposal for giving aid to developing countries and countries with low military expenditures have been made.

Two members of the Brookings Institution[33] proposed to transfer aid to developing countries in the same financial amount as that of the reduction of their military expenditures. This proposal is not attractive for developing countries: first, a country which has no military expenditure to reduce would receive no aid; second, the proposal does not consider the wars, conflicts or threats from which they try to defend themselves by increasing their military expenditures; third, the main problem in the current arms race is not developing countries but developed countries, and the idea that they would give aid to underdeveloped and often less-armed states in order to reduce their already low military expenditures tastes of irony and imperialism.

A study published by UNIDIR[34] proposed to help the initiatives among the poorest developing countries in favour of regional arms reduction by giving these states international development aid in order to reduce social and economic conflicts. This proposal did not receive support from the international community.

Because disarmament does not seem to be a realistic objective in the short run, it has also been suggested[35] that it would be possible, in order to aid the developing countries, to use for civilian purposes the enormous potential of the developed countries for the production of military goods or services. Because armies are able to build bridges or to give first aid in case of a catastrophe, developed countries could lend out military specialists for these civilian purposes. Such a proposal is very ambiguous and can be either dangerous or useless. If it results in substantial personnel transfers, a dependency problem may develop. If, on the other hand, it only produces occasional personnel transfers, it can be of little help for development.

Reduction of military expenditure

Since 1973 an important effort has been made to clarify the notion of military expenditure. This notion is ambiguous. In wartime, the military sector dominates society, which generally is not the case in peacetime. United Nations experts adopted a *stricto sensu* concept of military expenditure, based on the direct nature of the expenditure incurred.[36] The Soviet Union's proposal (1973) failed because the United States wanted to measure, to compare and to verify figures on military expenditure. The Soviet Union did not agree with this idea and asserted that the US demand was above all an expression of a lack of political will to reduce military expenditure.[37] At the second special session of the United Nations General Assembly devoted to disarmament, the United States took the important initiative of calling for the convening of an international conference on military expenditure.[38] Here, the Soviet Union was negative about the United Nations work on the reduction of military expenditure and particularly the report on disarmament for development.[39] This exercise in non-communication between the USSR and the USA dominates the debate on the reduction of military expenditures. Obviously only if the superpowers and other industrialized states decide to reduce their military expenditure will developing states accept such a policy. In the best case they will only follow. But even in this case, some of them could argue that their military expenditures are too low to be decreased, that the level of spending hardly ensures national security and that it must therefore be maintained at the present level.

One must also consider that the reduction of military expenditure by developed states needs to be managed very carefully, in the interest of these states and of the developing states. One must especially underline that any reduction of military expenditure should be done with much care for the strategic desequilibrium that it can induce in the world or in a region. Moreover, one cannot forget that in the short run disarmament could increase underemployment, painful industrial conversions and the reduction of wages in developed countries.[40] The conversion of military activities into civilian activities is not always economically feasible. It could be difficult for a developed country both to solve this initial problem of reduction of military expenditure and to give a part of this reduction to international aid.

Another important point is that developing countries must be cautious in receiving international aid. If they receive non-convertible currencies or products, they can become captive markets for developed countries, particularly if they receive goods or services which are either also produced domestically or which take the place of a national product. Moreover, each product embodies a particular culture, and some types of international aid increase foreign cultural and technological domination. If the developed countries must be careful in the short run about internal problems of conversion and transfers of financial resources to the poorest countries, developing countries must be careful in the long run about dependence and the effects of domination. Even in this case, international aid is not useful for a nation if it is not distributed to the whole economy and to all social categories.

As far as a reduction of military expenditures by Third World states is concerned, one must remember that—beyond huge political obstacles—there will be technical difficulties, for example, that of assessing their military expenditure.

International disarmament fund for development

Even if in both cases a fund can be created and aid given to developing states, the proposal of an international disarmament fund for development is different from the reduction of military spending. Disarmament would follow a reduction of military expenditures. In the proposal of a disarmament fund for development, disarmament comes first and gives rise to the fund and aid transfers. The resources for the fund could come from three main sources: resources released by disarmament, voluntary contributions and compulsory contributions.

1. The method of using resources released by disarmament is fully in line with the purpose of the fund. This approach is favoured by the experts who produced the report on disarmament for development. But it implies that the disarmament process is under way: this method could not be employed at the initial stage of the creation of the fund. *A priori*, the reduction of arms or military expenditure benefits only those states which decide to reduce their efforts on defence, and the developed countries, in the long run, must receive the best advantages. This is why it seems very important to compute, in the short and long run for every country, the advantages of the process in order to allocate the proper share of these resources to the developing countries. Another problem is that resources freed by disarmament are likely to provide only a transitory revenue to the fund rather than sustained resources. Since a real disarmament process is not presently under way, the method of released resources cannot be applied, and other avenues must be tried.

2. One alternative is the voluntary contributions method. This method[41] is simple, and it avoids the painful problem of verification. However, it leaves states free to decide whether or not to transfer resources to the fund and, moreover, it does not establish a clear link between disarmament and development. It would also face difficulties during a world economic crisis. Nevertheless, this method may be the simplest method for the initial stage of a

disarmament for development process and could facilitate the participation of states which do not accept the label 'overarmed'.

3. Another method is to levy taxes on armaments.[42] It encourages disarmament but gives rise to many difficulties: Which kind of weapons will be chosen? Is it possible to count one US aircraft against one Soviet aircraft without regard to their respective qualities? How many weapons are possessed by any particular state?

The three methods could be used simultaneously, but even if the question 'who will pay and how' were resolved, other problems would appear, such as the process of establishing the fund, its structure and the distribution of resources.[43] Another method has been suggested to use disarmament for development specifically against the arms race in the Third World. In 1978, France proposed that resources from the international disarmament fund for development be given to the least developed and armed states; underdeveloped but over-armed states would not obtain aid from the fund. In principle that would be a stimulus to reduce their military expenditure and devote more efforts to social and economic development. This method is compatible with the principle that the arms race is due to the behaviour of the superpowers. Moreover, it is compatible with the fact that military expenditures in the Third World vary greatly. Only a few over-armed states would be excluded from the benefits of the fund. Nevertheless, several difficulties remain, such as the definition of over-armed countries and the relation between security and development: there must be clear criteria for deciding whether a state, bearing in mind its present military capability, will receive aid. One can easily conceive of various criteria—the amount of military expenditure, the number of a certain kind of weapons, and so on—but how can one take into account the position of states involved in wars and conflicts? Furthermore, it is necessary to appreciate the situation of each state as a whole, its military power and its social and economic position. Thus there exists no single, simple criterion for the definition of over-armament, security and responsibility in conflicts. The lack of a single criterion implies one more obstacle: it gives a greater role to the body in charge of the reallocation. Other questions then arise, such as those regarding the composition of this body.[44]

IV. Conclusions

There is now no world-wide acceptance of the interrelationship between disarmament and development. Beyond the technical difficulties, it is obvious that great powers find neither in the development of underdeveloped countries nor in their own economic welfare a sufficient reason to disarm. Security is always considered as the first priority. The pressure that can be exerted by the Third World is too weak to change that situation.

Until now the Third World has been concerned with proposals on disarmament for development almost solely as a beneficiary. Trying to use the idea of disarmament for development in order to limit arms races in the Third World would imply a major change in the overall perceptions and the removal of several important obstacles. The first and perhaps the most difficult of these obstacles is the principle that the superpowers and great powers lead the arms race and thus have a special responsibility in the field of disarmament. That means that they must disarm first. This very strong idea certainly has very good grounds—most of the Third World states are nearly unarmed and do not participate in the arms race—but it also legitimizes those in the Third World which participate in that race. The fact that the main conflicts since World War II have occurred in the Third World and that the great powers have made interventions undoubtedly encourages special attention to security and the belief that without a sufficient amount of arms there will be no real independence.

How can it be possible to convince the developing states that they must not create their own military industry when they see that developed states have such industries? In that context, the arguments used to demonstrate to them that military industry cannot be considered as a valuable means to promote industrialization and development sound false and are seen as aimed at keeping the developing states in a position of dependence. This, in turn, favours the unity of the Third World in order to defend its interests against the great powers. Undoubtedly this unity can be used as a shelter by those states in the Third World which try to obtain military power. There exists a vicious circle. But only the great powers, especially the two superpowers, can break this vicious circle by stopping the arms race and beginning the disarmament process.

Notes and references

[1] For a brief account of proposals made in the UN framework, see Preparatory Committee for the International Conference on the relationship between disarmament and development, document A.CONF/130/PC/INF 8 (Feb. 1986).

[2] On Edgar Faure's plan, see Colard, D., Fontanel, J. and Guilhaudis, J. F., 'Le désarmement pour le développement: dossier d'un pari difficile', Fondation pour les Etudes de Défense Nationale (Paris), *Les Sept épees*, no. 19, pp. 85–92.

[3] UN General Assembly document A/S–10/AC 1/28, 1978.

[4] President Mitterrand's statement, UN General Assembly, 28 Sep. 1983, in *Document d'actualité internationale, La Documentation Française*, no. 23, 1983; and UN Disarmament Commission document A/CN 10/57/add 1 (1984).

[5] UN General Assembly document A/9191. The Soviet Union proposed to reduce military budgets in 1956 (DC/SC 1/41) and 1958 (A/C1/L207).

[6] UN General Assembly resolution 3093 (XXVIII) A (Soviet proposal) and B (Mexican proposal), 1973.

[7] UN General Assembly, Fifth Session, Fifth Committee, document PV 377 (1950).

[8] UN Disarmament Commission document DC 209, Annex 1, Section F (1964).

[9] UN General Assembly document A/S–10/PV 17 (1978) and Disarmament Commission document A/CN 10/57/add 1 (1984).

[10] UN Disarmament Commission document A/CN 10/57/add 6 (1984).

[11] UN Disarmament Commission document A/CN 10/57/add 13 (1984).

[12] UN General Assembly document A/40/PV 44 (1985).

[13] UN General Assembly document A/9191 (1973).

[14] UN General Assembly document A/S–10/28 (1978).

[15] UN General Assembly, Final Document of the first special session on disarmament, Res S–10/2.

[16] See the French position expressed by C. Cheysson, UN General Assembly, A/S–12/PV 9 (1982).

[17] See note 9.

[18] See note 10. In favour of contributions coming from all states, see UNIDIR, *Establishment of an International Disarmament Fund for Development* (UNIDIR: Geneva, 1984). See also Japan (A/CN 10/57/add 16); Italy (A/CN 10/57/add 11).

[19] Fontanel, J. and Saraiva-Drummond, J., 'Industries d'armement et développement', in Fontanel, J. and Guilhaudis, J. F., 'Le désarmement pour le développement', *Arès: La course aux armements et le désarmement* (Grenoble, 1986).

[20] Deger, S., 'Military expenditure in Third World countries, the economic effects', *International Library of Economics* (Routledge & Kegan Paul: London, Boston and Henley, 1986).

[21] Smith, R., Humm, A. and Fontanel, J., 'The economics of exporting arms', *Journal of Peace Research*, vol. 2, no. 3 (1985).

[22] Fontanel, J. and Saraiva-Drummond, J., 'Les industries d'armement comme vecteurs du développement économique', *Etudes Polémologiques*, 1987.

[23] Deger, S. and Sen, S., 'Military expenditure, spin-off and economic development', *Journal of Development Economics*, vol. 13 (1983).

[24] Schmidt, C., 'Industrie d'armement et endettement dans les pays en voie de développement: les examples d'Israël, du Brésil, de l'Argentine et de la Corée du Sud', Congrès International de Economistes de Langue Française, Clermont-Ferrand, May 1984.

[25] Brzoska, M. and Ohlson, T. (eds), SIPRI, *Arms Production in the Third World* (Taylor & Francis: London, 1986); Lock, P., 'Arms production and the Third World', Working Group on Armaments and Underdevelopment at the Institute of Political Science, University of Hamburg, 1986.

[26] Basso, J. and Marsaud, J. L., 'Le Club de Londres et le transfert de technologie nucléaire', *Arès: Défense et Sécurité* (Grenoble, 1980), pp. 7–28; Pirotte, O., 'Réflexions sur quarante ans d'expérience en matière de non prolifération horizontale', *Arès: Défense et Sécurité* (Grenoble, 1984–85), pp. 149–79.

[27] Fontanel, J. and Colas, P., 'Le COCOM et le Commerce Est-Quest', in Cahiers du CEDSI, *Réflexions sur la sécurité internationale* (CEDSI: Grenoble, 1984), pp. 117–32; Bertsch, G. K., 'East–West Strategic Trade, COCOM and the Atlantic Alliance', Atlantic Institute for International Affairs, *Atlantic Papers*, Apr. 1983; Perez, Y., 'La dissuasion par les embargos, Les embargos américains contre l'URSS et leurs conséquences sur les relations transatlantiques', *Cahiers d'Etudes Stratégiques*, no. 9 (Cirpes: Paris, 1985).

[28] Brandt, W., *Nord–Sud: un programme de survié* (Gallimard: Paris, 1980).

[29] Fabius, L., 'Discours devant le Congrès du Parti Socialiste'. Toulouse, 12 Oct. 1985.

[30] See note 10.

[31] World arms transfers/world military expenditures for 1982 are, $26 billion/$765 billion = 3.4 per cent. Source: ACDA, *World Military Expenditures and Arms Transfers* (ACDA: Washington, DC, 1985).

[32] Fontanel, J., 'Le commerce international des armes', in *Le Supplément*, 'Violence et non-violence' (Cerf: Paris, Sep. 1985).

[33] Blechman, B. M. and Fried, E. R., 'Désarmement et développement: quelques propositions précises', *Journal de la Planification du Développement*, no. 12 (1978), pp. 157–77.

[34] Pipart, A. and Sada, H., *The Establishment of an International Disarmament Fund for Development, The Regional Approach* (UNIDIR: Geneva, 1984).

[35] French proposal, A/CONF 130/B.C./A (Mar. 1986).

[36] United Nations, 'Réduction des budgets militaires. Publication internationale des dépenses militaires. Désarmement', *Serie d'Etudes*, no. 4 (1981); 'Reduction of military budgets, Refinement of international reporting and comparison of military expenditures', *Disarmament*, Study Series 10 (1983); 'Reduction of military budgets, Construction of military price indexes and purchasing-power parities for comparison of military expenditures', *Disarmament*, Study Series 15 (1986). These experts groups carried out the practical test of a proposed reporting matrix and undertake the task of constructing price indexes and purchasing power parities for the military expenditures of participating states. They conclude that the construction of useful instruments for inter-temporal and international comparisons of military budgets is feasible. Unfortunately, socialist countries did not participate in this exercise.

[37] Fontanel, J., 'La réduction des dépenses militaires', *Cahiers du GRIP*, Brussels, 1985.

[38] Fontanel, J. and Guilhaudis, J. F., 'Le désarmement pour le développement, la réduction des dépenses militaires. L'affrontement des super puissances' in 'La crise du desarmement', *Arès*, Supplément no. 1, 1983.

[39] A/36/536. On the Soviet views, see A/S–12/13/add 1; and Guilhaudis, J. F., 'Le désarmement pour le dévelopement' in G. Fischer (ed.), *Armement–développement–droits de l'homme–désarmement* (Université René Descartes, Bruylant: Brussels, 1985).

[40] Fontanel, J., 'L'intérét d'un Fonds International de Désarmement pour le Développement', *Etudes Internationales*, vol. 16, no. 3 (Sep. 1985).

[41] Smith, R. and Fontanel, J., 'La création d'un Fonds International de Désarmement pour le Développement', Cahiers de la Faculté des Sciences Economiques de Grenoble, Université des Sciences Sociales, 1985: Fontanel, J., 'The International Disarmament Fund for Development', *Disarmament*, vol. 9, no. 1 (Spring 1986).

[42] Thee, M., 'Modalities for the establishment of an international disarmament fund for development', in UNIDIR, *Establishment of an International Disarmament Fund for Development* (Geneva, Nov. 1984).

[43] Sollie, F., 'International, technical and political aspects of an international disarmament fund for development', in UNIDIR (note 42).

[44] See note 42.

Paper 14.   The nuclear non-proliferation regime as a model for conventional armament restraint

JOHN SIMPSON[1]

I.   Introduction

International regimes to limit state activities can have two types of foundation: a voluntary decision by states to cede autonomy to an international agency in a specific area of activity, or the practical ability of one or a group of states to impose restraint on others. Two areas where states are most reluctant to cede autonomy are security and advanced technology: security, because the ability of a state to protect its citizens from external threat is one of its key attributes; and advanced technology, because this is seen as supportive both of security and the potential for economic growth and wealth production.

Nuclear energy is one area of activity where the existence of an international regime would be least expected, given the potential it represented to statesmen in the 1950s for advancing both state security and economic interests. Yet by the early 1960s formal international institutions and procedures were in existence in this area, and by the 1970s a comprehensive regime of restraint was starting to emerge.[2] This regime appeared to be mainly consensual in its nature, and during its existence no additional states have sought nuclear weapon status. Yet no comparable regime for conventional armament restraint, an issue area of more direct significance to many states than the nuclear one, emerged during this period. This paper therefore analyses the special features of the nuclear non-proliferation regime and discusses whether they might offer new directions for international policy on the control of conventional armaments.

Before proceeding further, some comments are necessary on the boundaries within which this paper was written. First, its focus will be on the production, transfer and deployment of weapons and their associated technologies: it will not address methods of restricting military expenditures and the size and disposition of military manpower. Second, it will not deal directly with basic questions about the motives of states in acquiring conventional arms or the roots of international conflicts. These have been variously argued to reside in the domestic political environment, in the international one and in the existence of armaments themselves.[3] Thus the paper examines only one component of a possible comprehensive regime to restrain conventional warfare, rather than attempting to explore such a regime in its totality.

II.   The nature of the nuclear non-proliferation regime

There exists an extensive literature on international regimes.[4] Such regimes have been seen to possess a number of key attributes, including *norms* which encapsulate their purpose; *rules* to operationalize these norms; *agreements*, *procedures* and *institutions* to implement the rules and verify that they are being upheld; and degrees of *universality of membership*.[5]

The *norms* of the non-proliferation regime can be either ethical or political in their nature. The ethical norm views nuclear weapons as devices of mass and indiscriminate destruction with unknowable after-effects, making both them and their use unacceptable to the international community. Use of nuclear weapons, particularly first use of them, could breach the laws of war, which are themselves a codification of what constitutes civilized international behaviour.[6] Unlike the situation with chemical weapons,[7] a norm of non-use of nuclear weapons has not yet been formalized in an international legal document.[8] Thus, from this perspective the regime's purpose is the global elimination of both nuclear weapons and their possible use.[9]

Three potentially conflicting political norms can be identified. One can be derived from the implementation of the ethical norm but could equally well be a substitute for it. This is the redistribution of political power away from the existing nuclear weapon states towards the rest of the world through nuclear disarmament. The second norm is the obverse of the first, namely, the freezing of the distribution of world power in favour of the existing nuclear weapon states. This implies sustaining their nuclear weapon status and making no concrete provisions for disarmament. Both norms rest on the assumption that the possession of nuclear weapons gives political power to a state. The third norm is that there should be a reciprocity of benefits and sacrifices within the regime.[10] This means that the non-acquisition of nuclear weapons will be rewarded by assistance with the development of nuclear energy for peaceful purposes and by the nuclear disarmament of the existing nuclear weapon states.

The *rule* of non-proliferation that follows from the ethical norm is that those states which possess nuclear weapons should dispose of their stockpiles and that all states should then agree not to acquire any new nuclear weapons or engage in nuclear weapon research.[11] Rules for the transition period from a partially disarmed (or armed) nuclear world to a fully disarmed one would include states without nuclear weapons making no attempt to acquire them and the nuclear weapon states ceasing to work on such weapons and destroying their existing stockpiles.[12]

The rules derived from the first political norm are identical to those for the ethical norm. In the case of the second political norm, the rules are similar to those applicable to the transition phase for the ethical norm, except that the nuclear weapon states promise only to negotiate an end to their nuclear energy activities rather than actively do so. In both cases, all nuclear energy activities in the disarmed part of the world would be by definition peaceful in character.

The rules derived from the third political norm would be that generous assistance should be offered with all nuclear activities, while the nuclear weapon states would actively engage in disarmament.

The *agreements*, *procedures* and *institutions* relevant to the ethical norm address two issues. First, there are those aimed at managing the disarmament of the existing nuclear weapon states. At present these consist of the multilateral Partial Test Ban Treaty of 1963 and the bilateral Anti-Ballistic Missile Treaty of 1972, together with the procedures for superpower consultation created through its linked Standing Consultative Committee. In addition, there are the bilateral Geneva negotiations; discussions on limiting various types of nuclear weapon and nuclear explosive testing; and the SALT II Treaty, the Threshold Test Ban Treaty and the Peaceful Nuclear Explosions Treaty, none of which has been ratified by the United States.

The second set of issues addressed is how to dissuade states from acquiring nuclear weapons. The major global agreement here is the Non-Proliferation Treaty (NPT) signed in 1968.[13] Under this treaty, non-nuclear weapon parties agree not to acquire nuclear weapons, and the nuclear weapon parties promise not to assist any state attempting to do so. In addition, all non-nuclear weapon states party to the treaty must sign an agreement with the International Atomic Energy Agency (IAEA) to allow it to monitor, under specified conditions, the disposition of all fissile materials in their peaceful nuclear energy programmes.

The IAEA is the only global international institution operating in the non-proliferation area, and it implements procedures, known as safeguards, which provide some assurance that fissile materials are not being covertly diverted to other uses. These procedures do not seek to discover whether a state is engaged in the full range of research, development and production work necessary to make a nuclear explosive device. Instead, they perform the more restricted task of accounting for all of the fissile material calculated to be in the possession of an NPT non-nuclear party. In Western Europe, this safeguarding task is delegated to the Safeguards Division of the European Atomic Energy Community (Euratom).

A further element of the NPT deals with general arrangements to regulate trade in nuclear materials and technology with both parties and non-parties.[14] This makes it a condition of supply for all NPT parties that any fissile materials and their associated production technology will be subject to IAEA safeguards in the recipient state. These items are contained in a list published by the IAEA.[15]

Each of the three political norms provides different perspectives upon the NPT, the IAEA and arrangements for nuclear trade. The first one regards the NPT as a flawed and discriminatory treaty because it contains no specific commitment by the nuclear weapon states to disarm. This led to certain participants in the treaty negotiations refusing to sign the final text and dominates the attitudes of many non-aligned states to it. From this perspective, the NPT is primarily a treaty to ensure the disarmament of its nuclear weapon parties, rather than its non-nuclear weapon ones, and its most critical element is Article VI on nuclear disarmament.[16]

The second norm, freezing the status of the nuclear weapon states, appears to permeate the actions of certain Western governments. They regard the NPT as primarily designed to prevent further states from acquiring nuclear weapons; hence their emphasis upon strengthening safeguards and restricting supplies of nuclear technology and materials. This goal also justifies dis-criminatory and covert actions by groups of suppliers. It resulted in the mid-1970s in the convening of meetings of an informal Suppliers Group, known as the London Club. These confidential and exclusive gatherings produced the supplier guidelines which inspired the IAEA list of export items triggering safeguards.[17] In addition regular bilateral meetings are now held between key supplier states to discuss ways of strengthening the existing barriers to prolifer-ation. The most significant of these are frequent meetings between Soviet and US government delegations.[18]

Arguments over the practical implementation of the third political norm take two forms and are usually articulated by Third World statesmen. One is that non-nuclear weapon parties to the NPT have sacrificed their right to possess such weapons in the expectation that the nuclear weapon powers would disarm. The failure of these states to do so has resulted in an un-balanced bargain. The second is that states exchanged a promise not to acquire nuclear weapons for the freedom to develop all aspects of nuclear technology and for access to material assistance in this.[19] The IAEA has a major role to play in fulfilling this bargain, in that it has the task of providing technical and other assistance for a state's nuclear programme. The suppliers' delib-erations are also relevant if they lead to states being denied access to technology.

The degree of *universality of membership* of the regime differs between its institutions. Although almost all states well advanced in nuclear technology are members of the IAEA, two of the nuclear weapon states and at least six of the states with significant nuclear facilities have not become parties to the NPT, nor is there any current likelihood that they will do so. The latter are thus not subject to mandatory safeguards over all the fissile materials in their posses-sion. The Suppliers Group consists of fewer than 20 states and thus is an exclusive gathering. This lack of universality reduces the effectiveness of the NPT, while the possible existence of nuclear suppliers operating outside of the supply guidelines also decreases their impact. This was recognized by the creation of the IAEA Committee on Assurances of Supply, which was intended to restore consensus between North and South on supplier guidelines.

The conclusion that can be drawn from this analysis of the nuclear non-proliferation regime is that, although there may be considerable consensus on its *rules* and general support for some of its *procedures* and *institutions*, there exist damaging limitations in its *universality of membership* and four different interpretations of its *norms* and *purposes*. What is surprising is that the regime has persisted despite these differences and that the membership of the NPT has been slowly expanding. A number of possible explanations can be offered for this.

The most convincing is that all parties to the NPT believe that they derive security benefits from the regime, although few of the Third World states are prepared to admit this publicly. In particular, nuclear proliferation and weapon use now seem most likely to occur in a situation of acute regional conflict, and Third World regional opponents are more probable targets than the territory or assets of existing nuclear weapon states. At the same time, the NPT and the IAEA provide convenient forums for Third World states to harry the superpowers over nuclear disarmament. Finally, the desire of many developing states to embark upon nuclear energy programmes has decreased as greater recognition has arisen of the limitations of reactors as power sources. In short, the failure to realize the ethical norm and the first and third political ones is not seen as sufficient reason to withdraw from the regime, because the implementation of the second, Western, norm has produced publicly unacknowledged but nevertheless very real security benefits to Third World states. Under current circumstances, the norm of nuclear disarmament will continue to be pursued vigorously by them, but never at the expense of the continued viability of the regime. By default, this leaves the second political norm of freezing the existing nuclear weapon situation in a dominant position.

III.   A model for a conventional arms control regime

The nuclear non-proliferation regime is the only comprehensive international arms control regime currently in existence. It has been suggested that its structure and the practical experience of the IAEA could form the basis for an international arms control regime.[20] However, there are some unique features in the nuclear non-proliferation area which make it difficult to transfer its institutions and procedures to areas such as conventional arms limitation.

One feature concerns the *norms* of a global conventional armaments regime. Four norms compete for domination within the nuclear non-proliferation regime, and at least six can be identified in the area of conventional arms limitation. Three of these are ethical norms. There is the pacifist view that the taking of another person's life cannot be justified under any circumstances; hence any use or possession of conventional weapons is unacceptable. There is the perspective that the taking of life in ways which produce excessive suffering is unacceptable, leading to a distinction between 'humane' and 'inhumane' weapons. Finally there is the proposition that expenditure on weapons is a gross misuse of scarce resources. This leads to demands to divert these resources to more productive uses.

Political norms similar to those applicable to nuclear non-proliferation also exist in this area. There are the attempts by states to change or sustain the existing global distribution of political power through limitations on conventional arms. A crucial difference between the two areas, however, is that East–West differences are fully operative in the conventional armament area whereas in the other they are suppressed. In the former there is no consensus on the *status quo* to be sustained or the new distribution to be sought; in the latter there exists a substantial measure of agreement concerning these issues.

A further comparable norm is that of reciprocity. One possible bargain of this type would be proportional reductions in arsenals on a global basis: another would be agreements that certain states would not increase their arsenals while other states were reducing theirs; a third would be to exchange disarmament for economic assistance. In all three cases those states with few armaments are in a weak bargaining position in relation to those with many. The global threat from states acquiring more conventional arms is qualitatively different from that of those same states acquiring nuclear armaments. Indeed the threat of the latter may trigger the transfer of more, not less, conventional armaments if this is the price demanded by a state not to go nuclear.

This discussion demonstrates that, whereas the norms relevant to the non-proliferation regime are relatively few in number, those that might form the basis for a conventional arms limitation regime are both more numerous and more diverse in their nature. Consequently, there exists a much smaller area of potential overlap between these latter norms to serve as the basis for agreement on a minimal set of rules.

The rules of any system of conventional arms limitation would be much more complex than in the nuclear case because many types of weapon and several distinct technologies and development and production processes would be involved. Nuclear non-proliferation involves safeguarding three nuclear materials and the banning of one specific use of them. By contrast, many choices over modalities would be involved in conventional arms limitation. First, there would be the option of total bans or mere limitations. Second, there would be the question of focusing upon a single weapon, a family of weapons or all weapons. Third, there would be the issue of whether the restrictions were to be qualitative or quantitative in nature, or a combination of the two. Fourth, there would be the question of whether limitations were to be universal or regional in scope, or based upon some other discriminatory geographic, ideological or political criteria. Fifth, there would be the question of whether the restrictions were to apply to the deployment, transfer or manufacture of weapons, and to research, ·development and prototype production. Sixth, there would be a need to distinguish between legitimate civil and illegitimate military applications of technology, or alternatively a willingness to ban all applications of a particular technology or all development work in a particular scientific area. Finally, there is the question of whether limitation should be based on approaches linking these modalities in a rigid or flexible way. Examples would be to base restraint on financial criteria or concepts such as particularly threatening or offensive weapons.[21]

Rules based on ethical norms appear at first sight to be easy to specify. The pacifist rule would be that the global development, production and possession of all weapons would be banned. In practice, however, an agreed definition of a weapon and what activities are military would be needed to implement the rule. A rule based on the concept of an 'inhumane' weapon runs into similar problems of definition, but the existence of a partial ban on such weapons demonstrates that these problems are not insuperable and that the ban could be extended to cover new types of weapon.[22] A rule based on the misuse of scarce resources for weapons would either be similar to the pacifist one or attempt to base itself on the idea that a state or states had 'excessive' armaments. However, 'excessive' seems incapable of universal definition in a world where nation-states claim the right to make autonomous decisions on what they require for their own security.

Rules based on the first two power-politics norms would be variants on the theme of 'attempt to limit the (most threatening) armaments of your potential enemies while leaving yourself and your friends free to both acquire all the weapons you think you need and to export to those states which might be persuaded to become your friends'. The application of such a rule is complicated by it operating in four directions: North–South, South–South, East–West and West–West. This makes the area for consensus very small and creates a situation of considerable East–West and West–West competition in arms exports, often producing a buyer's market.

In both the consensus case or the more likely situation where groups of states attempted to apply the rule in a partisan and discriminatory manner, decisions would be necessary on those military artifacts and technologies to be limited and whether transfers or production or both were to be involved. Weapons might be limited on a quantitative or qualitative basis. The type of weapons to be limited could include long-range bomber aircraft and missiles; precision-guided munitions and electronic countermeasures equipment; modern supersonic fighters and anti-tank and anti-aircraft missiles; modern land and sea mines; night and all-weather fighting equipment; and submarines and anti-ship missiles.[23] A more subtle form of limitation would be to allow transfers but to withhold the training necessary to exploit the capabilities inherent in such equipment.

Rules based on the third power-politics norm are easy to envisage but much more difficult to operationalize. Proportional reductions on a global or regional basis would necessitate agreement on the base from which reductions were to occur,[24] acceptance of a common concept of security and the creation of some type of armaments register.[25] This would open up debate on what constituted an equal military balance, how military capability was to be evaluated, how data was to be authenticated and how compiling the register could be distinguished from spying. It might also involve rules for modernization of arsenals, possibly based on 'build-down' principles.[26] Similar problems would also be encountered over an agreement that certain states would not increase their armaments while others decreased theirs.

Rules to implement a norm based on exchanging a reduction in conventional armaments for an expansion of economic assistance are more difficult to envisage. The simple analogue to the nuclear case would involve exchanging reductions in the arsenals of Third World states for offers of development assistance from a multilateral fund. These states would thus in theory gain the double benefit of the opportunity costs involved plus counterpart funds from international sources.

Such a development depends on a radical change in the global security environment and would be rejected by many non-aligned states on the basis that it weakened their military position in relation to the militarily advanced states and thus was a discriminatory bargain. Their non-co-operation over such proposals could be guaranteed; moreover, experience suggests that attempts to control national industries will only encourage indigenous production.[27] To them, a suitable exchange would involve the superpowers and their allies reducing defence expenditure and transferring it to development assistance. Yet this would be regarded as a discriminatory bargain by the advanced states, as the benefits they would obtain from this reduction are unclear. It would also raise similar problems of implementation to those studied at length in the context of proposals to reduce military budgets and increase development assistance.[28] There thus seems to be no common ground for a rule of reciprocity in the conventional armaments area similar to that discerned in the nuclear area.

No global agreements similar to the NPT on limiting conventional weapons exist at present. No state has denounced the use of these weapons or agreed formally not to assist other states to acquire them. As a consequence there are no procedures or institutions to assure signatories that such an agreement is being respected and no international institution devoted to the task of monitoring arms production and transfers. Thus, the issue of universality of membership does not arise.

A viable global agreement for conventional weapon limitation would be unlikely to involve the total disarmament of all conventional weapons, if only because complex problems of definition, and a revolution in the nature of the internal management of states and the state system, if not human nature, would have to precede it. What might be possible is a partial agreement, involving a ban or limits on activities with at least three dimensions: specific weapon systems or technologies; a global or regional focus; and some combination of research, development, production, deployment or export. It might also have to tackle the distinction between civil and military activities both in relation to the stages of weapon acquisition and when in use.

The potential for such an agreement will be directly linked to the ease with which it might be implemented and verified. In the nuclear area this is facilitated by the focus on one specific and clearly delineated weapon and a set of equally unique production facilities. In the conventional armament area implementation is likely to be facilitated if weapons with high visibility and few suppliers are involved. This suggests that prime candidates for limitation are advanced weapons which are complex, expensive and few in number rather than artifacts such as pistols, rifles, grenades and mortars which many states own and manufacture. A further issue here is that private dealers conduct a non-governmental trade in many of these small arms, whereas in nuclear energy and advanced weapon technology governments make vigorous efforts to prevent any unauthorized transfers of materials or technology across state borders.

Any ban or limit on research, development, production and export of advanced conventional weapons will have global consequences because no more than a handful of states are actively involved in these activities. It is almost certainly going to be restricted to the superpowers and their major advanced industrial allies: states such as the Federal Republic of Germany, France, Japan, Italy and the United Kingdom. But support for such a ban from these states is unlikely if it limits their ability to provide for their own defence, especially if the new systems would enable them to reduce their reliance upon the deterrent function of nuclear weapons. Yet to refuse to impose any limit on production of such systems for their own needs, while at the same time denying them to other states, will have a hostile reception in the Third World. It will be seen there as both discriminatory and linked to attempts to ensure that developed states retain the ability to mount effective military interventions and conduct power politics in their region. It is therefore unlikely to be fertile ground for any producer–recipient agreements of the NPT-type.

The implementation of such a ban would be dependent upon East–West agreement on which systems and technologies should not be exported and to whom. The superpowers attempted to negotiate an agreement on this during the late 1970s through their bilateral Conventional Arms Transfer (CAT) Talks, but these were suspended after encountering insurmountable diffi- culties within the US Administration (see paper 7). Alternatives to formal negotiations would include regular private consultations and informal under- standings, similar to those that have been implemented over nuclear non-proliferation.[29]

The political realities of the current world are such that significant superpower co-operation appears unlikely in this area, in contrast to the position on nuclear energy. Moreover, the problem encountered in the latter arena of whether it is problem-technologies or problem-states that need to be constrained is much more central to conventional arms limitation discussions. Disagreements on problem states arc likely to be so acute that they will preclude East–West consensus: while both sides can agree to constrain exports of nuclear technology to states such as Libya, similar agreements on conven- tional armaments seem most unlikely.

Two possible structures for a global conventional armament limitation regime emerge from these considerations. One would be imposed on the world by the major suppliers and would focus on specific, high-value weapon systems and involve a measure of East–West agreement on the rules of limitation, if not its purposes. It would be predominantly an arms transfer regime, with little or no restriction on the weapon procurement activities of the supplier states. Its success is likely to be limited as long as the East–West conflict persists and no attempt is made to obtain the agreement of recipients to its rules.

A second and more durable basis for such a regime would be a treaty of the

NPT type in which recipient states agreed not to seek particular types of weapon in return for the suppliers agreeing to limit or ban them from their own armouries. This raises the practical question of whether there actually exist technologies, weapons or families of weapons in this category. Suppliers would have to exercise a global monopoly over their production and believe that diffusion to the rest of the world would have a catastrophic effect upon security. While this seems a reasonable proposition in the abstract, it is much more difficult to give concrete examples of weapons or technologies that fall into this category.

Such a treaty might have a system of safeguards to ensure implementation linked to it, although it is unclear what it would be focused upon, as there would be no relevant civil industrial activities in the majority of the recipient states, unlike the nuclear area. One possibility, however, would be to set up an international system of end-user certificates for weapons[30] and an inspection arrangement to ensure that their conditions were being respected.

IV. An ideal conventional weapon limitation system

Outlining an ideal set of agreements, processes and institutions to place comprehensive restrictions on conventional armaments is not difficult: providing states and statesmen with a motivation for both negotiating about them and preventing discussions from becoming stalemated by the inherent problems of definition is another matter. Agreements could define the weapons or technology to be limited and the point or points in the weapon acquisition process at which this would be done. They could set out ad hoc procedures for destroying those weapons which already existed and create more permanent procedures and institutions to monitor and safeguard those civilian technologies and artifacts which could be diverted to create replacements for the banned weapons. These procedures could involve accountancy methods, seals, remote monitoring, on-site inspections at short notice and many other procedures already used in the nuclear non-proliferation regime.

Such limitations might be more viable on a regional rather than a global basis, taking the form of the conventional weapon equivalent of the Latin American nuclear weapon-free zone treaty. The prime issue would be the degree of unity within the region, the degree to which it could insulate its security concerns from the rest of the world and the ability of its leaders to agree on a self-denying ordinance not to seek or develop particular types of weapon or technology. It seems probable that these conditions may exist only in Latin America.

All arms limitation agreements are political, not technical, in their motivations and in their judgements on what is an acceptable package. This opens up the prospect of agreements covering several weapon types. Such packages could be based on reducing the forces which were seen as most threatening to individual states, thus avoiding the necessity for symmetry in perceptions. Agreement on a package between a small number of states or groups of states can be envisaged, but it is difficult to see how this technique could form the basis for global agreements, unless they were imposed on the world by a few dominant suppliers.

Bargains which link together state security and other issues, however desirable this may be, also pose difficulties. Attempts have been made in the United Nations to link together disarmament and Third World economic development, but there is no inherent logic to this other than a crude concept of opportunity cost. Yet its simplicity gives it considerable political appeal, and some linking of restraints on arms transfers with increases in development aid might be an attractive proposition to some supplier states and to civilian governments in the Third World. However, given political realities, it hardly seems to be an idea which would appeal to their military counterparts, and there would be just as much debate on how restraint was to be measured in the Third World as on how military budgets were to be evaluated in the First and Second Worlds.

This thus returns to the issue of norms: of why restraint should be undertaken at all. In the nuclear area there are unambiguous ethical, pragmatic and power-political answers to this question, and considerable international acceptance of them. There also exists agreement on a set of rules which bridge any East–West differences over norms. In the area of conventional arms there are no such unambiguous answers, except perhaps ethical ones based on the concept of inhumane and excessively injurious weapons. While it is possible that some limited agreements might emerge among suppliers to limit transfers of specific weapons and technologies on ad hoc prudential grounds, the cross-cutting effect of the East–West conflict and the lack of overriding common interests, in contrast to the case of nuclear proliferation, make superpower collaboration in this area extremely difficult. Recipient agreements on a regional basis may be possible, as may political-package deals in which both producers and recipients link together a number of weapon technologies or security and other areas, but these seem likely to be inherently difficult to negotiate.

One is thus left to conclude that an attempt to extend the scope of the 1981 Convention on Inhumane Weapons may be the most promising path for global conventional arms control, if only because it is based on a clear vision of *why* it is desirable to ban the weapons under discussion; on a relatively clear criterion for deciding which weapons to include and exclude and an absolute logic that weapons possessed by all states should be banned rather than limited. A matter for further investigation would be whether such bans should be monitored by an international safeguards organization modelled on the IAEA. Any judgement on this would depend on the weapons and technologies to be limited, their industrial context and how intrusive safeguards are likely to be. Such a strategy could not hope to confront or resolve the major issues of international conflict which lead states to acquire weapons for their security. But precisely because resolution of these conflicts appears to be a pre-requisite for generating the consensus on norms or rules that would enable any other type of conventional arms limitation regime to be created, it appears to be the only hopeful contemporary basis for further negotiations.[31]

Notes and references

[1] This is a product of the University of Southampton's Ford Foundation research project on North/South Security Relations in the 1990s. The author wishes to acknowledge the support he has received from the Ford Foundation and the useful comments and assistance received on earlier drafts of this paper from Darryl Howlett and Jo Spear, together with other colleagues and research students.

[2] The Statute of the IAEA was agreed in 1957, although it was not until the mid-1960s that the USSR started to take an active part in its proceedings. The NPT was signed in 1968 and came into force in 1970, making it mandatory to subject all the nuclear materials and their associated facilities in non-nuclear weapon states party to the treaty to the IAEA's materials accountancy and monitoring procedures. For a short account of this process see Potter, W. C., *Nuclear Power and Nonproliferation* (Oelgeschlager, Gunn and Hain: Cambridge, MA, 1982), pp. 36–50.

[3] The classic analysis of the first two causes is found in Waltz, K., *Man, the State and War* (Columbia University Press: New York, 1959).

[4] The most notable example of this literature is probably Krasner, S. D. (ed.), *International Regimes* (Cornell University Press: Ithaca and London, 1983).

[5] This approach is based on ideas found in Robinson, J. P., *Chemical Warfare Arms Control: A Framework for Considering Policy Alternatives*, SIPRI Chemical and Biological Warfare Studies No. 2 (Taylor & Francis: London, 1986), pp. 11–12; and more particularly Schiff, B. N., *International Nuclear Technology Transfer* (Rowman & Allanheld: Totowa, NJ, 1983), pp. 22–30.

[6] For a short discussion of the evolution of recent attempts in the international community to codify these ideas see Goldblat, J., SIPRI, *Agreements for Arms Control* (Taylor & Francis: London, 1982).

[7] In the chemical weapon field, signatories to the Geneva Protocol of 1925 have agreed not to initiate the use of chemical weapons, although many signatories have reserved the right to use them in response to such an attack. See Goldblat (note 6), pp. 49–51; and Robinson (note 5), pp. 13–16.

[8] The main reason for this is that the NATO states regard themselves as being threatened in Western Europe by a significant Warsaw Pact superiority in conventional forces and regard the freedom to initiate the first use of nuclear weapons as an essential element in deterring any attack from the East. The Soviet Union has made a unilateral pledge that it will not be the first to use nuclear weapons, while in 1978 all the nuclear weapon states made a pledge not to use nuclear weapons against non-nuclear weapon states in the context of the Final Declaration of the United Nations Special Session on Disarmament. But there does not exist any equivalent to the 1925 Geneva Protocol on chemical weapons in the nuclear area.

[9] Some profound philosophical issues are raised by the distinction between use and possession of nuclear weapons. In both the chemical and nuclear weapon area, the current position of governments seems to be that possession is linked to conditional intent. This doctrine justifies the possession of weapons for deterrent purposes, but not if a serious intent to use them in an unprovoked manner exists. Once the justification is shifted to use for retaliation, the argument becomes much more complex and problematic. It is further confused by the practical need felt by military organizations to rehearse procedures for use and offensive doctrines in order to make a deterrent threat credible.

[10] Schiff (note 5), pp. 23–26.

[11] Unfortunately, this latter rule could prove difficult to operationalize. The NPT, for example, does not explicitly prevent states from working on the *non-nuclear* aspects of nuclear weapon designs, such as implosion mechanisms and fusing. Theoretically, they could then rapidly produce a non-nuclear assembly and insert a fission core into it once the decision to breach the Treaty had been made. The allegations made about Swedish 'defensive' weapon design work are a good illustration of this problem. See Johansson, T. B., 'Sweden's abortive nuclear weapons project', *Bulletin of Atomic Scientists*, Mar. 1986, p. 31.

[12] This might not be an easy task, as the practical problems of engaging in a process of nuclear disarmament have been insufficiently explored, and studies have mainly concentrated on delivery systems. For an attempt to examine this issue in a British context, see Simpson, J., *The Independent Nuclear State* (Macmillan: London, 1983), pp. 206–16.

[13] For the text of this treaty see Goldblat (note 6), pp. 156–58.

[14] Article III.2.

[15] The main items of technology involved in the Zangger list, named after one of its main architects, are those related to chemical plants to enable plutonium or U_{233} to be extracted from irradiated nuclear reactor fuel and facilities to enable either uranium to be enriched in the isotope U_{235} or plutonium in the isotope Pu_{239}. There has also been hostility to the export of materials and technology which would enable heavy water and graphite-moderated reactors to be built in certain countries, on the grounds that these reactors can produce materials for weapons. Both the contents of this list and the rules for nuclear trading have been the subject of considerable controversy. Several supplier states feel that trade should be denied to NPT non-parties until they agree to join the treaty or at least accept safeguards on all their nuclear facilities. Others argue that certain types of nuclear technology should be denied to all non-nuclear weapon states. Yet others want to distinguish between 'reliable' trading partners who could be supplied with sensitive technology and 'unreliable' ones to whom it should be denied. For a description of these differing views see Jones, W. J. et al., *The Nuclear Suppliers and Nonproliferation* (Lexington Books: Lexington, MA, 1985).

[16] This states: 'Each of the Parties to the Treaty undertakes to pursue negotiations in good faith on effective measures relating to cessation of the nuclear arms race at an early date and to nuclear disarmament, and on a treaty on general and complete disarmament under strict and effective international control.'

[17] For an account of these activities from the perspective of a British participant see Wilmshurst, M. J., 'The development of current non-proliferation policies' in J. Simson and A. McGrew (eds), *The International Nuclear Non-Proliferation System: Challenges and Choices* (Macmillan: London, 1984), pp. 28–33.

[18] *Washington Post*, 1 Dec. 1984.

[19] Contention has often arisen in this context over the distinction between assistance *at a price* and *at no cost*. During the NPT negotiations, for example, Britain, among others, made it clear that Article IV was not intended to be an obligation to provide free and unlimited assistance for developing states in the civil uses of nuclear energy.

[20] An interesting and realistic example of this literature is Fischer, D. A. V., 'Safeguards—a model for general arms control?', *IAEA Bulletin*, vol. 24, no. 2 (June 1982), pp. 45–49.

[21] The idea of 'particularly threatening' forces is found in the United Nations *Study on Conventional Disarmament* (UN: New York, 1985), p. 32, para. 113. There exists a basic disagreement between Soviet policy makers and those of some other states over the notion of offensive weapons. Their position is that all weapons have the potential to be either offensive or defensive: the crucial issue is how they are deployed.

[22] This is the Convention on the Prohibitions or Restrictions on the Use of Certain Conventional Weapons which may be deemed to be Excessively Injurious or to have Indiscriminate Effects, signed in 1981 and entered into force in 1983.

[23] Such a list could be based on the idea that there existed certain weapons which were inherently offensive. A good illustration of the type of guidelines necessary for implementing such a policy can be found in the Annexes to Protocol No. III to the 1948 Brussels Treaty of Collaboration and Collective Self-Defence among Western European States, signed in 1954. These were the Protocols which permitted the rearmament of FR Germany but limited the types of armament it could acquire.

[24] An indication of the magnitude of this type of problem is provided by the fact that the states of Europe have been trying unsuccessfully for some 13 years to agree on this point in the MBFR negotiations.

[25] The League of Nations gathered and published such data from 1925 onwards in their *Armaments Year-Book* and *Statistical Year-Book*, but the UN was unable to continue this work. A number of its member states have taken the position that they would supply such information only if actively engaged in negotiations or if required to do so by treaty.

[26] This technique has been suggested in the nuclear area and involves allowing modernization on condition that numbers of units are reduced at the same time. An example would be a rule allowing combat aircraft above a certain weight to be replaced on a 3:2 basis.

[27] South Africa is a classic case of this.

[28] *Reduction of Military Budgets of States Permanent Members of the Security Council by 10 per cent and Utilization of Part of the Fund Thus Saved to Provide Assistance to Developing Countries* (UN: New York, 1974). This was followed by UN studies and reports on the same topic in 1976, 1977 and 1980.

[29] A similar idea involving more states is suggested in Pierre, A., *The Global Politics of Arms Sales* (Princeton University Press: Princeton, 1982), pp. 292–94.

[30] Such a system can be argued to exist in embryo form already in the shape of the COCOM arrangements for the control of exports of sensitive materials and technologies to communist countries. The nuclear suppliers group had similar origins as it grew out of arrangements to deny nuclear materials and technology to the USSR. In addition there exists a disparate collection of national and international arrangements to control the export of military materials. Britain, for example, imposes its own national export controls, the Export of Goods (Control) Orders, under the provisions of the Import, Export and Customs Powers (Defence) Act 1939. These Statutory Instruments list the items requiring a licence to export, and include a section headed Aircraft, Arms and related material, Ammunition, Military Spares and Appliances and Paramilitary Police Equipment. The European Community operates a system for controlling the export of five chemical weapon precursors and operates a ban on sales of them to Iran and Iraq. There also exists a wider Western group chaired by Australia for controlling similar exports. Such co-ordination could therefore act as a basis for a more coherent system of control over selected conventional weapons.

[31] This conclusion should not be taken to exclude the possibility of temporary pragmatic agreements being reached not to export military equipment to combatants in a war, but such agreements remain difficult to make and sustain, especially in the Middle East, where the 'enemy of my enemy is my friend' syndrome is prevalent.

Assessment

THOMAS OHLSON

The contributors to this volume have examined the possibilities for limiting the transfer of conventional weapons and arms-manufacturing technology to the Third World. Not surprisingly, they are not very optimistic in their assessments of the possibilities.

However, new attempts to limit arms transfers will be able to gain from the experience of past failures. Among the lessons learned is the fact that agreements have to be in the interests of the participating parties. Various proposals have been made, such as those for supplier or recipient restraint; unilateral, bilateral or regional/global multilateral measures; quantitative or qualitative limitations, and so on. Among these proposals, the most promising are those that: (*a*) combine diverging interests; (*b*) help to change or re-evaluate interests; or (*c*) provide countervailing interests. In other words, the practicable way forward is via a search for realistic and feasible limitation proposals within the framework of a broader attempt—in the Third World and in the industrialized countries—at re-examining their security needs in the light of the costs and consequences that arise. This concluding assessment addresses the partially contradictory and tension-creating need for both realism and basic changes of attitude called for in the contributions.

I. Is the arms trade out of control?

Looking at the realities, it is important to note that the arms trade is not entirely unlimited or uncontrolled. Many states apply some form of *unilateral export control*. Japan and Norway, for example, have made it their policy not to export arms to Third World countries. Hagelin points out that Sweden, a leading third-tier supplier, exercises restraint both with respect to the types of weapon supplied and to the character and security environment of the recipient. Pearson's paper shows that similar control is exercised by the commercially oriented second-tier suppliers in Western Europe, most notably the FRG. The papers by Klare and Krause show that both the USA and the USSR control their arms exports more rigorously than most other states, mainly because arms exports from the superpowers are wholly integrated parts of their foreign and security policies.

Second, there is at least one example of a relatively well-functioning *multilateral arms export control* agreement, namely, the arms embargo on South Africa. There are also examples of more implicit restraint. In 1965, the

USA and the UK co-ordinated their arms embargoes on both belligerents during the Indo-Pakistani War. Both superpowers refrained from delivering advanced jet fighters and sophisticated surface-to-air missiles to the Korean peninsula until the early 1980s. Similar superpower restraint could be observed in Central America, at least up to 1987.

Third, there are several examples of *unilateral arms import limitations*. As pointed out by Varas, such limitations may to a large extent result from external pressures related to debt burdens and so on, but there are also cases where considerations of arms control, development and security play a role. Hettne mentions Costa Rica as the classic case. The arms import reductions initiated by the civilian government in Argentina in 1983–84 and the reluctance of the Mozambican Government—at least in part in order to avoid becoming overly dependent on one supplier—to request sophisticated weapons despite the country's severe security predicament are other examples.

Fourth, proposals for *multilateral arms import limitations* were recently re-initiated: in the Lima Declaration of 1985, seven Latin American heads of state recommended cuts in military expenditures and arms imports.

Thus, although real efforts have been made to control and restrain the international arms trade, they are highly limited and very weak. Furthermore, these vestiges of restraint are seemingly being eroded by the current structure of the arms market and by specific current factors, such as the Iraq–Iran War. Somewhat ironically, however, fading prospects for control may—just as in the 1920s and 1930s—pave the way for a growing interest in multilateral limitation efforts. As noted in the introduction to this book, the commercialization and privatization of the arms market generate effects that are not always conducive to the long-term national self-interest of arms suppliers and arms recipients.

II.   The feasibility of future arms transfer limitations: pre-conditions and proposals

In his famous study of the global arms trade, Andrew Pierre concluded that the best approach for restraining the flow of arms to the Third World would be a *supplier-initiated*, regionally oriented one.[1] The trends in the arms market in the late-1980s suggest that the prospects for supplier-initiated multilateral restraint have decreased, if not vanished. One main conclusion from the contributions in this volume is that *the initiative must come from the recipient side*. There are two important qualifications to this conclusion. First, it must be recognized that if such an initiative is launched, the eventual goal is the establishment of a dual arms transfer control regime, involving joint supplier/recipient action and responsibility. Second, unilateral efforts for arms transfer limitations—by suppliers or recipients—are still very important. Owing to the multitude of suppliers available and the continuing demand, unilateral efforts will not produce immediate or significant effects on the level or direction of the arms flows. But someone has to begin. Successful unilateral measures can strongly influence others to follow the lead.

Recipient-initiated restraint efforts on a regional basis thus offer the best long-term possibilities, for the simple reason that arms transfers are so closely related to regional security. It appears virtually impossible to get all suppliers to agree on supplier initiatives for arms transfer control, given the present competitive atmosphere between an ever-growing number of producers/suppliers of arms. There is simply no way in which supplier constraints could work on a buyer's market. Moreover, the history of past attempts at arms transfer control shows that joint supplier action did not work even when the arms market was a seller's market. Most importantly, even if it were possible to achieve some form of multilateral supplier control, this would not *per se* improve relations between the recipients of arms. Conflicts and tensions within and between Third World countries arise mainly from local or regional problems, even if they are often enmeshed in and fuelled by the competition between the major powers, especially between the USA and the USSR. Therefore, the logical starting point for constraining trade on a buyer's market is not to cut supply; it is to *reduce demand*.

There is, however, no unambiguous evidence that recipient-induced restraint will come about any more easily; this is clear from the recipient-oriented papers by Alagappa and Sopiee, Muni, Subrahmanyam and Varas. In fact, if realism and short-term political feasibility had been the sole guiding principles for the study, this concluding assessment would have to end here. However, authors were asked to take a longer-term perspective in their search for possible ways forward. It is therefore necessary to briefly consider whether and under what conditions it would be possible to decrease the demand for arms, recognizing the longer-term goal as being a dual arms transfer control regime.

Hettne, Muni and Smith—along with most other contributors—argue that real progress towards arms transfer restraint will depend on the ability of the world community to establish a more effective system of collective security than that embodied in the UN Charter. Nations are not likely consciously to weaken their defences unless they receive a reliable guarantee that the rule of law rather than the use of force will prevail in mutual relations, and that their sovereignty and territorial integrity will not be placed in jeopardy. Furthermore, a gradual reduction in tension among and within Third World countries depends on local economic and political reform, and on some form of restructuring of the international system and its regional sub-systems so that they become more economically equitable and less military-dominated than is currently the case. In this last respect, the industrialized countries continue to bear a great responsibility for the continuation of conflict and high level of armaments in the Third World.

A process which modifies the international system in the way described above is fundamentally dependent on improved relations between the United States and the Soviet Union. Present tensions in the international system—in part resulting from the continued military dominance of the superpowers combined with their decreasing economic and ideological/normative power—would be reduced if they adopted less threatening postures towards each other. More specifically, their ability and will to intervene militarily in the Third World is a formidable obstacle to recipient-side restraint. Active, hegemonic superpower policies towards the Third World mean that the countries in the Third World can exercise less control over their own destiny—therefore at least the dominant Third World powers try to counter this with arms buildups of their own. In the longer run, less militaristic superpower postures in the Third World appear to be the only rational responses to the increasing global importance and influence of many Third World states. Whether such postures will be adopted depends on domestic politics in the USA and the USSR and on the benefits they perceive from more co-operation.

On a second level, it is hard to conceive of any substantial efforts at arms export limitations among the primarily commercially oriented suppliers in Europe and the Third World. As noted by Pearson, restrictiveness in arms exports will depend on the buoyancy of Third World markets, superpower détente and, in particular, the determination of West European states to stay in the weapons technology race. The economic and political importance of domestic arms industries in countries like Britain, France, the FRG and Italy indicates that the economic pressures to export arms will remain. At best, it can be hoped that the implications of an arms sale for regional security are understood by individual exporters before the sale is finalized.

However, if there is political will to agree on arms transfer limitations on a regional basis among Third World countries, the primary task of arms suppliers in such a process is, first, to respect such regional arrangements and, second, to reduce the overcapacity in arms production and thus reduce the economic pressures to export arms. For example, compensation schemes would have to be devised for arms industries that convert parts of their capabilities to high-technology activities in the civilian sphere—such as energy, environment or communications. The alternative defence and security concepts discussed in Smith's paper could play a role in such a process, although prospects for the near future are illusory.

On the recipient level, where most activity should be found, little is in fact happening. As noted by Simpson, the situation in Latin America appears most promising. However, if the described changes in superpower relations and in the global security environment were to occur, arms transfer limitations on a regional or sub-regional level in the Third World could find support in an international system which is more susceptible to such limitations. Adjustments in traditional security thinking would be facilitated, and it would be easier for Third World countries to accept their share of the responsibility for the level of armaments in the world.

The need for confidence building

Progress on different levels in the manner described above will, at best, be a slow process. Today, in the late-1980s, such progress does not appear possible for the near-term future. The international system is not highly prone to such changes—mutual confidence is low. Many contributions to this volume therefore highlight the immediate need for confidence-building measures that could be undertaken within the existing security environment without endangering security on any level. Such measures could include those listed below:

1. All states could seek to adopt an arms export law or some corresponding form of binding export guidelines, subject to public scrutiny. Without possibilities of legal sanctions, it seems impossible to effectively punish individuals, companies and others for violation of, say, international embargoes or voluntary restraint efforts.

2. All states could be urged to carry out the national studies on national military economics, disarmament and development recommended by the 1982 UN report on this subject. Such national in-depth studies may produce economic arguments that, for example, could enhance alternative security thinking.

3. The United Nations could establish a register on production of and trade in conventional weapons. This long-standing suggestion is still the best confidence-building measure on the agenda. Secrecy promotes suspicion, and suspicion promotes rearmament. More openness would furthermore stimulate public debate which, in turn, could facilitate political re-examinations of the arguments in favour of arms production and arms trade. Initially, such a register could cover, for example, especially sophisticated or offensive weapons.

4. Regional or sub-regional conferences could be convened in order to discuss confidence-building measures among the recipient nations. It seems especially important to study how different states in a region formulate their security needs and how they perceive the external threats to their own security.

If these and other confidence-building measures were to be carried out, it is conceivable that the necessary modifications of attitudes towards such concepts as armaments, disarmament, development and security could be facilitated. The non-aligned movement could, theoretically, assume a more significant role in advocating regional attempts at arms transfer limitations than predicted in the paper by Muni. The freeze on arms imports which he discusses could then become more than just a remote possibility. The same could be true for regional organizations, such as the Contadora and Andean groups in Latin America, OAU, ECOWAS and SADCC in Africa, and SAARC and ASEAN in Asia. In an environment characterized by higher degrees of confidence, and only then, could it be possible to proceed from confidence building to actual arms limitations.

The very complex problems involved in arms transfer control—as compared to nuclear weapon proliferation—discussed by Simpson could be at least partially solved by conventional CBMs. With respect to actual limitations it must be recognized that in many regions the accumulation of small arms contributes substantially to insecurity and conflict. Logically, however, an eventual *production-cum-transfer* limitation process should start with the most advanced as well as the most destructive weapons. These could be weapons particularly effective in offence, particularly threatening to the civilian population, particularly inhumane or particularly suited to provide incentives for a conventional first strike.[2]

To sum up, old suggestions for arms transfer limitations could—in revised form and in the context of a new overall security framework—become more attractive, desirable and politically feasible than before, for all states concerned. The contributors to this volume have no high hopes in that direction. On the contrary, they are pessimistic. They underline the necessity of a lengthy process of mutual confidence building on all levels as a precursor to actual arms transfer limitations. They also agree, however, that the directions outlined above probably constitute the only alternative to 'business as usual' in the arms trade with the Third World.

Notes and references

[1] Pierre, A., *The Global Politics of Arms Sales* (Princeton University Press: Princeton, 1982), p. 310.

[2] Long-range surface-to-surface missiles, long-range strike fighters and bombers, heavy tanks, landing ships or fragmentation bombs are a few examples of such weapons.

Select bibliography

Arms transfer limitations

Betts, R. K., 'The tragicomedy of arms trade control', *International Security*, vol. 5, no. 1 (Summer 1980), pp. 80–110.

Blacker, C. D. and Duffy, G. (eds), *International Arms Control: Issues and Agreements* (Stanford University Press: Stanford, 1984).

Blechman, B. M., Nolan, J. E. and Platt, A., 'Pushing arms', *Foreign Policy*, no. 46 (Spring 1982), pp. 138–54.

Brzoska, M., 'Third World arms control: problems of verification', *Bulletin of Peace Proposals*, vol. 14, no. 2 (1983).

Cahn, A. H., 'Arms transfer constraints', *Arms Transfers to the Third World: The Military Build-up in Less Industrial Countries*, eds U. Ra'anan, R. Pfaltzgraff, Jr and G. Kemp (Westview Press: Boulder, 1978).

Cahn, A., Kruzel, J., Dawkins, P. and Huntzinger, J., *Controlling Future Arms Trade* (McGraw-Hill: New York, 1977).

Canizzo, C., 'Prospects for the control of conventional arms transfers', *The Gun Merchants*, ed. C. Canizzo (Pergamon: New York, 1980), pp. 187–96.

Evron, Y., 'The role of arms control in the Middle East', *Adelphi Papers*, no. 138 (International Institute for Strategic Studies: London, 1977).

Franko, L., 'Restraining arms exports to the Third World: will Europe go along?', *Survival*, vol. 21, no. 1 (Jan./Feb. 1979), pp. 14–25.

Haftendorn, H., 'Der internationale Rüstungstransfer: Motive, Folgen, Kontrollmöglichkeiten', *Europa-Archiv*, vol. 33, no. 11 (June 1978), pp. 331–40.

Hammond, P. Y., Louscher, D., Salomone, M. D. and Graham, N., *The Reluctant Supplier: US Decisionmaking for Arms Sales* (Oelgeschlager, Gunn & Hain: Cambridge, MA, 1983).

Harkavy, R. E., *The Arms Trade and International Systems* (Ballinger: Cambridge, MA, 1975), chapter 7.

Kearns, G., 'CAT and dogma: the future of multilateral arms transfer restraint', *Arms Control*, vol. 2, no. 1 (1981), pp. 3–23.

Kolodziej, E. A., *Making and Marketing of Arms: The French Experience and the International System* (Princeton University Press: Princeton, 1986).

Kozyrev, A., *The Arms Trade: A New Level of Danger* (Progress Publishers: Moscow, 1985).

Krause, J., *Der Internationale Handel mit Konventionellen Waffen und Rüstungsgütern: Strukturen, Entwicklungen, Perspektiven* (Stiftung Wissenschaft und Politik: Ebenhausen, Aug. 1985).

Pearson, F. S., 'The question of control in British defence sales policy', *International Affairs*, vol. 59, no. 2 (Spring 1983), pp. 211–38.

Pearson, F. S., 'US arms transfer policy: the feasibility of restraint', *Arms Control*, vol. 2, no. 1 (1981), pp. 25–65.

Pierre, A., *The Global Politics of Arms Sales* (Princeton University Press: Princeton, 1982), part 4.

Prospects for Multilateral Arms Export Restraint, Staff Report of the Committee on Foreign Relations, US Senate, 96th Congress (US Government Printing Office: Washington, DC, 1979).

SIPRI, *The Arms Trade With the Third World* (Almqvist & Wiksell: Stockholm, 1971), chapter 2.

Smith, R., Humm, A. and Fontanel, J., 'The economics of exporting arms', *Journal of Peace Research*, vol. 2, no. 3 (1985), pp. 239–47.

Taylor, T., 'The evaluation of arms transfer control proposals', *The Gun Merchants*, ed. C. Canizzo (Pergamon: New York, 1980), pp. 167–86.

Väyrynen, R., 'Curbing international transfers of arms and military technology', *Alternatives*, vol. 4, no. 1 (July 1978), pp. 87–113.

Wulff, H., *Arms Transfer Control: The Feasibility and the Obstacles*, Paper presented at the International Colloquium on Defence, Security and Development, Birkbeck College, University of London, Mar. 1986.

Related issues: disarmament, development and security

Ayoob, M. (ed.), *Regional Security in the Third World* (Croom Helm: London, 1986).

Blomley, O., 'The Arms Trade and Arms Conversion', discussion paper (Council for Arms Control: London, 1983).

Buzan, B., *People, States and Fear: The National Security Problem in International Relations* (Wheatsheaf: Brighton, 1983).

Buzan, B. and Rizvi, G. et al., *South Asian Insecurity and the Great Powers* (Macmillan: London, 1986).

Common Security: A Programme for Disarmament, Report of the Independent Commission on Disarmament and Security Issues—The Palme Commission (Pan Books: London and Sydney, 1982).

Deger, S., *Military Expenditure in Third World Countries: The Economic Effects* (Routledge, Kegan & Paul: London, 1986).

DeSouza, P., 'The other side of the defense coin', *Defense & Foreign Affairs*, Mar. 1983.

Fontanel, J. and Smith, R., 'The creation of an international disarmament fund for development', Paper presented at the International Colloquium on Defence, Security and Development, Birkbeck College, University of London, Mar. 1986.

Gasteyger, C., *Searching for World Security: Understanding Global Armament and Disarmament* (Frances Pinter: London, 1985).

Graham, M., Jolly, R. and Smith, C., *Disarmament and World Development* (Pergamon Press: Oxford, 1985).

Harkavy, R. E. and Neuman, S. (eds), *The Lessons of Recent Wars in the Third World*, vols. 1 and 2 (D.C. Heath: Lexington, 1985 and 1987).

Hettne, B., *Approaches to the Study of Peace and Development: A State of the Art Report*, EADI Working Papers, No. 6, Tilburg, 1984.

Interaction Council, Final Statement adopted at the Third Session, IAC74, Paris, 25–27 Apr. 1985.

Kaldor, M., *The Baroque Arsenal* (Will and Wang: New York, 1981).

Klein, J., 'Arms sales, development, disarmament', *Bulletin of Peace Proposals*, vol. 14, no. 2 (1983), pp. 157–63.

Kolodziej, E. A. and Harkavy, R. E. (eds), *Security Policies of Developing Countries* (Lexington Books: Lexington, MA, 1982).

Krasner, S. D. (ed.), *International Regimes* (Cornell University Press: Ithaca and London, 1983).

Mehta, J. S. (ed.), *Third World Militarization: A Challenge to Third World Diplomacy* (L.B. Johnson School of Public Affairs: Austin, 1985).

North–South: A Programme for Survival, The Report of the Independent Commission on International Development Issues under the Chairmanship of Willy Brandt (Pan Books: London and Sydney, 1980), chapter 7.

O'Neill, R. and Horner, D. (eds), *New Directions in Strategic Thinking* (Allen & Unwin: London, 1981).

Reduction of Military Budgets of States Permanent Members of the Security Council by 10 per cent and Utilization of Part of the Funds Thus Saved to Provide Assistance to the Developing Countries (UN: New York, 1974), and subsequent reports 1976, 1977 and 1980.

Senghaas, D., 'The cycles of war and peace', *Bulletin of Peace Proposals*, vol. 14, no. 2 (1983), pp. 119–24.

Subrahmanyam, K., 'Insecurity of developing nations and regional security', *Strategic Analysis*, vol. 9, no. 11 (Feb. 1986), pp. 1152–64.

Thorsson, I., *In Pursuit of Disarmament: Conversion from Military to Civilian Production in Sweden* (Liber: Stockholm, 1984).

Two Decades of Non-Alignment: Documents of the Gatherings of the Non-Aligned Countries, 1961–82 (Ministry of External Affairs: New Delhi, 1983).

UNIDIR, *Establishment of an International Disarmament Fund for Development*, UNIDIR/84/08, Geneva, Nov. 1984.

United Nations Disarmament Year Book (Department for Disarmament Affairs: New York, annually since 1975).

United Nations, *Economic and Social Consequences of the Arms Race and of Military Expenditures*, Department for Disarmament Affairs, Report of the Secretary-General, A/37/386 (New York, 1983).

United Nations, Preparatory Committee for the International Conference on the Relationship Between Disarmament and Development, *Relationship Between Disarmament and Development: A Bibliographical Survey of Recent Literature*, and *Addendum*, A/CONF 130/PC/INF 4 (New York, Feb. 1986 and Feb. 1987).

United Nations, *Relationship Between Disarmament and International*

Security, United Nations Centre for Disarmament, Report of the Secretary-General, A/36/597 (New York, 1982).

United Nations, *Study on All the Aspects of Regional Disarmament*, Report by the Secretary-General, A/35/416 (New York, 1981).

United Nations, *Study on Conventional Disarmament*, Department for Disarmament Affairs, Report of the Secretary-General, A/39/348 (New York, 1985).

United Nations, *Study on the Relationship Between Disarmament and Development*, Report of the Secretary-General (Inga Thorsson chairman), A36/356 and A/40/618 (New York, 1982 and 1985).

Varas, A., *Militarization and the International Arms Race in Latin America* (Westview Press: Boulder, 1985).

Wolpin, M. D., *Militarization, Internal Repression and Social Welfare in the Third World* (Croom Helm: London and Sydney, 1986).

Index